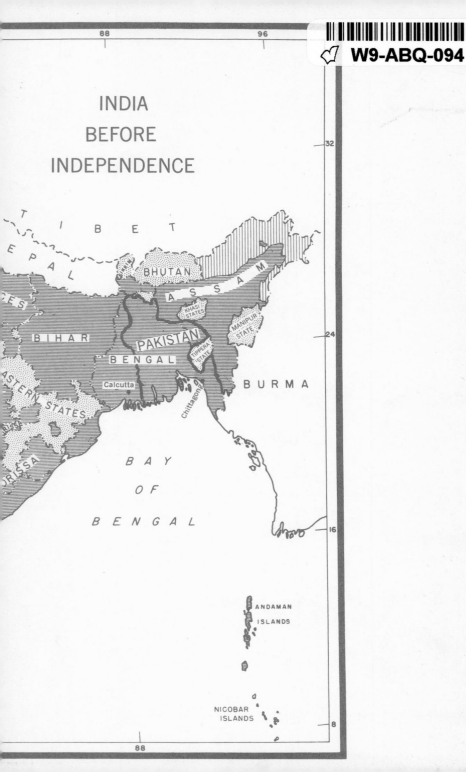

INDIA
BEFORE
INDEPENDENCE

TIBET

NEPAL

BHUTAN

ASSAM

KHASI STATES

MANIPUR STATE

BIHAR

PAKISTAN

BENGAL

TIPPERA STATE

Calcutta

Chittagong

BURMA

EASTERN STATES

ORISSA

BAY

OF

BENGAL

ANDAMAN ISLANDS

NICOBAR ISLANDS

Gandhi and

Modern India

Gandhi and
Modern India

PENDEREL MOON
FELLOW OF ALL SOULS COLLEGE,
OXFORD

W·W·NORTON & COMPANY·INC·
NEW YORK

Contents

Gandhi and

Modern India

I

Introduction

Gandhi was both a politician and a saint, a combination of roles that was not unusual in earlier epochs but is almost unique in the twentieth century. He alone among the front-ranking political figures of our times claimed constantly and in public to be doing God's bidding, to be acting at the prompting of the "inner voice"; he alone sought to cast out devils and to win over opponents by prayer and fasting; and he alone made prayer meetings a main avenue of approach to the public.

Such a throwback to a bygone age could not have emerged as a great political leader in a modern industrialized society, but only in one still basically medieval in organization and outlook. India under British rule was such a society—ancient, custombound, as yet scarcely touched by the industrial revolution, worshiping God without attempting to define Him, and accepting without question traditional moral values.

Comparable societies existed in the first half of this century in Russia and China, but they produced no political leaders comparable to Gandhi. Men of a very different character dominated the scene—ruthless, amoral, atheist, iconoclastic, intent for the most part on executing the decrees of Marx rather than the Will of God. These men—the representatives of an innovating middle class who, discarding traditional values, aimed at con-

verting their backward countries into modern industrial states—
were not, and could not afford to be, saints. Saintliness was
incompatible with their aims, and with the power that they
exercised. If India had been free, similar unsaintly men would
probably have taken charge of her destiny. But India's subjection to foreign rule, combined with the medieval outlook of
most of her people, gave scope for the saint-*cum*-politician.
Gandhi, who neither shared the aims nor was saddled with the
responsibilities of the Russian and Chinese leaders, could flour-
ish under the mild British rule as a saintlike political agitator.
The tolerant British did not suppress him and, so long as British authority continued, his own more mundane and moderniz-
ing colleagues did not cast him aside. They realized that the
saint-*cum*-politician, however unfitted for directing the affairs of
a modern state, was admirably fitted for directing agitation
against the British. With the coming of independence his political influence inevitably declined, and within six months of the
departure of the British he had been assassinated, the victim of
his own insistence on moral principles. But for about twenty-
five years the saint and utopian dreamer maintained his position
as the unquestioned political leader of India—truly an amazing
achievement, reflecting his tremendous force of personality and
his unbounded faith in himself and his mission.

As a politician Gandhi's main goal was clear enough—to free
India from British rule—in association with the British if possible; if not, in opposition to them. But he saw this goal in a
wider context of national regeneration. Indians, he perceived,
had been demoralized by political subjection. He wished to
restore their self-respect and self-confidence, to improve their
moral fiber, to remove the sense and the stigma of inferiority, to
instill in them pride in Indian culture and civilization, and to
mold them into a people who would exemplify Indian rather
than Western values. In pursuit of this wider aim the politician
became merged in the social reformer. The background to his
thinking as a politician was a consciousness of India's past,
fostered by his upbringing in a princely state, and a belief in the
superiority of Indian to European traditions and values; for,
in his view, Indian civilization was "permeated with faith in

God," whereas Western civilization was godless.

Gandhi's background as a saint is perhaps less familiar to the ordinary reader; it was essentially Hindu. With a typically Hindu eclecticism, Gandhi absorbed something from other religions, especially Christianity, but he was always dominated by the Hindu philosophical tradition, and a Hindu scripture, the Bhagavad Gita, became his bible.

The Gita teaches renunciation of desire and nonattachment to the things of this world, but not withdrawal into a life of inactive contemplation. A man should act and strive to do his duty in the service of his fellow men, but he should remain as indifferent to the fruits of his action as to the promptings of desire. Renunciation, nonattachment, and acts of service without regard to their fruits are the stepping stones to deliverance from the bondage of life and death and to reunion with the universal spirit or God—a state of bliss or nothingness which is the ultimate goal of all living creatures. Such reunion is to be achieved fully, if ever, only after countless cycles of lives, for the soul in search of salvation continually takes on new forms and ever strives to rise from the lower to the higher. But even in this life some partial approximation to reunion can be attained through strict discipline of the senses and conquest of desire. Gandhi certainly aspired to attain it. He may not have been successful, but the mastery he gained over himself in the attempt gave him a mastery over others.

Renunciation and nonattachment tend to be conducive to self-centeredness, and a common criticism of Hinduism is that it assigns insufficient value to positive love for one's fellow men. In Gandhi's case this deficiency was overcome by his absorption of the Christian teachings of the New Testament. But if Hinduism itself does not advocate love, it does advocate reverence and respect for other humans and indeed for all sentient life in that it is, like ourselves, part of the universal spirit with which reunion is sought. This belief in the unity of all life and reverence for it is a prominent feature of Hinduism, and is sometimes carried to absurd lengths. The Jains, a Hindu sect strongly entrenched in Gandhi's home province of Gujarat, take elaborate precautions to avoid killing the most trivial insect. Jain influences in his childhood may account for the deep impression this particular aspect of Hinduism made on Gandhi. The obligation to refrain from taking life is part of the more general obligation to refrain from causing harm to other living creatures. From this springs the principle of *"ahimsa"* (non-violence) that Gandhi preached and practiced throughout his career. Although as a practical politician he was compelled occasionally to permit or acquiesce in deviations from the strict rule of nonviolence, there is no doubt that he had a sincere and almost fanatical belief in it. Rightly understood, it was, in his view, the cure for all evils, and it was India's destiny to proclaim the message of nonviolence to the world.

The spiritual ideas that Gandhi derived from Hinduism were for him a living faith, never far removed from his consciousness and constantly renewed by prayer, meditation, and fasting. As a politician Gandhi had some of the defects of the politician, but as a saint he had the power that belongs to saints. The multitude revered him as a holy man—and rightly, for he really was one; even the sophisticated Jawaharlal Nehru felt awe at Gandhi's moral quality. G. K. Gokhale, his earliest political mentor, considered him to be "of the stuff of which heroes and martyrs are made" and to possess "the marvellous spiritual power of turning ordinary men around him into heroes and martyrs." In addition to these unusual gifts, Gandhi was endowed with an acute and original mind, a great capacity for hard work, exceptional moral courage and fearlessness (which he tried to impart to others), and above all a remarkable personal charm which, combined with a strong sense of humor, captivated almost everyone he met—except, alas, the Muslim leader, Jinnah. Nehru, who described this quality as "amazing and irresistible," has written, "His smile is delightful, his laughter infectious, and he radiates light-heartedness. There is something childlike about him which is full of charm. When he enters a room he brings a breath of fresh air with him which lightens the atmosphere."

This charm, which no words can adequately convey, was part of the secret of his success.

II ∿

Birth and

Education

Gandhi was born on October 2, 1869, at Porbandar, the capital of a small principality of that name on the coast of Kathiawar in what is now the state of Gujarat. He was the youngest of three sons born to his father by his fourth wife. His father's three previous wives had all died.

The Gandhis belonged to the not very elevated Bania caste and were, it seems, originally grocers. But for two generations the family had been of some consequence in Kathiawar. Gandhi's grandfather, his father, and his uncle were each in turn diwan, or prime minister, of the petty princely state of Porbandar, and his father was later prime minister of two other similar states in the region, Rajkot and Vankaner. None of these states was subject to direct British rule and so Indian customs and traditions were more respected and more fully preserved there than in most parts of British India.

Gandhi's mother was a saintly, deeply religious woman addicted to prayer and fasting. She went daily to the temple and would "take the hardest vows and keep them without flinching." She was illiterate, but, according to Gandhi, a woman of considerable intelligence and strong common sense.

Gandhi spent the early years of childhood at Porbandar and went to school there. But when he was about seven his father moved to Rajkot and it was there that over the next ten years he completed his schooling. From the age of twelve he attended the high school along with his two elder brothers. He was a shy boy and rather aloof, but diligent, well behaved, and well liked by his teachers. He says that he had no high regard for his own abilities and was astonished when he won prizes and scholarships, but he was very proud of his character and felt deeply pained if a teacher had reason to find fault with him.

At school he was "taught all sorts of things except religion," but he obtained religious instruction from his parents, who were devout Hindus. They took him regularly to the temple, and he listened to Gujarati translations of the Bhagavad Gita and Ramayana being read aloud to his father when he was ill. He also heard his father's Muslim and Parsee friends talking about their faiths and thus at an early age he learned to be tolerant of other religions—with the exception of Christianity, which, as a boy, he disliked because Christian missionaries preached near the high school and poured abuse on Hindus and their gods. At this time he did not have "a living faith in God," but one thing took deep root in him: "the conviction that morality is the basis of things." A Gujarati stanza also made a great impression on him; it ended with the lines

> But the truly noble know all men as one,
> And return with gladness good for evil done.

Following the custom of the day, Gandhi was married at the age of thirteen to a girl of the same age named Kasturbai. She was illiterate, and although Gandhi was very anxious to teach her to read, "lustful love left me no time." Nor was Kasturbai herself a very willing pupil. His efforts to instruct her were, therefore, a failure, and private tutors who were engaged later did not do much better. A child was born to them when they were sixteen, but survived only a few days. Other children were born later. From the start Gandhi was, by his own admission, a very jealous husband who tried to keep Kasturbai in virtual imprisonment. This led to bitter quarrels. "Refusal to speak to one another," Gandhi records, "became the order of the day with us, married children."

At school Gandhi made friends with a boy older than himself who told him that Indians were weak and easily ruled by the English because the English were meat eaters and the Indians vegetarians. This boy recited a doggerel verse that was current in the school:

> Behold the mighty Englishman,
> He rules the Indian small;
> Because being a meat eater
> He is five cubits tall.

He assured Gandhi that many of their teachers and many well-known persons in Rajkot were secretly eating meat and that this was the beginning of a desirable "reform" because if everyone in the country started eating meat the Indians would be able to throw off the English yoke.

Gandhi was impressed by these arguments. Moreover, his friend, who ate meat regularly, seemed to be a living proof of its invigorating effects; he was strong, athletic, and daring, while Gandhi by comparison was feeble, hardly able to jump or run, and prone to childish fears of ghosts and snakes. Gandhi wanted to emulate his friend so that he would be fit to help defeat the English and make India free, but this would mean deceiving his parents to whom, as strictly orthodox Hindus, meat eating was absolutely abhorrent. With some compunctions, Gandhi reconciled himself to this deception and for about a year joined his friend in surreptitious meat feasts. Gradually, however, he came to the conclusion that although there was a duty to eat meat and take up food "reform" in the country, "deceiving and lying to one's father and mother is worse than not eating meat." So he resolved to give it up—at any rate during his parents' lifetime—and, having once given it up, never went back to it again.

The friend who persuaded him to eat meat also prevailed on

him to visit a brothel. On this occasion he was saved from faithlessness to his wife only "by the skin of his teeth." He himself describes the episode:

> [My friend] sent me in with necessary instructions. It was all prearranged. The bill had already been paid. I went into the jaws of sin, but God in His infinite mercy protected me against myself. I was almost struck blind and dumb in this den of vice. I sat near the woman on her bed, but I was tongue-tied. She naturally lost patience with me, and showed me the door, with abuses and insults.

A few more visits to houses of ill-fame at later stages of his life ended in much the same way, but he regarded them "from a strictly ethical point of view . . . as moral lapses."

Gandhi was fifteen and still studying at the high school in Rajkot when his father died. Two years later he passed the matriculation examination and was sent to the Samaldas College at Bhavnagar to study for a B.A. degree. After he had been there only one term, an old friend of the family, a shrewd Brahman named Kewal Ram Dave, advised Gandhi's mother and elder brother that a B.A. degree at Samaldas College would only qualify him for a post at sixty rupees a month and that in the changed times, if he were to become a diwan like his father, or something better, he should study in England, where in three years' time and at no great expense he could become a barrister at law. With such an educational background he could go far.

Gandhi, who had been finding his studies at the college very difficult, jumped at the idea, but his mother and brother were in two minds. They wanted to send him to England, for they realized that he, although the youngest son, was the member of the family with the best chance of achieving his father's position in life. But how were they to pay for it? And how in far-off England, severed from his family, could a young Indian be kept from going astray?

Gandhi offered to sell his wife's ornaments to provide the funds. This proved unnecessary, as his brother said he would manage to find the money somehow. But his mother's doubts and anxieties remained. She had heard many accounts of young men taking to meat and alcohol in England, and the more inquires she made, the more hazardous the project appeared.

Another family adviser, a Jain monk, set her anxieties at rest, "I will get your boy solemnly to take three vows," he said, "and then he can be allowed to go." So Gandhi solemnly vowed not to touch wine, woman, or meat. His mother was satisfied. She trusted her son to keep these vows and gave her blessing to his departure. He sailed for England from Bombay on September 4, 1888. His wife, with a baby a few months old, remained behind at Rajkot.

For a young man barely nineteen who, except for one short term at college, had spent his entire life with his parents, leaving home and family to spend three years in a far-off foreign country must have been somewhat daunting. Gandhi himself confesses that for the first few nights after his arrival in London he shed copious tears and longed to be back at home. He felt utterly lost in a strange land among a strange people, and there was no one with whom he could share his miseries, for there were no close relatives or friends of the family in England at that time. During the voyage he had experienced some of the difficulties and embarrassments that confronted him in England. Nearly all the passengers were English and he did not have sufficient command of the English language to talk with them. He did not know how to use a knife and fork, and he was too shy to inquire which of the dishes on the menu were free of meat. Consequently he was reduced to eating in his cabin and his meals consisted mainly of fruit and sweetmeats that he had brought with him from Bombay. Indeed, he spent most of the day in his cabin, only venturing on deck when there were few passengers about.

Gandhi, though shy and exceedingly naïve, was by no means deficient in grit and spirit. He was, moreover, determined to make good use of his time in England and not waste the family money that was being spent on him. An Indian gentleman, Dr. P. J. Mehta, to whom he had a letter of introduction, kindly arranged for him to stay for a month with a friend of his in Richmond and then with a family in West Kensington. This was fairly inexpensive, but Gandhi's vegetarian vow posed a problem. A constant diet of porridge, boiled potatoes, and cabbage was not very appetizing, and the two or three slices of bread provided were insufficient to satisfy his hunger. His host at Richmond repeatedly urged him to give up his vow; it was ridiculous, he said, for Gandhi, who had eaten meat in India where it was quite unnecessary, to refuse to eat it in England where it was quite essential. And what was the value of a vow made to an illiterate mother, and in ignorance of conditions in England? But Gandhi was not to be moved. "A vow is a vow," he said, "and cannot be broken." Throughout his stay in England he kept faithfully the triple vow that he had made to his mother.

Gandhi realized that in England vegetarianism, besides being an inconvenience, was a social handicap, and he resolved to make up for this and other social defects by acquiring a number of accomplishments that would fit him for polite society and make him an "English gentleman." He took lessons in dancing, French, and elocution, and he bought a violin for three pounds and tried to learn to play it. These experiments, except learning French, lasted only a few months. He soon discovered that he could not afford all these extras and that, expense apart, they would be of little real utility. He had come to England primarily to study, not to turn himself into an English gentleman. He began to ask himself how he could best employ his time.

The bar examinations, he learned, were not difficult and would not require much study and he thought, therefore, that he should also try to pass some literary examination. This would help improve his English, which was still weak, and also add to his stock of general knowledge. Courses at Oxford or Cambridge, he found, would take too long and be too expensive. A friend suggested that he try to pass the London Matriculation, which, although it would mean hard work, would entail almost no extra expense. But a modern language and Latin were compulsory. The modern language presented no very serious problem as he had already started to learn French, but how was he to manage Latin as well? Gandhi was dismayed. Encouraged, however, by his friend, who said that Latin would be useful to a lawyer and would give him a better command of English, he decided to learn it, no matter how difficult it might be. He joined a private matriculation class and settled down to the life of a serious student.

In order to cut down expense he gave up lodging with a family and moved to a room of his own. He studied books on simple living and found that by installing a stove in his room and having porridge and cocoa for breakfast, bread and cocoa for dinner, and lunch at a cheap restaurant, he could live on a little more than a shilling a day. His total expenses were only seventeen shillings a week; he was delighted.

There had appeared to be a danger—Dr. Mehta's friend, who had tried to argue him out of vegetarianism, had been very much aware of it—that he would fritter away his time on fads and experiments and become a mere crank. But he was too conscientious and had too keen a sense of duty and service and too much ability to allow that to happen. In London he settled down very quickly to a routine of plain living and intensive study. He failed in Latin in his first attempt to pass the London Matriculation, but six months later he tried again and passed. The bar examinations were much less exacting; they were almost a formality and of little practical value. However, Gandhi took them seriously and even went to the length of reading Roman law in Latin. He attended the requisite number of dinners, although he usually merely sat through them or, if he ate, had only bread, potatoes, cabbage, and fruit.

Despite his concentration on his studies, Gandhi was able to indulge to some extent his penchant for fads and cranky theories, some of which remained with him throughout his life. During his early weeks in London when his vow not to eat meat was giving him trouble, he roamed the streets in search of a vegetarian restaurant and at last found one in Farringdon Street. The mere sight of it gave him a thrill of pleasure, and he had his first hearty meal since his arrival in England. In one of the windows of the restaurant, among a number of books exhibited for sale, his eye fell on Salt's *Plea for Vegetarianism*, which he bought for a shilling. Hitherto he had refrained from meat because of his vow, not because he himself objected to it; on

the contrary, he had wished to make every Indian a meat eater.
But after reading Salt's book he became a vegetarian by choice
and conviction and henceforward regarded the spread of vegetarianism as his mission. He joined the Vegetarian Society of
England, subscribed to its weekly journal, became a member of
the Executive Committee, and met all the leading lights of
vegetarianism in England.

Gandhi's interest in vegetarianism led him to the dietetic
studies and experiments that were to preoccupy him throughout
his life. From a conviction that one should consume only things
that sustain the body, he gave up tea and coffee and substituted
cocoa, which also had the advantage of being very cheap. At
one time he lived on bread and fruit alone and for a short
period he tried a diet of cheese, milk, and eggs as an experiment. He persuaded himself that eggs could not be considered
meat, as no injury is done to living creatures by eating eggs. His
conscience soon pricked him, however, because he knew that
his mother's definition of meat included eggs, and within a
fortnight he gave up the experiment as incompatible with his
vow.

Another of his interests was religion. During his second year
in England he met two Theosophist brothers who were reading
the Gita in Sir Edwin Arnold's translation—*The Song Celestial*
—and who invited him to join them in reading the original.
Gandhi was ashamed to confess that he had never read it in
English or Sanskrit or even in his mother tongue, Gujarati, although he had heard bits of it read aloud to his father. He
gladly joined them in reading it in Sanskrit along with Arnold's
English translation. At their instance he also read Arnold's
Light of Asia and Madame Blavatsky's *Key to Theosophy*,
which roused in him a desire to learn more about Hinduism.

A vegetarian acquaintance who was also a keen Christian
urged him to read the Bible. He plowed through the Old Testament "with much difficulty and without the least interest or
understanding," but the New Testament, especially the Sermon
on the Mount, appealed to him and invited comparison with the
Gita. He resolved that, when he was free from examinations, he
would read more books about religion and acquaint himself

with all the principal religions of the world. As was natural for one born and bred as a Hindu, he was greatly attracted by the idea that "renunciation [is] the highest form of religion."

Throughout his life Gandhi claimed to set the highest value on truth, but when, as a boy, he had eaten meat, he had thought for a while that "the mere hiding the deed from his parents was no departure from truth." During his stay in England he was for some time guilty of a similar deception. It was quite common for Indian students in England who had been married at an early age to pose as bachelors. Gandhi did not hesitate to follow the herd and pass himself off as unmarried, although of course he was married and the father of a son. This dissemblance proved embarrassing. On a visit to Brighton he made friends with an elderly widow staying at his hotel who, on their return to London, asked him to come and dine with her every Sunday and introduced him to a number of young ladies. Gandhi at first was shy and tongue-tied, but gradually he became more at ease and began to look forward to Sunday dinner and the company of the young ladies. Then it dawned on him that perhaps the old widow was hoping that he would become engaged to one particular young lady, with whom he often found himself alone. He was in a quandary. "How I wish I had told the good lady that I was married!" he said to himself. There was no alternative now but to purge himself of "the canker of untruth," embarrassing though this might be. So after much thought he wrote her a letter:

Ever since we met at Brighton you have been kind to me. You have taken care of me even as a mother of her son. You also think that I should get married and with that in view have been introducing me to young ladies. I must confess that I have been unworthy of your affection. I should have told you when I began my visits to you that I was married. I knew that Indian students in England dissembled the fact of their marriage and I followed suit. I now see that I should not have done so. I must add that I was married while yet a boy, and am the father of a son. I am pained that I should have kept this knowledge from you for so long. But I am glad God has now given me the courage to speak out the truth. Will you forgive me? . . .

If on receipt of this you feel that I have been unworthy of your hospitality, I assure you I shall not take it amiss. You have laid me under an everlasting debt of gratitude by your kindness and solicitude. If, after this, you do not reject me but continue to regard me as worthy of your hospitality, which I will spare no pains to deserve, I shall naturally be happy and count it a further token of your kindness.

The old widow, of course, forgave him, as she could hardly fail to do after such a disarming letter, and their friendship continued unimpaired. But Gandhi had deviated significantly from truth.

While in England Gandhi overcame his shyness to some extent, but he still found it difficult to converse freely in any large group and remained quite incapable of making a speech in public. As a member of the Executive Committee of the Vegetarian Society he punctiliously attended every meeting but never could pluck up the courage to utter a word. On one or two occasions, when he felt that some important matter was at issue, he wrote down what he wanted to say, but he was too nervous to read it aloud himself and got someone else to do so. On the eve of his departure for India he gave a farewell dinner at the Holborn Restaurant for some of his vegetarian friends. Speeches were made, but when his turn came he had such a fit of nerves that he quite forgot what he was going to say and sat down abruptly after saying, "I thank you, gentlemen, for having responded to my invitation."

This extreme nervousness did not augur well for a barrister. But this was the career on which he was now to embark, for he had duly attended his dinners, passed his examinations, and been called to the bar; it was time to return to India and start work. His family was eager to welcome him home. They expected great things of him as a barrister-at-law.

III

Early Years
in South Africa

Gandhi was called to the bar on June 10, 1891, and on June 12 he sailed for India. He was met at Bombay by his elder brother, who gave him the news, of which he had received absolutely no forewarning, that during his absence in England his mother had passed away. This was a severe shock, but, Gandhi says, "I did not give myself up to any wild expression of grief. I could even check my tears, and took to life just as though nothing had happened."

His brother fully expected him to build up a lucrative practice in Bombay and had done what he could to prepare the ground for him. Gandhi himself had serious misgivings about his ability to earn a living as a barrister. These proved to be well founded. His studies in England of English and Roman law had given him no knowledge of Indian law and no practical experience in how to conduct cases in court. Conscious of his deficiencies, he was content to remain for a while a briefless barrister. At last he plucked up courage to appear for the defendant in a simple case in the Small Causes Court, but when he rose to cross-examine the plaintiff's first witness, he could think of no question to ask! He sat down again in confusion, told his client's agent to engage another counsel, returned the fee of thirty rupees that had been paid to him, and hurried from the court.

After this experience he decided not to take any more cases and applied for a post as a teacher of English in a well-known high school. His application was not accepted. He was in despair. His six-month stay in Bombay had brought him no income at all. There was nothing for him to do but close his establishment there and move to Rajkot, where his brother, along with a partner, had a fairly well-established legal practice and might be able to give him some drafting work.

At Rajkot, according to his own account, he "got along moderately well" and managed to earn about three hundred rupees a month drafting applications and memorials for his brother's poorer, less important clients. But he soon became depressed by the political intrigue that was inevitably prevalent in a petty Indian state like Rajkot, and a quarrel with the Political Agent—the British official in charge of the Kathiawar states—in whose court much of his work would lie, appeared to dim the prospects of his practice. He had met this official in England and, presuming on this acquaintance, sought an interview with him in order to put in a good word for his brother, who had somehow incurred the man's displeasure. The British official resented Gandhi's intervention and told him that if his brother had anything to say he should say it himself. When Gandhi tried to press the matter further, the official asked him to leave, and, when Gandhi hesitated called his *peon* to show him out. As Gandhi still seemed disclined to go, the *peon* finally more or less pushed him out.

Gandhi felt insulted and wanted to "proceed against" the Political Agent, but he did not know how to go about it, and his friends advised him that he would gain nothing by legal proceedings and would probably ruin himself. Gandhi had to pocket the supposed insult and keep quiet. He had learned a lesson, however, and resolved "never again to place myself in such a false position, never again . . . to try to exploit friendship in this way."

"This shock," he says, "changed the course of my life." The incident was no doubt a factor predisposing him to seize an opportunity to leave Rajkot. One of the partners of a Muslim firm in Porbandar, Dada Abdulla & Co., which had business in South Africa, wrote to Gandhi's brother saying that they had a big lawsuit with respect to a claim for forty thousand pounds pending in court in Pretoria and suggesting that Gandhi come to South Africa for a year to assist them in instructing their counsel. They offered to meet all his expenses and pay him a hundred guineas.

Gandhi realized that he would be going to South Africa as an employee of the firm rather than as a barrister, but it was a tempting opportunity to see a new country and gain new experience, and he wanted to leave Rajkot. With his brother's concurrence he accepted the offer and in April 1893, at the age of twenty-four, sailed from Bombay for South Africa, leaving his wife and two children in the care of his brother at Rajkot.

Gandhi landed in Durban dressed in a frock coat and a turban and with a full sense of his own importance. He noticed at once that Indians were treated in a rather contemptuous manner, and this stung him. As yet he had no idea of the grave insults to which they were habitually subjected, and he was only too quick to take offense. A day or two after his arrival, Seth Abdulla, the principal partner of the firm for which he had come to work, took him to the Durban court to watch the proceedings. The magistrate, after staring at Gandhi for some time, asked him to remove his turban. The magistrate was merely enforcing a rule of the court and intended no insult, but Gandhi was offended by this request, refused to comply with it, and walked out of the court. He then wrote to a newspaper about the incident. His letter provoked unfavorable comment and he was described as an unwelcome visitor.

Worse was to follow. The lawsuit was coming up for hearing at Pretoria and it was decided that Gandhi should go and help the lawyer there in the preparation of the case. A first-class seat was booked for him, but when the train reached Pietermaritzburg at about 9:00 P.M. a passenger objected to his traveling in a first-class compartment. Railway officials were summoned. Gandhi showed them his first-class ticket, but they said he must get out and go to the van compartment. He flatly refused to do so. A constable was then called and Gandhi and his luggage were pulled out onto the platform. He refused to get into the other compartment, and the train steamed away without him. He went into the waiting room. It was bitterly cold and there was no light. Shivering in the darkness, he debated whether he should cancel his engagement with Dada Abdulla & Co. and return at once to India rather than endure the insults to which, quite unexpectedly, he found himself subjected. After some reflection he decided that to go back to India would be cowardly and that he must proceed to Pretoria and fulfill his obligations to the firm, no matter what insults he might have to face. He also made up his mind to try, if possible, to redress the wrongs of the Indian community in South Africa.

This resolution, formed late at night in the waiting room of the Pietermaritzburg station, was to have momentous consequences. The attempt to redress Indian wrongs kept him in South Africa for over twenty years and enabled him to gain experience and make a name for himself which paved the way for his subsequent leadership in India.

On this first journey to Pretoria he had some further humiliations to put up with. Telegrams sent to Seth Abdulla and to the general manager of the railways procured for him a first-class berth on the train leaving the next evening. But at Charlestown, where the line ended and from where he had to travel to Johannesburg by stage coach, the guard made him sit outside on the box instead of inside the coach and when Gandhi remonstrated, gave him a severe pommelling. At Johannesburg the hotel would not admit him, and on the journey from Johannesburg to Pretoria he was only saved by the intervention of another passenger from being turned out of a first-class compartment by the guard.

Gandhi began to realize that such treatment was nothing unusual, and he resigned himself to enduring it. When, after he had been in Pretoria a while, he was kicked off a footpath by a policeman, he took no action, although an English friend had witnessed the assault and offered to give evidence against the assailant. To Indians of the laboring class such incidents seemed, of course, to be part of the order of nature, and Indian traders frankly confessed that they were in the country to make money and were prepared to ignore insults. But to Gandhi it was intolerable that Indians should be treated so contemptuously. His mind became more and more occupied with the question of how to improve their position.

But his first duty was to attend to the case of Dada Abdulla. Mr. Baker, the firm's attorney, who had welcomed him most cordially and procured him lodgings in Pretoria, told him that there was no work for him as a barrister, since the best counsel had already been engaged, but that he could be useful in assembling all the necessary information. Gandhi threw himself into the work heart and soul, sifting and marshaling all the facts, studying bookkeeping, and looking up law cases. It all ended happily. From the outset Gandhi had wished to bring about a compromise, and eventually the parties were persuaded to go to arbitration. The arbitrator found in favor of Dada Abdulla, and the latter, under pressure from Gandhi, agreed to accept payment by installments. Both parties, having saved themselves from ruinous litigation, were satisfied with the result. As for Gandhi:

> My joy was boundless. I had learnt the true practice of law. I had learnt to find out the better side of human nature and to enter men's hearts. I realized that the true function of a lawyer was to unite parties riven asunder. The lesson was so indelibly burnt into me that a large part of my time during the twenty years of my practice as a lawyer was occupied in bringing about private compromises of hundreds of cases. I lost nothing thereby, not even money, certainly not my soul.

Gandhi felt that his year's stay in Pretoria was the most valuable experience of his life. There he outgrew his earlier diffidence, acquired a practical knowledge of legal work, and gained the assurance that he would not fail as a lawyer. There, too, he had his first opportunity to perform public work and realized that he had some capacity for it. And it was there that "the religious spirit within me became a living force."

Mr. Baker, besides being an attorney, was a lay preacher and interested in missionary work. At his first meeting with Gandhi he questioned him about his religious views. Gandhi said that although he was a Hindu by birth he was uncertain about his religious beliefs and intended to make a careful study of Hinduism and of other religions as well. Mr. Baker was delighted to hear this and invited him to a prayer meeting, where he introduced him to several of his religious co-workers. Thereafter a very earnest effort was made to induce Gandhi to embrace Christianity. He was given the Bible and a number of other books to read; prayers were offered for his conversion; and he was taken by Mr. Baker to a big religious convention in the hope that the enthusiasm and religious exaltation of those attending it would influence him to become a Christian.

Gandhi appreciated the sincerity of their faith. He had long discussions with them. He read the books they gave him. He read others obtained from Christian friends in England, some of which seemed to him to support Hinduism, and was deeply impressed by Tolstoy's *The Kingdom of God Is Within You.* He also read the Koran and made a study of Islam, and he obtained books from India on Hindusim.

The "mental churning," as he calls it, that started in Pretoria went on for some years. But although he was influenced by Christianity, he could never accept it "as a perfect, or the greatest, religion." Gradually, as the years passed, he was drawn more and more closely to Hinduism, and the Bhagavad Gita rather than the Bible became his infallible guide. "Though I took a path my Christian friends had not intended for me," he says, "I have remained ever indebted to them for the religious quest that they awakened in me."

Gandhi's public work in Pretoria arose out of his desire to raise the status and improve the lot of his fellow countrymen in South Africa. His first step was to call a meeting of all Indians living in Pretoria. The speech he made at this meeting may be considered his first public speech. He stressed the importance of truthfulness, cleanliness, and unity, and suggested in conclusion the formation of an association to make representations to the authorities regarding the hardships of Indians in South Africa.

His speech made a considerable impression, as was to be expected, for Gandhi was a man of great charm and in education and natural ability he was in a class by himself compared with other Indians in Pretoria. Further meetings were held at more or less regular intervals, as a result of which Gandhi got to know every Indian in Pretoria and became thoroughly acquainted with the social, economic, and political conditions of Indians in the Transvaal and the Orange Free State.

But what was the value of this knowledge? Gandhi was due to go back to India after only a year's stay in Africa. Early in 1894, on the successful conclusion of the Dada Abdulla case, he left Pretoria for Durban and began to prepare for his return home. Seth Abdulla insisted on giving a farewell party in his honor. During the party Gandhi happened to see a newspaper article headed "Indian Franchise," from which he learned that a bill was about to be introduced in the local legislature disfranchising all Indians in Natal. Gandhi's nationalist feelings were immediately aroused. He suggested to Seth Abdulla and others present that the bill ought to be strenuously resisted as it would be the beginning of the end of such few rights as the Indians enjoyed. They agreed, but said that if the bill were to be resisted, Gandhi must cancel his passage and stay on a month to direct the fight against it. Gandhi consented to this, and so, in his own words, "the farewell party was turned into a working committee. . . . Thus God laid the foundations of my life in South Africa and sowed the seed of the fight for national self-respect."

The "working committee" moved quickly. Funds were raised and volunteers enrolled. Gandhi drafted a petition for presentation to the Legislative Assembly. The volunteers prepared copies and translations of it and collected signatures. The Speaker of the Assembly was requested to postpone further discussion of the bill and he agreed to a postponement of two days. Quite a stir was created—the petition attracted newspaper comment and was discussed in the Assembly. Although the bill was duly passed, it had become apparent that the Indian community was no longer prepared to take everything lying down.

A much longer petition was now drawn up for submission to Lord Ripon, a former Viceroy of India who was at this time Secretary of State for the Colonies. Ten thousand signatures were obtained in two weeks. Printed copies of the petition were widely distributed not only in South Africa, but also in India and England. The London *Times* supported the Indian cause.

Eventually the Disfranchising Bill was disallowed, a considerable moral triumph for Gandhi's first essay in organized agitation.* Long before this result was known, Gandhi had yielded, not unwillingly, to pressure to stay in Natal permanently and watch over the protection of Indian interests. He was keen to set up a permanent organization to serve this purpose and to foster a sense of national self-respect in the Indian community. But how was he to make a living? To accept a regular salary for public work of this kind seemed objectionable; so it was arranged that about twenty leading Indian merchants would give him retainers for legal work. Despite some opposition from the Law Society of Natal, he was admitted as an advocate of the Natal Supreme Court. Waiving his previous objection, he gracefully complied with the rule requiring him to remove his turban when appearing in court.

His law practice brought him his bread and butter; but in his own mind only public work for the Indian community could justify his stay in Natal, and it was on this that he concentrated most of his attention. There were about eighty thousand Indians in Natal at this time, and they were divided into three classes—indentured laborers, ex-indentured laborers, and free Indians. Indentured laborers had been brought from India since 1860 to work in European plantations. They were bound to serve their employer for five years and during this period were in a condition of semislavery since they could be imprisoned if they left his service. When, however, the five years were up they were entitled to return home or to stay on in Natal and

* The practical effect was somewhat diminished by the passage of another bill disfranchising Indians and other Asiatics not as such but as natives of countries that had not hitherto enjoyed elective representative institutions.

make a living as free laborers, agriculturists, or traders, subject to certain restrictions. Quite a few had elected to stay and had settled in the country. The free Indians, a much smaller class, probably numbering a little over ten thousand, were merchants and traders who along with their clerks and accountants had come to Africa on their own initiative. Many of them had earned large profits.

The permanent organization, which Gandhi set up to ventilate Indian grievances and protect Indian interests and which, borrowing from India, he named the Natal Indian Congress, drew its members predominantly from the free Indians, as the minimum subscription of five shillings a month was beyond the resources of the indentured laborers and of most of the ex-indentured, few of whom had risen above the level of unskilled wage earners. Gandhi, who had a deep, instinctive sympathy for the oppressed, wanted above all that the Congress should be of service to these humbler folk. He soon had an opportunity to take up the cudgels on their behalf. First there was an individual case. An indentured laborer appeared before him in tears and with bleeding mouth and broken teeth. He had been assaulted by his employer. Gandhi took him before a magistrate, who issued a summons against the employer. Gandhi did not want to proceed to extremes and was satisfied when the employer agreed to transfer the indenture to someone else. But news of the case ran like wildfire through the ranks of indentured laborers and percolated to far-off Madras, whence most of them came. A regular stream of them began to pour into Gandhi's office. He "hailed this connection with delight."

A general issue also arose at this time. Europeans were becoming alarmed at the increasing number of Indians in the colony and, with a view to checking this increase, proposed that an indentured laborer should return to India on the expiration of his indenture and that if he refused to leave he should pay an annual tax of twenty-five pounds. Negotiations were opened with the Government of India with a view to getting it to approve these revised terms. Gandhi and his Natal Indian Congress immediately organized a fierce campaign against the proposed tax. The Viceroy, possibly influenced to some extent by this agitation, considered the tax exorbitant, as indeed it was, but he agreed to a tax of three pounds. Although something had been achieved, Gandhi was by no means satisfied. "The £3 tax," he wrote, "was an open sore. There could be no peace until it was abolished." But it remained.

The activity of the Natal Indian Congress soon attracted attention not only in South Africa but also in India and England. Gandhi wrote pamphlets on the condition of Indians in Natal and on the franchise question which were widely circulated. At the same time he endeavored, through lectures and discussions, to impress upon Indians the need to improve their standards of hygiene and, in the case of the well-to-do, to live in a style more suited to their means, so as to remove the European complaint that Indians were dirty, slovenly, and miserly.

In 1896, after three years in Africa, Gandhi went home to India for six months to get his wife and children and then return to South Africa, where he planned to settle permanently. He had established a fairly flourishing legal practice and the opportunity for public work had been amply demonstrated.

On arriving in India Gandhi went to Rajkot and wrote another pamphlet on the condition of Indians in South Africa. It was widely quoted and commented on in the press. He also met several of the leading political figures in India, including Sir Pherozeshah Mehta, G. K. Gokhale, and B. G. Tilak, and addressed meetings at Bombay, Poona, and Madras. Summaries of his speeches and of the comments on his pamphlet were cabled by Reuters to England and from there transmitted in abbreviated and rather misleading form to Natal. They aroused considerable resentment among Europeans there.

At the end of the year he returned to Africa with his wife and two boys. They sailed from Porbandar in a ship belonging to Dada Abdulla & Co. Another ship sailed from Bombay about the same time and the two vessels, with a total of about eight hundred Indian passengers, reached Durban on the same day. The Europeans in Natal were already very angry with Gandhi because of the news reports from India of his vilification of them there, and when they learned he was on one of the ships bringing eight hundred Indian passengers they protested that he was leading an "invasion" of Natal designed to swamp the country with Indians. A resolution was passed that the passengers on both steamers, including Gandhi, should be prevented from landing.

There was as yet no law restricting immigration, and many of the Indian passengers were old residents of South Africa. The Government of Natal could not, therefore, prevent them from landing. But there had been an outbreak of bubonic plague in India that year and on this pretext the ships were detained in quarantine for five days. Threats and inducements were then offered to the ships' owners to take the passengers back to India, and the passengers themselves were threatened with being pushed into the sea if they landed—all to no avail. After five days the ships were permitted to enter the harbor and the passengers to disembark. There was no trouble. The threats proved illusory.

Gandhi, on the advice of the Attorney General, an old acquaintance, did not land. He sent his family ashore to the home of a Parsee friend, Seth Rustomji, but he remained behind to be taken off in the evening under police escort. An English friend, Mr. Laughton, counsel for Dada Abdulla, on finding him still on board and learning the reason, said that he did not like the idea of Gandhi entering the city furtively and volunteered to accompany him to Seth Rustomji's house. Gandhi accepted his offer, but as soon as they landed a number of boys hanging about the wharf, recognizing Gandhi by the distinctive style of his turban, began shouting, "Gandhi, Gandhi, seize him, thrash him." A crowd gathered and followed Gandhi and Mr. Laughton along the street, throwing stones and jostling them. Gandhi became separated from Mr. Laughton; his turban was pulled off and he was kicked and punched and began to feel faint. At this point a Mrs. Alexander, the wife of the Superintendent of Police, happened to come along the street. Seeing Gandhi in difficulty she went up and opened her parasol over him and thus protected him from further molestation, and soon a party of police arrived and escorted him to Seth Rustomji's house, where a doctor attended to his bruises.

Night was now coming on. An ugly crowd gathered outside

Seth Rustomji's house, shouting for Gandhi and threatening to
burn the place down. Mr. Alexander, the Superintendent of
Police, arrived and tried to pacify them, encouraging them to
sing "We'll hang old Gandhi on a sour apple tree." Meanwhile,
he sent word to Gandhi to leave the house in disguise. Gandhi
put on an Indian constable's uniform and, accompanied by two
detectives, slipped out of the house into a bylane without being
noticed and went to the police station. The crowd, on learning
that he had eluded them, dispersed peacefully.

When news of this episode reached England, Joseph
Chamberlain, Secretary of State for the Colonies, cabled to the
Natal Government to prosecute Gandhi's assailants. Gandhi,
however, told the Attorney General that he had no wish to
prosecute anyone and that he could not blame his assailants as
they had been inflamed by exaggerated reports of his speeches
in India. In an interview with a representative of a Durban
newspaper he was able to show convincingly that in India he
had made no false accusations against the whites nor said anything that he had not already said more forcibly in Africa.
Public opinion swung in his favor and in a few days he was able
to go to his home and resume his law practice, which benefited
from the publicity he had received.

Although the Europeans' wrath against Gandhi personally
was assuaged, they were more than ever resolved that the
Indian community should be held in check. Two bills were
introduced in the Natal Legislative Assembly, one designed to
restrict Indian immigration and the other to curb the activities
of Indian traders. These bills were not expressly directed against
Indians—the disallowance of the Disfranchising Bill had precluded further legislation based openly on racial discrimination
—but they were so drafted that in practice they would chiefly
affect Indians. Gandhi, working through the Natal Indian Congress, had the bills translated into Indian languages and made
the Indian community aware of their real implications. Their
passage through the local legislature could not be prevented,
but an appeal was made to the Colonial Secretary to reject
them. He declined to intervene and the bills became law.

The demonstration against Gandhi, and the subsequent passage of the bills, convinced Indians that they must unite to defend their own interests. Membership of the Natal Indian Congress increased, as did the funds at its disposal, allowing the Congress to acquire property which was vested in trustees and yielded enough income to meet current expenses.*

During the next two or three years, until the outbreak of the Boer War, Gandhi had sufficient leisure from his law practice and political work to indulge his propensity for fads and pet projects. His "longing for humanitarian work" led him to serve as a dispenser for two hours each day in a hospital where the majority of patients were indentured laborers. He studied the nursing of babies and took care of those which Kasturbai continued to present to him, and even assumed the responsibility for delivering one of them. He also undertook the education of his older children, with the aid of an English governess, instead of sending them to school. (Not all of them were grateful for this service.) To save money he bought a book on washing, equipped himself with a washing outfit, and taught himself and his wife to do their own laundry. He claimed to be "an expert washerman so far as his own work went." He learned to cut his own hair, although he was not very proficient at first. "What's wrong with your hair, Gandhi?" his friends would ask. "Have rats been at it?" "No," he replied, "the white barber would not condescend to touch my black hair, so I preferred to cut it myself, no matter how badly."

The outbreak of the Boer War in 1899 afforded Gandhi an opportunity to demonstrate his loyalty to the British Empire. In those days, he says, although he was not unaware of the defects of British rule he believed that it "was on the whole beneficial to the ruled" and that "India could achieve her complete independence only within and through the British Empire." He therefore "vied with Englishmen in loyalty to the throne." He had laboriously learned the tune of the national anthem and joined in singing it whenever the occasion arose. So, although his personal sympathies were with the Boers, he felt it his duty

* Much later this property became the subject of litigation and convinced Gandhi that "a permanent fund carried in itself the seed of the moral fall of the institution."

as a British citizen to participate in the defense of the British Empire, and he also thought that it was in the interest of Indians to do so. "If we desire to win our freedom and achieve our welfare as members of the British Empire," he said, "here is a golden opportunity for us to do so by helping the British in the war by all the means at our disposal."

Many other Indians in South Africa thought that, despite their grievances, their best course was to do their bit in the war. Under Gandhi's leadership an Indian Ambulance Corps, nearly eleven hundred strong, was organized and its services offered to the Government. At first the offer was declined with thanks, on the ground that the corps was not needed. But the initial successes of the Boers and the heavy casualities suffered by the British forces soon caused the Government to change its mind and the Indian Ambulance Corps, with Gandhi as one of its members, was employed for six weeks in connection with General Buller's abortive attempt to relieve Ladysmith, where a British force was besieged by the Boers. Its work was mentioned appreciatively in Buller's dispatches and its leaders were awarded medals.

As a result of this unexpected display of Indian loyalty a much greater feeling of friendliness sprang up between British and Indians in Natal, and the Indians thought that after the war was over many of their grievances would be redressed. Gandhi seems to have been of the same opinion. He began to feel that his mission in South Africa was over, that others could carry on the work that he had started, and that he should return to work in his own country. But he also felt that he could not leave South Africa without the willing consent of the Indian community. So, on the conclusion of his war duty, he informed his co-workers of his intention to take up public work in India and requested them to release him. With some difficulty they were induced to grant his request, but only on condition that he would be ready to come back to South Africa, if, within a year, they found that they needed him.

Gandhi was given a tremendous farewell. Costly presents were showered upon him, including a necklace, worth about fifty pounds, for Kasturbai. Gandhi was embarrassed: it would be churlish to refuse these presents, but how could he accept them when he had been training his family to a life of service and a belief that service is its own reward? He decided to put them in trust for the benefit of the community. Knowing that Kasturbai would not readily agree to this, he astutely got the children on his side and confronted her with a unanimous view that to keep the presents would be wrong. There followed a dialogue between husband and wife, revealing both in itself and for the frankness with which Gandhi has recorded it.

KASTURBAI: You may not need these gold and silver ornaments. Your children may not need them. Cajoled, they will dance to your tune. I can understand you not permitting *me* to wear them. But what about my daughters-in-law? They will be sure to need them.

GANDHI: The children are not yet married. And surely we shall not have for our sons brides who are fond of ornaments? And if, after all, we have to provide them with ornaments, I am there and you can ask me then.

KASTURBAI: Ask you? I know you by this time. You deprived me of my own ornaments. Fancy you offering to get ornaments for the daughters-in-law! In any case what right have you to the necklace meant for me?

GANDHI: Has the necklace been given you for your service or for mine?

KASTURBAI: Service rendered by you is as good as rendered by me. I have toiled and moiled for you day and night. Is that no service? You forced all and sundry on me, making me weep bitter tears, and I slaved for them.

Gandhi admits that some of these thrusts went home, but he was determined to return the presents. Kasturbai was overruled, or a reluctant consent extorted from her. She was not even permitted to keep her necklace. In later years, according to Gandhi, she saw the wisdom of his decision.

IV ∽

Preparation

for Satyagraha

Gandhi arrived back in India in time to attend the 1901 annual session of the Indian National Congress in Calcutta, his first actual experience of the working of the great political organization after which he had named his own organization in Natal. He was disconcerted by the wide use of English in the conduct of its affairs, and he was disgusted by the unsanitary conditions of the camp that had been prepared for the meeting and by the general slackness and disorder that seemed to prevail. He himself seized a broom and cleaned out one of the latrines for his own use. He also offered his services to the two Congress secretaries and was given a pile of unanswered letters to dispose of. He had been granted permission to present a resolution about the rights of Indians in South Africa, but it was hurried through with little attention or understanding. Gandhi was allowed five minutes to speak on it, but after he had spoken for three minutes a bell was rung to warn him that only two minutes were left, and he promptly sat down.

During the session he came into contact with most of the prominent Congress leaders, several of whom he had also met

during his earlier stay in India in 1896. G. K. Gokhale, a highly
respected and moderate leader of Indian nationalism, was particularly kind to him and, after the session was over, invited
him to stay with him in Calcutta. He was impressed by
Gandhi's diligence, regularity, and self-reliance, and suggested
that he should settle down as a barrister in Bombay and help
him in his work for the Congress. However, since Gandhi still
had painful recollections of his previous failure in Bombay and
was by no means confident of proving successful as a barrister
there, he preferred to start work at Rajkot. He traveled third
class from Calcutta to Rajkot in order to acquaint himself with
the hardships of third-class passengers. In later years this was to
become his habitual mode of travel, but in 1902 the experience
was novel and unpleasant. The compartments were dirty and
overcrowded and the passengers dirty and disorderly.

At Rajkot his old well-wisher, Kewal Ram Dave, who had
been responsible for his going to England, got him three cases
right away, all of which Gandhi won. In spite of this success,
Gandhi was diffident about moving to Bombay, until Kewal
Ram told him bluntly that he must not vegetate in Rajkot but
should start practice in Bombay and enter public life. He assured Gandhi that he would be successful.

So in the spring of 1902 Gandhi moved to Bombay. His
South African connections brought him work and, though he
secured no cases in the High Court, he did better than he
expected and was able to pay his way. Gokhale continued to
keep a friendly eye on him, calling on him in his chambers two
or three times a week and introducing him to his friends. He
obviously regarded Gandhi as a promising disciple.

Shortly after the move to Bombay Gandhi's second son, ten-
year-old Manilal, contracted typhoid fever, which occasioned a
typical Gandhian episode. The doctor advised that medicines
would be of little use, but that the boy should be given eggs and
chicken broth. Because of his vegetarianism (which he somewhat inaccurately represented to the doctor as being based on
religious scruples), Gandhi would not agree to this, and decided
to treat the boy himself with hydropathic remedies. The boy, of
course, was easily persuaded to say that he did not want eggs or

chicken broth and preferred the hydropathic treatment, and for three days he was fed orange juice and given frequent hip baths. But the treatment did no good. The boy got worse; his temperature rose to 104 degrees, and at night he was delirious. Gandhi began to get anxious. What right, he belatedly asked himself, have parents to inflict their fads on their children? What would people say of him if he was found to have sacrificed his son to his own whims and theories? These were disturbing questions, but he sought comfort in the reflection that the thread of life is in the hands of God. "Why not trust it to Him and in His name go on with what I believed as the right treatment?"

The boy's body was parched and burning hot and Gandhi resolved to try a wet-sheet pack. He wrapped Manilal completely in a wet sheet, put a wet towel on his head, and covered him with blankets. Then, leaving him in charge of Kasturbai, Gandhi went out for a short walk during which he kept repeating to himself in an agony of suspense, "My honor is in Thy keeping, oh Lord, in this hour of trial." On his return the boy had broken out into a profuse perspiration and his temperature was coming down. The next morning the danger had passed and he was on the road to recovery. Gandhi's obstinate adherence to his fads had been crowned with success. Certainly it seemed that God was on his side. For his own part he was sure that God had saved his honor.

A few months after settling in Bombay Gandhi received a cable from South Africa: "Chamberlain expected here. Please return immediately." He had promised to go back to South Africa if his presence was required there within a year. The call had come. Without hesitation he closed his office in Bombay and took the first available boat to South Africa. Thinking that he would not be detained there for more than a year, he left Kasturbai and the children in India.

Gandhi reached Durban at the close of 1902 and was immediately required to draft a memorial for submission to Mr. Chamberlain on behalf of the Indians of Natal and to accompany the deputation which waited on him. Mr. Chamberlain was not unsympathetic to their grievances, but bluntly told them that the Imperial Government could do little to modify the anti-Indian legislation of which they complained, since it had almost no control over a self-governing colony like Natal.

From Natal, Mr. Chamberlain proceeded to the Transvaal. Gandhi was asked to prepare a memorial for the Indians residing there and also to accompany their deputation. Because of the dislocation caused by the Boer War, a permit was required under the Peace Preservation Ordinance for entry into the Transvaal. Europeans could obtain permits without difficulty, but a separate Asiatic Department had recently been set up for dealing with the affairs of Indians, just as there was a special department for Africans, and permits were being issued to Indians only on the recommendation of this new department. Gandhi guessed that he would not get the necessary permit in time, and perhaps not at all, if he applied for it through these bureaucratic channels, so he enlisted the help of his old friend, Mr. Alexander, the Superintendent of Police in Durban, who prevailed upon the Permit Officer to issue him a permit, bypassing the Asiatic Department.

The officials of this department doubtless regarded Gandhi as a troublesome busybody and had probably intended to prevent his entry into the Transvaal, and were puzzled and chagrined at his arrival in Pretoria without their knowledge. But they had no power to send him back again, and could only gain a petty revenge by not allowing him to be a member of the deputation that was to meet Mr. Chamberlain on the grounds that Gandhi was not a local resident and that Mr. Chamberlain had already seen him in Durban. Another Indian barrister therefore had to be found to lead the deputation and to deliver the memorial Gandhi had drafted.

The task for which Gandhi had been summoned back to South Africa had now been completed and he was free to return to India, but he did not elect to do so. Although he was attracted by the prospect of public life in the wider field of India, he believed that the new Asiatic Department, far from protecting Indian interests in the Transvaal, was going to be a "frightful engine of oppression" and that the Indian community was in danger of being "hounded out of the country, besides being thoroughly robbed." For the present, therefore, he

felt that his work lay in South Africa and that he should estab-
lish himself in the Transvaal rather than, as before, in Natal.
He set up an office at Johannesburg, got himself enrolled in the
Transvaal Supreme Court, and, after a year, sent for his family.

At that time there were between ten and twelve thousand
Indians in the Transvaal. They had begun to enter the territory in the 1880's, but in 1885 the Boer Republic passed
a law that precluded them from holding land and enjoying
rights of citizenship and required them to register themselves at
a cost of twenty-five pounds. Under pressure from the British
Government, the registration fee was reduced to three pounds
and Indians were granted permission to acquire landed property
in a few limited and unfavorable locations, but their presence in
the Transvaal was very much on sufferance. They had been
abruptly expelled from the adjoining Orange Free State, and
President Kruger himself bluntly told the Transvaal Indians
that as descendants of Ishmael they were bound from birth to
slave for the descendants of Esau and must, therefore, be content with such rights as might be granted to them.

The Indians had expected that after the war, under British
administration, their position in the former Boer Republics
would be improved. Indian grievances had figured among the
alleged causes of the war and the British Agent at Pretoria had
often said that if the Transvaal became a British colony these
grievances would be redressed. The hopes thus aroused proved to
be illusory. The Europeans in the Transvaal, English as well as
Boer, were obsessed with the fear that the country would be
given over to "hordes of Asiatics," and they had no wish to
make conditions easier for Indian residents. The anti-Indian
legislation of the Boers not only remained on the statute book
but was enforced more rigorously than it had been under the
relatively lax Boer regimes; and the permit system, originally
justified as an emergency measure, was continued *sine die*, thus
placing a positive curb on Indian entry into the Transvaal which
had not previously existed.

The Indians at this time were really asking for very little. In a
memorial submitted in 1904, which may well have been drafted
by Gandhi himself, they agreed that the British should be the

dominant "race" in South Africa; they accepted the principle of restricting the influx of cheap labor; and they disclaimed any demand for political power. All they asked for was "freedom for those that are now settled and those that may be allowed to come in future to trade, to move about, and to hold landed property without any hindrance save the ordinary legal requirements; and . . . for abrogation of legislation that imposes disabilities on them because they wear a brown skin."

These modest requests deserved to be treated sympathetically, especially in view of the British Government's own professions and promises. But the Asiatic Department, which was responsible for the enforcement of laws affecting Indians, was lacking in imagination, bureaucratic in outlook, and also, it appears, deeply tainted with corruption.* Gandhi believed that at its hands Indians would be subjected to the maximum harassment, and perhaps would be squeezed out of the Transvaal altogether, and he was determined to resist such treatment. Ostensibly this was his reason for staying on in the Transvaal, but personal pique might have been part of his motivation: he had not forgotten his discomfiture by the Asiatic Department over the deputation to Mr. Chamberlain.

Gandhi's sojourn in the Transvaal lasted about eleven years and eventually brought him into direct and prolonged conflict with the Government, but several years elapsed before the battle was joined. During this period, besides practicing law and trying to mitigate the harshness of the Asiatic Department, he embarked on several other activities which, in slightly varying forms, were to occupy him for the rest of his life.

One of these was journalism. In 1904 he assisted a Gujarati friend in Durban, Shri Madanjit Vyaraharik, in publishing a weekly journal called *Indian Opinion,* in both English and Gujarati.† Gandhi was never actually the editor of the paper, but for a long time he financed it and was responsible for its policies. "Week after week," he says, "I poured out my soul in

* At Gandhi's insistence, two of its members were prosecuted for corruption and, although acquitted by a jury, were dismissed from service.
† At first it was also published in Hindi and Tamil.

its columns." Through these articles and the considerable correspondence they evoked, Gandhi extended his hold over the
Indian population in South Africa, and in the subsequent struggle with the Government, *Indian Opinion* played a crucial part,
keeping the progress of events and the issues involved prom-
inently before the Indian community. Indeed, Gandhi believed
that without it *satyagraha* * would have been impossible in
South Africa. *Indian Opinion* was the forerunner of other similar journals, for instance *Young India* and *Harijan*, which
Gandhi published later after his return to India, enabling him
to express his views, often original or eccentric, on a wide variety
of topics throughout the rest of his life.

Associated with *Indian Opinion* was another typically Gandhian project. At a vegetarian restaurant in Johannesburg where
he ate regularly, Gandhi became acquainted with a journalist,
H. S. L. Polak, who lent him a book by Ruskin, *Unto This Last*.
Gandhi was fascinated by it; it seemed to express his own deepest convictions, but it also suggested to him an idea that greatly
appealed to him—that the life of the tiller of the soil and the
handicraftsman is the life really worth living. He wanted to put
this idea to the test at once.

He read the book on his way to Durban to check on the
affairs of *Indian Opinion*. Albert West, who was the part owner
of a small printing concern and whom Gandhi had also met at
the vegetarian restaurant, had recently assumed charge of the
press where *Indian Opinion* was printed at a monthly salary of
ten pounds and a share of the profits. Mr. West had reported
that expenses were mounting and that, far from there being any
profits, a loss might be expected. On his arrival in Durban,
Gandhi, his mind full of *Unto This Last*, proposed to Mr.
West that they move the press to a farm where everyone would
do farm work for the same basic living wage of three pounds a
month and attend to the press and the publication of *Indian
Opinion* in their spare time. The good-natured Mr. West, who
might well have felt vexed at having been misled about the
profitability of *Indian Opinion*, readily agreed to take part in

* "Passive resistance," literally "truth-firmness." Also see page
52.

this seemingly harebrained venture.

Gandhi advertised for land near a railway station and succeeded in acquiring a hundred acres at Phoenix, about fourteen miles from Durban, for one thousand pounds. The press was installed in a large shed and from 1904 on *Indian Opinion* was regularly produced and published at Phoenix. The land was divided into three-acre plots and allotted to settlers, all of whom were expected to learn typesetting. Gandhi took one of the plots, and after the outbreak of the Zulu rebellion in 1906 his family lived there for some time. At first he had planned to retire gradually from his law practice and support himself at the Phoenix settlement by manual labor, but other activities proved more attractive and he—the originator and founder—only stayed there for short periods. A number of his relatives and friends, however, who had come to South Africa to try their luck, settled there, as did Mr. West, who looked after the press on a monthly allowance of three pounds instead of the ten-pound salary originally promised to him. And Mr. Polak, who was delighted with the results of lending Ruskin's book to Gandhi, also settled at Phoenix for a while.

Phoenix was the first of several centers at which, over the next forty years, groups of Gandhi's disciples or co-workers, as he called them, gathered together to live an austere and strenuous community life, devoted to some form of work or activity of which Gandhi approved.

One of Gandhi's lifelong avocations was nursing the sick, and an outbreak of plague in an unsanitary Indian "location" in Johannesburg not long after he had settled in that city afforded him an opportunity of practicing it. His service at this time and his public castigation of the municipality for its negligence aroused interest among Europeans as well as Indians, and was the direct cause of his restaurant acquaintances, Mr. West and Mr. Polak, seeking closer association with him.

A further opportunity for nursing came in 1906 with the outbreak of the Zulu rebellion. Gandhi at that time still believed that "the British empire existed for the welfare of the world," so once again he offered the authorities the services of an Indian ambulance unit. This time the Governor of Natal

promptly accepted the offer. Gandhi was given the temporary
rank of sergeant major and, with a staff of twenty-four, was on
active service for over a month. Although Gandhi was voluntarily serving the Government out of "a genuine sense of loyalty," his "heart was with the Zulus" (as it had been with the
Boers), and he was delighted that the main work of his unit
was nursing wounded Zulus. Most of them had not been
wounded in battle, but were suspects who had been arrested
and severely flogged which resulted in sores that festered. Gandhi's unit filled a real need, as Europeans were disinclined to
dress the wounds of the Zulus. The unit was mentioned in
dispatches and each member was awarded a medal.

During the weeks spent nursing the Zulus Gandhi began to
feel that service to humanity—such as he was then engaged
in—was inconsistent with the pleasures of family life and the
propagation and rearing of children. For instance, he could not
have gone off with his ambulance unit to nurse the Zulus if
Kasturbai had been expecting a baby. He resolved, therefore, to
take a vow that he had long been thinking about—the vow to
observe *brahmacharya* * for life. As soon as the ambulance work
was finished he went to the Phoenix settlement and discussed
the merits of this vow with some of his co-workers there, who,
on the whole, applauded his intention. Kasturbai, the one person most immediately affected, was not consulted at all until it
was time to take the vow, but she raised no objection. Gandhi
himself had great difficulty in making the final resolve. "The
elimination of carnal relationship with one's wife seemed a
strange thing," he tells us, "but I launched forth with faith in
the sustaining power of God." The vow was taken at Phoenix in
1906.

During his years in the Transvaal Gandhi continued his dietetic experiments. He read of the formation of a "No Breakfast Association" in Manchester, was intrigued by the idea, and
decided to give up breakfast himself. At one time he gave up
salt and legumes for one year and dragooned Kasturbai, who
was ill, into doing the same as a means of recovery. He wrote an

---

* Conduct that leads one to God; hence self-restraint, and, particularly, mastery of one's sexual desires.

account of these dietetic experiments which appeared as a series of Gujarati articles in *Indian Opinion* and were subsequently published as a booklet titled "Guide to Health." After he had taken the vow of *brahmacharya* he no longer pursued his dietetic experiments on the grounds of health or vegetarianism, but on the basis of a *brahmachari:* Now what diet is most conducive to the keeping of that vow? Complete fasting at regular intervals was, he found, an aid to self-restraint, and he began to accustom himself to such fasts. Six years of experimentation convinced him that milk was superfluous and stimulated animal passions, and that the *brahmachari's* ideal food is fresh fruit and nuts. This was the diet he adopted some years later, because he found that "restraint of the sexual and other passions becomes easy for a man who lives on such food." In 1912 he took a positive vow to give up milk altogether, partly because he felt it was unnecessary and partly because he had read somewhere that cows in Calcutta were subjected to the most cruel treatment in order to extract the last drop of milk from them. But this vow, although he had adhered to it against great pressure when he was ill with pleurisy in England, ultimately proved to be an occasion for his faltering in his resolve. Some years later in India when he was seriously ill and the doctors advised him to drink milk, he beguiled himself into thinking that his vow applied only to cow's milk and buffalo's milk but not to goat's milk, and so he began drinking goat's milk.

It is an odd coincidence that the Zulu rebellion which afforded Gandhi an opportunity of serving the Government of Natal "out of a genuine sense of loyalty" immediately preceded his first open defiance of the neighboring and kindred Government of the Transvaal. It also appears to have been a coincidence, although a more appropriate one, that the vow of *brahmacharya* was taken just when he was about to embark on a long career of public service—or political agitation—which could not fail to be disruptive of family life, and, in his own words, demanded self-purification. The remainder of Gandhi's life in South Africa—that is, from the end of 1906 to 1914—was intimately bound up with the *satyagraha* struggle.

V

Satyagraha:
First Phase

It was the policy of the British Administration to limit strictly the entry of new Indian immigrants into the Transvaal. A first essential was the effective registration of existing Indian residents so that newcomers could not slip into the country by pretending to be someone else. The permits initially issued by the British Administration to Indian residents, bearing the signature or thumbprint of the holder, were felt to be insufficient, and it was decided that Indians should be required under the Peace Preservation Ordinance to take out new permits which would include more details and also a photograph. The Indian community objected to these new regulations, but were eventually persuaded to reregister and to take out permits in the new form.

This reregistration was substantially completed by 1906, but the authorities were still dissatisfied. They felt that the existing laws did not adequately prevent the surreptitious infiltration of Indians into the Transvaal or provide for deporting unauthorized residents. In order to close all loopholes they decided to introduce new legislation. A draft of the Asiatic Law Amendment Ordinance was published in the Transvaal Government *Gazette* at about the time Gandhi was released from his ambulance work. It caused a commotion among Indians in the Transvaal, and they sent letters and telegrams to Gandhi urging him to come there at once. As soon as he was free, he hastened to Johannesburg, read through the draft ordinance carefully, and translated it into Gujarati for *Indian Opinion*. He was aghast at the stringency of its provisions and thought that if it was meekly accepted it "would spell absolute ruin for the Indians in South Africa."

Under the proposed ordinance every Asiatic—man, woman, and child—above the age of eight who was entitled to reside in the Transvaal was required to surrender his old permit and obtain a new certificate of registration from the Registrar of Asiatics who, besides recording particulars of caste, age, and so forth, would take the applicant's fingerprints and note important marks of identification. Anyone failing to register would forfeit his right of residence and render himself liable to fine, imprisonment, or deportation. Certificates of registration were required to be produced on demand by the police, who were also empowered to enter private houses to inspect certificates, and the certificates could also be demanded in courts and government offices. Failure or refusal to produce a certificate on demand was made an offense punishable with fine and imprisonment.

Gandhi said that he had never known legislation of this nature being directed against free men in any part of the world. This may have been so, but by present-day standards the legislation was not very harsh. The powers given to the police could, of course, be used to harass Indians, even to the point of making them leave the country. Gandhi certainly thought that this was the intention. In his view the legislation was "designed to strike at the very root of [Indian] existence in South Africa," and he argued that an Indian trader, with assets running into thousands of pounds, could be deported and faced with ruin under the ordinance. These fears appear to have been exaggerated. There was no reason why a bona fide Indian resident in possession of a valid permit should ever have been troubled at all. It seems unlikely that the authorities had any other object than to make absolutely certain that further influx of Indians into the Transvaal would be effectively controlled and unauthorized residents detected and expelled. They knew by experience how likely it was for Asiatics to evade regulations, and they were determined to make such evasion impossible.

Though their intentions may not have been as sinister as Gandhi imagined, the timing and some of the details of the ordinance showed great want of tact. Gandhi himself, always quick to resent as insulting treatment that most of his compatriots in South Africa were prepared to accept without protest, objected strongly to the compulsory fingerprinting, as though, he said, all Indians were criminals. Others did not feel so keenly about this, but all were aggrieved at being required to register themselves again, so soon after they had just done so, and, since many Indian women were in *purdah*, there was widespread indignation because the ordinance applied to women as well as men. Gandhi fanned the general discontent. At a small meeting of leading Indians he said the ordinance was humiliating not only to Indians in South Africa but to India, and declared that it was the first step toward hounding them out of South Africa altogether. At a subsequent public meeting held on September 11, 1906, all those present solemnly swore not to submit to the "Black Ordinance" if it became law, and to suffer all the consequent penalties. The community's enthusiasm, according to Gandhi, "knew no bounds."

There was, however, no immediate occasion to proceed to extremes. The "Black Ordinance" was not yet law and, under Gandhi's guidance, the Indians resolved to exhaust all legal and constitutional methods open to them to prevent it becoming so. Memorials were addressed to the local government and a deputation met with the minister concerned. He promised to exempt women from the provisions of the ordinance, but, with this exception, it was passed very much as originally drafted. The Government claimed to have exempted women on its own initiative, independently of the Indian agitation. The Indians believed that the exemption was a result of their firm stand and were all the more encouraged in their attitude of defiance.

Constitutional remedies, however, were not yet exhausted, for in 1906 the Transvaal did not enjoy responsible government. It was still a Crown Colony, and the royal assent to its legislative measures was by no means a formality, but might be withheld. A deputation consisting of Gandhi and a Muslim, H. O. Ali, was therefore sent to England to present a memorial to the Secretary of State for the Colonies, urging that assent to the ordinance be withheld. Before leaving for England Gandhi requested leading Indians to pledge themselves again—this time in writing—not to submit to the ordinance. He thought that this evidence of the determination of the Indian community would have some weight with the Secretary of State. Many signed the pledge, but quite a few of those who had orally sworn to resist the ordinance hesitated to give a pledge in writing.

Gandhi and Mr. Ali spent about six weeks in England. They saw Lord Elgin, a former Viceroy of India, who was at that time Secretary of State for the Colonies, and Lord Morley, Secretary of State for India, and they interviewed Members of Parliament and other influential persons. They were everywhere sympathetically received, and Lord Elgin appeared to be friendly, although he made no immediate decision on their case. However, during their return journey they received a cable at Madeira intimating that Lord Elgin had advised the King not to assent to the ordinance.

Their satisfaction at this good news was short-lived, for they soon discovered that the disallowance of the ordinance was little better than a fraud. On January 1, 1907, the Transvaal was granted responsible government and ceased to be a Crown Colony. Lord Elgin had made it clear to its political leaders that if the newly constituted Transvaal legislature passed a new bill in exactly the same terms as the ordinance he would not be able to advise His Majesty to withhold assent. So a new bill was introduced in March 1907, hurried through the new Parliament at a single sitting, and duly received the formal sanction of the Crown. The "Black Ordinance" had become the Black Act, effective from July 1. It required Indians to apply for registration by July 31.

The Indian community now had to make plans for carrying out their pledge not to submit to this legislation. Gandhi had at first described the movement he was about to inaugurate as "passive resistance," but he soon became dissatisfied with this description. He disliked an essentially Indian movement being known by an English name, and he discovered that the term "passive resistance" gave rise to what seemed to him to be "terrible misunderstanding." At a public meeting in Johannesburg a Mr. Hoskens, a European sympathizer, had spoken of passive resistance as a "weapon of the weak" to which Indians, having failed to secure redress by other means, were compelled to resort, because they were few in number and without arms and without votes. Gandhi contradicted this interpretation of the movement. He denied that the Indians were weak or passive and defined their passive resistance as "soul-force," which is far stronger than brute, physical force.

A prize was offered in *Indian Opinion* for the best suggestion for a name for the movement. The word *"sadagraha,"* meaning firmness in a good cause, was judged the best suggestion, but Gandhi adopted a slightly different word, *"satyagraha,"* the meaning of which he explained as follows: "Truth (*satya*) implies love, and firmness (*agraha*) engenders and therefore serves as a synonym for force. I thus began to call the Indian movement 'Satyagraha,' that is to say, the Force which is born of Truth and Love or non-violence."

Gandhi was at pains to make clear that *satyagraha* differs from passive resistance in that it abjures physical force altogether, not just from expediency but as a matter of principle. In ordinary passive resistance, physical force is eschewed because it appears to offer no hope of success, but it might be used if suitable occasion arose for it. In *satyagraha* physical force is altogether forbidden even in the most favorable circumstances. Gandhi maintained that *satyagraha* also differed from passive resistance because in the latter there is always present the idea of harassing the other party, whereas "in *satyagraha* there is not the remotest idea of injuring the opponent. *Satyagraha* postulates the conquest of the adversary by suffering in one's own person."

These somewhat esoteric distinctions meant a great deal to Gandhi. Brought up from childhood on the doctrine of *ahimsa,* his own reflections on moral problems had confirmed his belief in its cardinal importance. Nonviolence and the avoidance of hurt to another were therefore of the essence of *satyagraha* as he conceived it. But he admitted that the *satyagraha* which he described was an ideal. He depicted it as it ought to be, not as it proved to be. Few *satyagrahis* lived up to the ideal, and so there was not much practical significance in the distinction which he sought to draw between *satyagraha* and passive resistance. It is, in any case, hard to see how the conduct of *satyagrahis* could fail in practice to be harassing to those who opposed them, even if such harassment was in no way deliberately intended. As for Mr. Hoskens' remarks, they seem to have contained at least a grain or two of truth. For Gandhi, while maintaining that the weakness of Indians had nothing to do with the organization of *satyagraha,* admitted that if they had possessed arms or the franchise, they would probably not have resorted to it.

The first move made by the Indians in defiance of the Black Act conformed to the principles of *satyagraha* in letter and spirit, but it also revealed how easily the purity of *satyagraha* might be tainted. Registration offices were opened on July 1, 1907. Volunteers were organized to picket these offices and politely request any weak-kneed Indians who might be inclined to apply for permits not to do so, and to hand them a printed paper explaining the injuries which submission to the Black Act would entail. Each volunteer was also instructed to behave politely and respectfully to the police if they tried to interfere with the picketing.

Everywhere the approved volunteers worked "with boundless enthusiasm." But a number of Indians also appeared who were not authorized volunteers and who privately intimidated persons who were willing to take out permits. This was to Gandhi "a most painful development" and steps were taken to stop it, but without complete success.

Polite, peaceful picketing, along with some measure of intimidation, achieved its purpose. The last date originally fixed for registration, July 31, was extended from time to time, but by November 30, which was the date finally fixed, only about five hundred Indians had registered. The authorities believed that a considerable number, knowing that they were illegally resident in the Transvaal, had quietly slipped away. Even so, it was reckoned that about nine thousand had deliberately refused to register as required by law.

Such determined resistance by the Indians had not been expected. To Lord Selborne, the British High Commissioner in South Africa, it appeared ominous. Educated Africans were watching the struggle and might well perceive that they had "an instrument in their hands—that is, combination and passive resistance—of which they had not previously thought." What would happen if large numbers of Africans began to use this instrument? And what could the Transvaal Government do with even the few thousand Indians who had so resolutely refused to register? They decided to make arrests. To begin with they arrested a man named Ram Sundara, a person of no consequence who turned out to be a runaway indentured laborer, and sentenced him to one month's imprisonment. This brought no advantage to the Government. Not a single additional Indian applied for registration and Ram Sundara, on release, was congratulated and fêted.

General Smuts, the minister primarily responsible for dealing with the Indian agitation, now decided "to strike at the head, not at the tail." Orders were given to proceed against the leaders and in Christmas week of 1907 Gandhi and a number of prominent Indians, together with a Mr. Quinn, the leader of the small Chinese community, were called upon to show cause why, having failed to apply for registration, they should not be ordered to leave the Transvaal. All of them were duly ordered by the magistrate to leave within specified periods and on failure to comply were brought before him again and sentenced to varying terms of imprisonment. Gandhi himself received the comparatively mild sentence of two months' imprisonment, although he requested the magistrate to award him at least the three-month sentence with hard labor and a heavy fine that had been imposed on some of the others.

During January the number of *satyagrahi* prisoners rose to over 150 and seemed likely to go higher, for neither the Government nor the Indians were as yet by any means exhausted. For some time, however, Smuts had been under pressure from Lord Selborne and influential friends in England and South Africa to reach a settlement with the Indians, and soon after Gandhi's imprisonment he opened negotiations through Albert Cartwright, editor of the Transvaal *Leader*, with Indian leaders who were still at liberty. They expressed a desire for a compromise, but said that its terms must be settled with Gandhi. They also sent a message to Gandhi that he should accept any suitable compromise. Mr. Cartwright came to see Gandhi in jail and reached a provisional settlement with him, the substance of which was:

1. Indians over the age of sixteen should register voluntarily within three months instead of under the compulsion of the act;
2. the details to be entered in the registration certificates should be settled in consultation with the Indian community, and exemption from fingerprinting should be allowed for certain classes;
3. the provisions of the act should not be applied to those who so registered, but their voluntary registration should, if necessary, be validated.

A letter embodying these terms—signed by Gandhi and by the Chinese leader, Mr. Quinn—was conveyed to Smuts on January 28, 1908. Smuts felt able to accept the terms and arranged for Gandhi to be brought from jail to see him at Pretoria. Their meeting was cordial. Smuts congratulated Gandhi on the firmness shown by the Indians. He said that the Europeans wanted the law (the Black Act), but that he accepted the proposed settlement, and added, according to Gandhi, that he had also consulted General Botha and would repeal the Asiatic Act as soon as most of the Indians in South Africa had registered voluntarily. Further, he said he would send Gandhi a copy of

the bill legalizing such registration for Gandhi's criticism, and
he hoped there would be no more trouble. "I wish to respect
the feelings of your people," he concluded.

Gandhi himself was released then and there and proceeded
straight from General Smuts' office to Johannesburg. The remaining prisoners were released the next morning. A meeting
was immediately held to explain the settlement to the Indian
community, where it was criticized a good deal because nothing
they had been fighting for appeared to have been gained. The
Black Act had not been repealed; there was only a promise that
it would be. A small group of Pathans were particularly critical.
Would they have to be fingerprinted under the settlement?
they asked. Gandhi replied equivocally, "Yes and no." He intended to allow himself to be fingerprinted and thought everyone should do so, but there would be no compulsion on those
who had any conscientious objection. The Pathans were not
satisfied. How did his present attitude square with all that had
gone before? He had made a great fuss about the fingerprints,
saying that they were only required of criminals and that the
struggle centered around them, yet now they were expected to
give them. Gandhi replied that it would have been a sin to give
them under the terms of the Black Act, but to do so in the
altered circumstances was "the hall-mark of a gentleman."

These Hindu subtleties were beyond the comprehension of
the Pathans. They concluded that Gandhi had been bribed by
General Smuts—a sum of fifteen thousand pounds was mentioned—and declared that they would allow neither themselves
nor anyone else to be fingerprinted, and would kill the first man
who applied for registration. In spite of this outburst, the settlement was ratified with only two Pathan dissentients.

The Registrar of Asiatics was soon ready to begin registrations
under the new voluntary arrangement. A new form of certificate had been devised in consultation with the *satyagrahis*.
In order to set a good example, Gandhi and a few prominent
Indians decided to be the first to register themselves. On their
way to the Registrar's office one of the Pathans, Mir Alam, an
old client of Gandhi's, met them and asked them where they
were going. Gandhi replied that they were going to take out

certificates of registration and that he himself intended to give
his ten fingerprints. He had scarcely finished speaking when he
was struck a heavy blow on the head from behind and, with the
words "*He Rama*" (O God!), fell unconscious to the ground.

He was picked up and carried to a nearby office where he
recovered consciousness and agreed to be taken to the house of
a friend and staunch supporter, the Reverend J. Doke, a Bap-
tist minister. Though in considerable pain, he insisted on being
the first to register, and the Registrar brought the papers to the
house. A doctor stitched up the wounds on Gandhi's cheek and
lip and said there was no serious injury and that he would be all
right in about a week. Gandhi issued a reassuring statement to
the Indian community, requesting them not to prosecute his
assailants and bidding the Hindus not to take it amiss that the
assault was committed by Muslims. Before he lay down to rest
the Dokes' little daughter stood at the door of his room and
sang to him his favorite English hymn, "Lead Kindly Light."

So, on this rather sanctimonious note, all ended happily, except that, contrary to Gandhi's wishes, Mir Alam and one of his
Pathan companions were prosecuted by the Government and
sentenced to three months' imprisonment with hard labor.

Criticism of the settlement was not confined to the Transvaal. Indians in Natal, though not directly affected, were also
critical, as Gandhi learned from correspondence reaching him
through *Indian Opinion*. As soon as he had recovered from his
injuries, he went to Durban—his family was in Phoenix—and
sought to remove misunderstandings by holding public meetings and writing articles for *Indian Opinion*. He was unable
to conciliate the Pathan element, which heckled him severely
in Durban, but with few exceptions the Transvaal Indians accepted the settlement and by the middle of May almost all of
them had voluntarily registered. The Indians had kept their
side of the bargain.

But now came another shock. General Smuts introduced into
the legislature a bill validating the voluntary registrations and
removing from the purview of the Black Act those who had
voluntarily registered, but not repealing the act itself. Gandhi
was astounded. He regarded the failure to repeal the act as a

clear breach of faith. Smuts flatly denied the accusation.

Here was fresh ammunition for Gandhi's critics. That it did not prove fatal to his prestige as a leader is a testimony to his personality and to the confidence and affection he inspired. His critics taunted him with credulity. He replied that what they called credulity was trust—trust that we should all have in our fellow men. In this instance the trust had proved misplaced, but who can prevent an adversary from breaking faith? They must now patiently consider how to resume the struggle, if the Government persisted in its refusal to repeal the Black Act.

Was Smuts guilty of a breach of faith? Undoubtedly Gandhi thought so at the time. But writing of these events about fifteen years later, he added a question mark to a chapter headed "General Smuts' Breach of Faith" and said: "I have placed a mark of interrogation after the phrase, as in point of fact the General's action did not perhaps amount to an intentional breach of faith." Defenders of Smuts can take their stand on the letter of January 28, signed by Gandhi and Mr. Quinn, which was the basis of the settlement. This letter contained no stipulation that the act should be repealed—its terms, in fact, implied exactly the contrary. On the other hand, Gandhi certainly was given the impression, either by Cartwright or by Smuts himself when he saw him at Pretoria, that the act *would* be repealed. It seems, indeed, probable that Smuts hoped and intended to repeal it and, without making any definite promise, said so to Gandhi, but later found himself unable to carry out his intention. The repeal of the act was bound up in Smuts' mind with another act, the Transvaal Immigration Act, which had been passed in 1907 soon after the Black Act, but to which the Indians had, at first, raised no objection. This act, though couched in general terms, was chiefly directed against Indians and in a roundabout way barred any new Indian immigrants. Smuts seems to have thought that once all existing Indian residents had been safely registered, the Black Act could be repealed and thereafter everything would be taken care of by the Immigration Act. But difficulties arose. A vital provision of the Immigration Act contained a reference to the Asiatic (Black) Act and would become ineffective in securing the

total prohibition of Indian immigration if that act were itself to
be repealed. This situation gave rise to a further difficulty. The
Indians, realizing that if the Black Act were repealed the Immigration Act would also lose its sting, did not initially include its
repeal or modification in their demands. Later they thought
that their silence might be misconstrued as implying their consent to a total bar of new Indian immigration. They therefore
decided that removal of such a total bar should also be covered
by the *satyagraha* movement and began to protest to the Government against the Immigration Act also. This greatly annoyed
General Smuts and made him declare that Gandhi was very
"cunning" and that there was no limit to his demands. This
annoyance hardened his attitude toward the Indians and contributed to his determination not to repeal the Black Act as he
had at one time contemplated.

Gandhi's feeling at the time that Smuts had deceived him on
the main issue—the repeal of the Black Act—seems to have
been due to a misunderstanding. But at bottom there was an
irreconcilable difference between them. Smuts and the Europeans were bent on stopping all new Indian immigration. Gandhi wanted educated Indians, with a good knowledge of English, to be treated more or less on a par with Europeans and
admitted into the country in reasonable numbers, a desire
prompted by feelings of national pride and self-respect. Why
should the Indian be penalized for his brown skin, if otherwise
he was as good as the European? This constant, unvarying
appeal to Indian pride was expressive of his own deep-seated
national feeling, and was also the secret of his success.

Gandhi resented Smuts' charge against him of submitting
new demands, for he claimed that it had been a point of principle to confine *satyagraha* to the demands in view at the beginning. "The minimum," he said, "is also the maximum." In
practice, however, he countenanced so many deviations from
this principle that to others it appeared to lose all significance.
Gandhi attributed the extension of the area of a *satyagraha*
struggle to the natural progress of events and the mistakes of
the Government rather than to himself. He defended his stand
by comparing *satyagraha* with the Ganges:

. . . as a *satyagraha* struggle progresses onward, many another element helps to swell its current, and there is a constant growth in the results to which it leads. . . . But I must explain how the law of progression comes into play when the minimum is also the maximum as in *satyagraha*. The Ganga does not leave its course in search of tributaries. Even so does the *satyagrahi* not leave his path which is sharp as the sword's edge. But as the tributaries spontaneously join the Ganga as it advances, so it is with the river that is *satyagraha*.

Probably Smuts—like most other people—would not have been able to appreciate the cogency of this comparison any more than the Pathans had understood why registration was one day a crime and the next day the mark of a gentleman. But Gandhi himself believed that he adhered rigidly to his principle of the minimum being the maximum.

VI ᕲ

Satyagraha:

Second Phase

The stage was now set for the resumption of the struggle. The first step taken by Gandhi was to send General Smuts a letter—described by Smuts as an "ultimatum"—stating that if the Government failed to communicate by a specified date its decision to repeal the Asiatic Act, the Indians would burn their registration certificates and "humbly but firmly take the consequences."

There was much discussion among the Indians as to whether it was politic to send such a letter. Although quite courteous in language it was strong and determined in tone. Would it not be regarded as insolent and only stiffen the Government's attitude? Gandhi was prepared to take the risk. He attached importance to the letter as it symbolized for him that "a slave was no longer saluting a master."

In renewing the struggle after it had been called off, Gandhi was at a disadvantage, for enthusiasm had to be rekindled. This was to some extent achieved by the ceremonial burning of certificates. A large African cauldron was set up in the grounds of

the Hamidia mosque in Johannesburg and on the afternoon of
August 16, 1908, before a huge gathering of Indians more than
two thousand registration certificates were thrown into this
cauldron and set ablaze amid resounding cheers. The corre-
spondent of the London *Daily Mail* compared the event to the
Boston Tea Party.

This defiant conflagration caused some temporary excitement
and enthusiasm. But in seeking to maintain the momentum of
the movement Gandhi was at another serious disadvantage, as
he was himself aware. "Merely burning the certificates," he told
his audience, "is no crime, and will not enable those who court
imprisonment to win it." Now that most Indians in the Transvaal had voluntarily registered themselves and been taken out of
the purview of the Black Act, defiance of it was possible on only
a limited and not a mass scale. Transvaal Indians who had
burned their certificates could court arrest in two ways. In order
to obtain a hawker's license it was necessary for an Indian to
show his registration certificate, so those who had burned theirs
could court arrest by hawking without a license. Alternatively
they could cross over into Natal and hope to be arrested by re-
entering the Transvaal without having any certificate to show.
But only small numbers could court arrest in this way, and the
authorities were liable to ignore them.

Another device, now that *satyagraha* also covered the Immigration Act, was to persuade English-educated Indians living in
Natal to violate that act by entering the Transvaal without
permission and refusing to leave it when ordered to do so. But
obviously only a very small number of Indians were prepared to
leave their businesses or professions in Natal for the sake of a
few months' imprisonment in the Transvaal.

While in some cases the Transvaal Government simply ignored the *satyagrahis,* in others they had recourse to a form of
punishment that was highly deterrent. The Asiatic Act and the
Immigration Act provided three penalties: fine, imprisonment,
and deportation. Deportation to neighboring African territories
held no great terrors, but deportation to India was a very different matter. India had become a strange land to many of the ex-
indentured laborers, while the more prosperous Indians, who

might accept with equanimity the martyrdom of a month or two in jail, were not at all keen to risk the forced abandonment of their businesses and property in South Africa. The Transvaal Government deported a large batch of *satyagrahis* to India as deck passengers, and though because of legal and other objections this policy could not be continued for long, the threat of such deportation had a demoralizing effect. This, combined with the difficulty and apparent futility of courting arrest, soon reduced the *satyagrahis* to a small band of stalwarts.

Gandhi himself underwent a second term of imprisonment, and during the next four years devoted most of his energies to maintaining a flicker of life in the movement. Only his persistence, his obstinate faith in himself and his cause, and his organizing ability saved it from petering out altogether. He himself admits that there were not enough *satyagrahis* to put up a strong fight and that he and his small band of faithful followers began to be looked upon as "fools." To the Government they were only a minor irritant.

Meanwhile, there were important political changes in South Africa. In 1909 discussions took place in London which led to the passage of the Union of South Africa Act in September of that year. Gandhi felt that Union would reinforce the anti-Indian tendencies of the individual colonies and that consequently the Indians would be worse off than before. It was resolved that a two-man deputation composed of Gandhi, who had finished serving his sentence, and a Muslim, Seth Haji Habib, should be sent to London to voice the interests of South African Indians, although Gandhi feared that "their small voice [would be] drowned in the loud roar of British and Boer lions."

Through the good offices of Lord Ampthill, an ex-Governor of Madras, Gandhi and his colleague were able to exert a certain amount of pressure on Botha and Smuts, who were anxious to be well thought of by the British. They made some practical concessions on details to the Indian community, but on their main principle, racial discrimination, they stood firm. They were not willing to amend the Immigration Act or to repeal the Asiatic Act.

Gandhi's Muslim colleague, who, on Gandhi's own admission, represented the majority, including the wealthier members of the Indian community, accepted the concessions for the present and said that he would, if necessary, fight for the principle later on. Gandhi said that he and his handful of *satyagrahis* were more interested in principle than in practical relief and would fight on for the repeal of the Asiatic Act and "hope to soften General Botha's heart by their self-suffering."

Gandhi returned to South Africa in November 1909 and during the voyage composed a pamphlet entitled "Hind Swaraj" (Indian Home Rule), "in order to demonstrate the sublimity of *satyagraha*." This pamphlet, which ranged over a fairly wide field, much of it far removed from South African *satyagraha*, is of importance as the first comprehensive, coherent expression of certain basic ideas that Gandhi never lost sight of throughout his subsequent political career. The core of the pamphlet is a denunciation of European civilization as representing a turning away from God to purely material values. Indian civilization, Gandhi claimed, was far superior to European, and *swaraj* did not mean, as most contemporary national leaders imagined, "English rule without the Englishmen" but "self-rule or self-control." This, rather than the pursuit of material ends, was the value that had been preserved and transmitted through India's long history, and this was the ideal at which India should aim. The pamphlet appeared in dialogue form in *Indian Opinion* and revealed Gandhi as primarily an idealist and moral reformer and only secondarily a politician.

Gandhi was aware on his return to South Africa that he was very much in a minority. Though he said that he was quite indifferent to the numerical strength of the *satyagrahis* and that his small party of "fools" or cranks had full faith in God, in their cause, and in the righteousness of the means they had selected to promote it, he went through a period of despondency. He was especially worried about finances. Funds were urgently required to support the families of *satyagrahis*, whose life of intermittent imprisonment precluded them from earning a regular livelihood.

A timely donation of twenty-five thousand rupees by the Parsee industrialist Sir Jamshedpur Tata restored his spirits and provided amply for immediate needs. He was dissatisfied, however, with the payment of monthly allowances to *satyagrahi* families, as this appeared to him to be an opportunity for fraud and injustice. He resolved, therefore, that they should all live together as members of a sort of cooperative commonwealth. But where could he find a suitable place for such a settlement? Phoenix, three hundred miles away, was too far; he needed some place in the Transvaal. A well-to-do German sympathizer named Kallenbach, an architect, came to his aid by donating, free of rent, an eleven-hundred-acre farm, abundantly stocked with fruit trees, only twenty-one miles from Johannesburg.

Here Gandhi gathered together his small band of faithful *satyagrahis*, had them build simple houses for themselves under Mr. Kallenbach's direction, and organized them into a more or less self-supporting vegetarian community. He had recently been in correspondence with Tolstoy and called the settlement Tolstoy Farm. The *satyagrahis*' families and, when they weren't in jail, the *satyagrahis* themselves worked on the farm and engaged in such activities as carpentry and sandal making. Gandhi, who learned to make sandals and later, in jail, made a pair for General Smuts, was altogether in his element. With his customary zest he attended to the sanitary arrangements of the settlement; he started a coeducational school for the children of the *satyagrahis* and along with Mr. Kallenbach bore the main burden of the teaching; he continued his dietetic experiments, with many of the *satyagrahis* as willing collaborators—it was at this time that he gave up milk and persuaded Mr. Kallenbach to do likewise; and he indulged to the full his skill as a "quack" doctor. Every evening prayers were read at the farm and hymns sung in English, Hindi, or Gujarati.

Thus the *satyagrahi* stalwarts, whose numbers Gandhi later reckoned at a maximum of sixty-six and a minimum of sixteen, settled down to a peaceful routine on Tolstoy Farm. Now and then they went to jail, but for long periods they showed no marked inclination to get themselves arrested, nor were the police anxious to arrest them. Critics said that they were sick of going to jail and were simply "enjoying themselves in their fruit garden away from the roar and din of cities." Gandhi, with the advantage of hindsight, maintained that by their peacefulness and self-restraint they were preparing themselves for "war" and that Tolstoy Farm "proved to be a centre of spiritual purification and penance for the final campaign." However this may be, it is probably true that the final mass phase of the struggle would have been impossible without the "elite" group of *satyagrahis* who had been trained at Tolstoy Farm.

The *satyagrahis'* uneventful existence was pleasantly broken in the autumn of 1912 by a visit to South Africa of Gokhale, who was at this time a member of the Viceroy's Legislative Council. Gandhi had been in constant correspondence with him all these years and had long been requesting him to come and study conditions on the spot. His visit was undertaken with the full concurrence of the Secretary of State for India and the Union Government of South Africa. Gandhi arranged his program and accompanied him throughout his tour, and everywhere Gokhale was given red-carpet receptions by both Europeans and Indians. Gokhale had intended to address Indian meetings in English since he had only a poor command of Hindustani, and his own mother tongue, Marathi, was known to very few Indians in South Africa, but Gandhi, always intensely nationalistic in the matter of language, persuaded him to address Indians in Marathi.

Gokhale's visit culminated in a two-hour meeting with Botha, Smuts, and other ministers of the Union Government. Gandhi briefed him on all the problems to be discussed, but did not accompany him to the meeting. The talks were cordial and constructive, and when they were over Gokhale told Gandhi that everything had been satisfactorily settled. The Black Act was to be repealed, the restriction of Asian immigration was to be based explicitly on social and economic grounds and not on race, and even the old grievance of the three-pound annual poll tax on ex-indentured Indians in Natal was to be removed. Gandhi expressed skepticism, but Gokhale assured him that all this would happen and told him that he must return to India within a year, as the problems of Indians in South Africa had been solved.

Gokhale's confidence was to some extent justified. The Union Government, which took over from the provinces responsibility for Indian affairs, repealed the Black Act and modified the immigration restrictions. The original objectives of *satyagraha* were thus secured. But the three-pound tax was not abolished. Gandhi claimed that failure to abolish it was a breach of pledge. It was to his advantage to make this claim, for it provided him "with the welcome opportunity of including the despicable impost as a cause of 'war.'" With the abolition of the tax as a plank in his platform it was possible to revive his moribund *satyagraha* and give it the character of a mass movement. He began to prepare for a fresh and more intense campaign and wrote to Gokhale that the Indians in South Africa "would fight unto death and wring a repeal of the tax out of the . . . unwilling . . . Government."

Gandhi's belief that there had been a breach of pledge was no doubt genuine, and it received a certain amount of support from Gokhale's own statements; but Gokhale himself seems to have admitted in the end that Botha and Smuts did not actually promise or pledge themselves to abolish the tax. They assured him that they would give most favorable consideration to his views on the subject and that they intended, if possible, to repeal the tax, but said that they would first have to consult members of Parliament from Natal. When this was done, there was found to considerable opposition, and so they gave up their original intention.

Satyagrahis, according to Gandhi, "would never go beyond the objective fixed when the fight began" or, as he put it in a passage already quoted, "in *satyagraha* the minimum is also the maximum." How then could he justify including the repeal of the three-pound tax among the objectives of *satyagraha* initiated only for the repeal of the Black Act? He had justified including the amendment of the Immigration Act among its objectives on the ground that this was new anti-Indian legislation enacted *after* the Black Act. But the three-pound tax had been paid ever since 1895! Gandhi explained that the minimum that was also a maximum could be expanded if, in the course of the struggle, the Government broke a promise, especially a

promise made to such a representative of India as Gokhale, for
such a breach constituted an insult to the whole of India.

Gandhi was a great stickler for his own principles, but he was
the sole interpreter of them, and his interpretation often
showed the same flexibility and sense of expediency as his interpretation of his vows. Just as his vow to his mother to abstain
from meat was interpreted, for a while, as not including eggs,
and his vow to abstain from milk was at last strained so as not
to include goat's milk, so too the minimum that was also a
maximum was interpreted from time to time as not being really
a maximum. It is hardly surprising that the South African
Government charged him with violating his own principles. He
was, however, most indignant at this charge.

Gandhi's tactics in the final campaign showed consummate
opportunism and astuteness. The demand for the repeal of the
three-pound tax had a considerable appeal to the many thousands of Indians of the laboring class who had to pay it, and so
opened a wide area for recruitment to Gandhi's "army." He
had always befriended these poor people—he had helped them
as a lawyer for little or no reward; he had voluntarily worked as
a dispenser at their hospital; he was widely known to be sympathetic to them—and so there was every chance that they would
follow his leadership. Other events played into his hands. "As if
unseen by anyone," he wrote, "God was preparing the ingredi-
ents of the Indians' victory." In March 1913 the Supreme Court
of the Cape Province delivered a judgment which seemed to in-
validate in South Africa all marriages not celebrated according
to Christian rites and to bastardize all Indian children whose
parents had been married according to Hindu, Muslim, or Zoro-
astrian rites. Gandhi requested the Government to have the
judgment set aside on appeal or, if it were believed to be a
correct interpretation of the law, to amend the law so as to
recognize the validity of Indian marriages. These were reasonable requests on which the Government, unreasonably, declined
to take any action.

Up to this time Gandhi had refrained from inviting women
to become *satyagrahis*, but "this insult offered to Indian
womanhood" swept away his hesitations. He now welcomed

their participation in the movement, foreseeing that their arrest and imprisonment would arouse passionate feelings. At first a select band of about twelve women from Tolstoy Farm courted arrest in the Transvaal by hawking without licenses, but when the police ignored them it was decided to use them to rouse the indentured laborers in the mines, and they were sent to Newcastle, a big coal-mining center in Natal, to stir up the Indian miners there to go on strike until the three-pound tax was repealed. Gandhi calculated that the Government was bound to arrest the women, if the miners responded to their appeal, and that that their arrest would fire the miners to still greater enthusiasm.

Meanwhile another party of sixteen women from the Phoenix settlement, including Kasturbai and other of Gandhi's close relatives, "invaded" the Transvaal, crossing the border without permits and refusing to disclose their identity.

These moves met with complete success. The Phoenix party was arrested and sentenced to three months' imprisonment with hard labor in September 1913 and in the following month the Tolstoy party, which had induced a large number of miners to stop working, was arrested and given the same sentence.

The women's imprisonment, according to Gandhi, "worked like a charm upon the labourers in the mines near Newcastle" and thousands of them now went on strike. It also caused a considerable stir in India. A well-known Indian political leader, Sir Pherozeshah Mehta, who had hitherto been utterly indifferent to the *satyagraha* movement in South Africa, said that "his blood boiled at the thought of these women lying in jails herded with ordinary criminals, and India could not sleep over the matter any longer."

Gandhi proceeded to Newcastle and took over leadership of the miners. The coal owners had cut off light and water from their houses, and Gandhi advised them to leave their houses and "fare forth like pilgrims." They agreed to follow his advice and he gathered them all together—about five thousand men, women, and children—in an open camp and fed them rice and *dal*, which Indian traders at Newcastle willingly supplied. But Gandhi could not keep them indefinitely under the open sky, and there was a danger that the miners would drift back to their homes and the strike collapse.

Gandhi decided to solve the problem by marching his "army" to the Transvaal in the hope that they would be "safely deposited in jail like the Phoenix party" for entering the territory without permits. Accordingly on October 28 they all set out for the border at Charlestown, thirty-six miles from Newcastle, taking a minimum of clothes and rations of bread and sugar. Gandhi instructed them not to resist arrest if the police offered to arrest them, and to continue the march even if he himself was arrested. He also announced the names of those who should successively lead the army in his place.

On reaching Charlestown the army halted for a few days, hoping that the Government would arrest them there. But as the authorities made no move, it was decided to cross the border and march by eight stages to Tolstoy Farm, where Mr. Kallenbach had begun to construct mud huts for them. When all preparations were complete, Gandhi put through a last-minute phone call to General Smuts' secretary, saying that he would stop the march into the Transvaal if Smuts promised to repeal the three-pound tax. He was told that General Smuts would have nothing to do with him and he could act as he pleased. The next day, November 6, after offering prayers, the army set out on its march and crossed the border. The numbers had decreased considerably by this time, although there were, estimated to be no fewer than two thousand men, one hundred twenty women, and fifty children.

Gandhi was arrested that evening but was released the next morning on bail. He was rearrested on the eighth along with five of his principal lieutenants, but again released on bail. He was arrested for the third time on the ninth and sentenced on the eleventh to nine months' imprisonment. Meanwhile the army had proceeded under the leadership of Mr. Polak, but on the tenth they were all rounded up, put on special trains, and taken back to Natal. There they were sentenced to imprisonment and sent to work at the mines as prisoners.

But the movement was not to be easily crushed. The prisoners at the mines flatly refused to work, and all over the country

Indian laborers came out on strike in sympathy with them. In India there was an outcry and the Viceroy, Lord Hardinge, took the unprecedented step of publicly criticizing the Union Government and expressing "the sympathy of India, deep and burning . . . for their compatriots in South Africa in their resistance to invidious and unjust laws."

In face of this criticism and with other grave internal problems looming ahead, the Union Government shrank from keeping hundreds of nonresisting Indians in jail and decided to give in. To cover their retreat, they appointed a commission of three members to inquire into Indian grievances and immediately afterward released Gandhi unconditionally, along with his European coadjutors, Kallenbach, Polak, and West, who had also been imprisoned.

Gandhi welcomed the appointment of the commission, but demanded that one of its members should be nominated by the Indian community. When Smuts refused to agree, Gandhi announced that he would boycott the commission and court imprisonment again by leading another march of *satyagrahis* from Durban. However, better counsel prevailed. Gokhale cabled from India advising Gandhi to give up the march and cooperate with the commission, and although Gandhi replied that he and thousands of Indians had pledged themselves to boycott the commission and could not go back on their word, he was induced to seek an interview with Smuts and to create an atmosphere of good will by calling off the proposed march. The Union Government was confronted at this time with a great strike of European railwaymen, and Gandhi announced that he was not out to harass the Government and that, therefore, if he undertook the march at all, it would be after the railway strike had ended.

Smuts, for his part, amid the confusion caused by the strike, was only too anxious to settle the Indian question. He told Gandhi that the Government had decided to grant his demands, but that for political reasons it was, necessary to have a recommendation from the commission, which he had no doubt would be forthcoming. Smuts had no objection to Gandhi boycotting the commission and refusing to give evidence before it, but he felt that Gandhi should not prevent others from doing so and should suspend *satyagraha*. In the meantime all *satyagrahi* prisoners would be released.

On this basis a provisional settlement was reached during January 1914. The commission immediately set to work and without much delay produced a report recommending that the main Indian demands, i.e., the repeal of the three-pound tax and the validation of Indian marriages, should be accepted. The Government promptly gave effect to these recommendations in the Indian Relief Act, which was passed by Parliament in July. Thus, after nearly eight years, the *satyagraha* struggle was brought to a successful close.

Gandhi's work in South Africa was finished, and in July he sailed for England where he intended to meet Gokhale before returning to India. "The saint has left our shores," Smuts commented, "I sincerely hope for ever." This hope was fulfilled. Gandhi never returned to South Africa, where he had passed twenty-one of the best years of his life and where, he says, "I had realized my vocation." What he had achieved had no lasting effect on the position of Indians in South Africa. Discrimination against them continued. He himself confessed to feeling "as if all this suffering had gone for nothing," but reassured himself by claiming that without it Indians would have been driven out of South Africa altogether. The claim can hardly be sustained. The struggle had, however, revealed his capacity for leadership and the potentialities of *satyagraha*.

VII ✑

Return
to India

During the *satyagraha* struggle Gandhi had deliberately traveled third class, and he took a third-class passage to England. When the ship called at Madeira it was learned that war between England and Germany was imminent, and news of its actual outbreak was received as the vessel entered the English Channel.

On reaching London on August 6, Gandhi found that Gokhale had gone to Paris and that no one knew when he would return or how he could be reached. Gandhi began to think about where his loyalty lay regarding the war. As he was still hopeful of improving the status of Indians through the help and cooperation of the British, he concluded that, far from regarding England's necessity as India's opportunity, it was the duty of Indians "to win the help of the British by standing by them in their hour of need." He discussed these views with Indians residing in England and invited them to volunteer for ambulance work. About eighty responded and Gandhi offered their services to the Secretary of State for India. After some hesitation the offer was accepted, and arrangements were made to give them six weeks' training in first aid, and they were then put under a colonel for drill and military training. Unfortunately, a good deal of unpleasantness arose. Many of the volunteers were irked by the colonel's dictatorial manner, and Gandhi thought the colonel was not consulting him often enough, considering that Gandhi was chairman of the volunteer corps. After some rather strained correspondence with the colonel it was decided to offer what Gandhi described as "miniature *satyagraha*," with the result that some members of the corps refused to proceed to Netley Hospital when their services were requisitioned.

By this time Gandhi himself was ill in bed. Shortly before leaving South Africa he had seriously weakened himself by a fourteen-day fast, undertaken as a penance for the "moral fall" of two residents of the Phoenix settlement, and the exertions of military training when he had not fully recovered his strength brought on an attack of pleurisy. The Under-Secretary of State for India, visited him and persuaded him to accept a compromise whereby the recalcitrant members of the corps would agree to serve at the hospital, but under a different commanding officer. Gandhi, because of his illness, could not go there himself.

His recovery was slow and not helped by his refusal to drink milk. After some time he realized that in his weak condition he would never be able to join the ambulance corps at Netley and accepted friends' advice to return to India before the onset of colder weather. As soon as he reached the warmer climate of the Red Sea he began to regain strength.

He was returning to India after an absence of ten years. During this period he had made a name for himself. Though Gokhale felt that Gandhi's actual achievements in South Africa were not as meritorious as was popularly supposed, the novel *satyagraha* campaign had aroused the keenest interest and admiration in India, and Gandhi was already marked as one of the political leaders of the future. He had gained unrivaled experience in organizing political agitation and embarrassing a modern government. Through his association with the indentured laborers he had learned how to win the hearts of large masses of men, and Tolstoy Farm and the Phoenix settlement had shown that he could attract a faithful elite who would act as his principal lieutenants. *Indian Opinion* had taught him the art and the value of publicity. Life in Johannesburg had thoroughly familiarized him with the ways and attitudes of Europeans. It was a unique combination of qualifications. Above all he had acquired confidence in himself and an almost fanatical faith in the efficacy and righteousness of *satyagraha*. This political weapon, which he had employed in South Africa with, ultimately, such success, could, he firmly believed, also be successfully employed in India if the occasion arose.

An impartial observer might well have told him that there had been a large element of luck in the success of *satyagraha* in South Africa. The movement had become practically moribund by 1912 and its original objectives were secured not through the sufferings of the *satyagrahis*, but as a result of Gokhale's circumspect and soothing intervention. The opportunity to fan its dying embers into flame was presented by an accident—the unexpected failure of the Union Government to honor its assurance (which it need never have given) regarding the repeal of the three-pound tax. And the final triumph would not have been achieved so easily, if at all, had not the Government been unnerved by the prospect of a railway strike. To Gandhi these fortuitously favorable circumstances appeared as the hand of God, confirming the righteousness of the cause and of the means adopted to promote it. His strength lay in these convictions. His first essays in *satyagraha* in India served to confirm them.

Gandhi reached India early in 1915, and Gokhale arranged a reception for him. At another party given in his honor by Gujaratis a rising young Muslim lawyer and politician from Gujarat, Muhammad Ali Jinnah, made "a short and sweet little speech in English!" Other speeches were also made in English, but Gandhi, when his turn came to express his thanks, spoke in Gujarati and entered a "humble protest against the use of English at a Gujarati gathering." The protest was not ill received.

Gandhi had promised Gokhale to spend a year traveling around India and gaining experience and not to express opinions on public questions during this period. Political life in India was in any case at a low ebb during the first eighteen months of the war. Gandhi traveled third class, and as he now wore only a shirt, a *dhoti*, and a cheap Kashmiri cap, having discarded Western dress during the *satyagraha* campaign, he could mingle with third-class passengers and experience to the full their woes without attracting attention. His appearance was not as familiar to everyone in India as it soon was to be, but already his name was fairly widely known. On a visit to Hardwar, on the occasion of a big fair, he had to spend most of his time giving *darshan* * to pilgrims, and he records with some complacency, "I realised what a deep impression my humble services in South Africa had made throughout the whole of India."

During the first year after his return his principal concern was to start an *ashram*,† where he could settle down with the group of relatives and co-workers from Phoenix who had followed him back to India, and pursue certain activities very dear to his heart. Gokhale was sympathetic and helpful financially, and friends at Ahmedabad offered to meet expenses if he would establish the *ashram* there, to which he was quite agreeable. He was thus relieved of anxiety regarding funds. The *ashram* was founded in May 1915; at first it was located in a rented bungalow in a village near Ahmedabad, but later it was moved to a site on the bank of the Sabarmati River a few miles distant. It was largely run by Gandhi's cousin, Magan Lal, who had been one of the pillars of the Phoenix settlement. Forty men, women, and children lived there. Its name, Satyagraha Ashram, was significant, as it reflected Gandhi's desire "to acquaint India with the method I had tried in South Africa and . . . to test in India the extent to which its application might be possible."

Almost from the start the *ashram* became associated with two of the dominant themes of the rest of Gandhi's life, untouch-

* Sight of a venerated person or deity.
† A hermitage or center of community living.

ability and hand spinning. Within a few months of its foundation an application to join the *ashram* was received from a
family of Untouchables. The family was admitted, but Gandhi's Ahmedabad friends ceased their monetary help and there
was also a threat of social boycott. Gandhi met the situation
with characteristic courage. He resolved that in the event of
bankruptcy and social boycott the residents of the *ashram* should
all move to the untouchable quarter in Ahmedabad and live on
whatever they could earn by manual labor. A sudden, unexpected donation of thirteen thousand rupees by a sympathizer
made this plan unnecessary, and the social boycott never
materialized. So the *ashram* continued, and the presence in it of
an Untouchable family "proclaimed to the world that the
ashram would not countenance untouchability." Gandhi believed that the monetary help given by orthodox Hindus to an
ashram where it was the custom to dine with Untouchables was
a proof that "untouchability is shaken to its foundation." This
estimate was a little optimistic, but Gandhi had taken a typically bold, uncompromising step to break the tyranny of
untouchability.

A factor which had influenced him in settling at Ahmedabad
was the belief that as an ancient center of handloom weaving it
was likely to be a favorable area for the revival of hand spinning. He had long felt that handicrafts and cottage industries,
in particular handloom weaving and hand spinning, were the
panacea for India's poverty. They could provide the villagers
with supplementary income during the off-season when there
was little work in the fields and so would be a remedy for both
idleness and poverty. This had been one of the topics discussed
in his pamphlet "Hind Swaraj," although he confesses that at
that time he had probably never seen a handloom or a spinning
wheel! Handloom weaving soon became the principal activity of
the Satyagraha Ashram. At first the members' aim was to dis-
pense altogether with mill-woven cloth and to wear only cloth
woven by their own hands from Indian yarn. Then, in 1917,
they wanted to spin their own yarn. To find either a spinning
wheel or a spinner to teach them how to use it proved unexpectedly difficult, as in Gujarat the art had almost died out.

However, after a long search, spinners and spinning wheels were found. Members of the *ashram* learned the art of spinning and began to manufacture *khadi*—coarse cloth woven by hand from hand-spun yarn—and Gandhi soon wore nothing else. Here, then, in the Satyagraha Ashram were the beginnings of *khadi*, destined to become the symbol of the independence movement once Gandhi had taken over its leadership. In time the wearing of *khadi* and the plying of the spinning wheel (*charkha*) were accepted as part of the hallowed ritual of the Indian National Congress, although it was not always strictly observed.

Gandhi's *ashram* was subsidiary to his main work as a political leader even though it was connected with it. He had returned to India an acknowledged disciple of Gokhale and "in the ardent hope of merging myself in him." But this was not to be. At a critical juncture the advantage of Gokhale's moderating influence was lost, for within a few weeks of Gandhi's landing at Bombay Gokhale was dead. He had ridiculed several of the ideas Gandhi had expressed in "Hind Swaraj" and told him that after a year in India his views would be modified. Without Gokhale's guidance the modification never took place. Gandhi remained indissolubly wedded to his own nostrums, and struck out on a path very different from that which Gokhale would have followed.

Because he was a disciple of Gokhale and had repeatedly proclaimed his loyalty to the British Empire and had been awarded the Kaisar-i-Hind gold medal in 1915, Gandhi was considered a moderate. For some time, however, he took no very active part in the affairs of Congress or in the general politics of the country. He attended the annual meetings of Congress, but this, he says, was "nothing more perhaps than an annual renewal of allegiance to the Congress" and his share in the proceedings was confined to "the constructive advocacy of Hindi by making my speech in the national language" and to the presentation of the case of Indians overseas.

However, on several specific and mainly local issues he played a prominent part, in every case hinting at or actually adopting his chosen method of *satyagraha*. The first of these was a small matter, the removal of a customs cordon at Viramgan in Kathiawar that was causing considerable hardship. He saw Lord Willingdon, the Governor of Bombay, and was told that if the matter had rested with the Government of Bombay the cordon would have been abolished long ago. So Gandhi approached the Viceroy, Lord Chelmsford. There was very little trouble and shortly afterward the cordon was removed. Gandhi regarded the episode as "the advent of *satyagraha* in India." During a speech about this matter he had referred to *satyagraha* as a method of remedying grievances, and when an official of the Bombay Government criticized him for threatening the Government, remarking that a powerful government would not yield to threats, Gandhi replied as follows:

This was no threat. It was educating the people. It is my duty to place before the people all the legitimate remedies for grievances. A nation that wants to come into its own ought to know all the ways and means to freedom. Usually they include violence as the last remedy. *Satyagraha*, on the other hand, is an absolutely non-violent weapon. I regard it as my duty to explain its practice and limitations. I have no doubt that the British Government is a powerful Government, but I have no doubt also that *satyagraha* is a sovereign remedy.

Satyagraha was also on his mind when he confronted the next issue which attracted his attention—the abolition of the indenture system. Gandhi had had long experience of indentured labor in South Africa and was, of course, a keen advocate of the abolition of this system of "semislavery." In 1916, in response to Indian pressure, the Viceroy promised its abolition as soon as alternative arrangements could be made for emigrant Indian labor. This rather vague promise did not satisfy Gandhi. He thought that India ought to agitate for immediate abolition, and he found there was wide public support for this view. Might this be a fit subject for *satyagraha*? He had no doubt that it was, and early in 1917 he contemplated working up an all-India agitation for abolition by July 31, and resolutions to this effect were passed at meetings held at Bombay, Calcutta, and other centers. But he was knocking at an open door. The Viceroy, with whom he discussed the matter, was accommodating, and the abolition of the indenture system was announced before July 31. Gandhi, however, felt that "potential *satyagraha* hastened the end."

In the meantime, his attention had turned to a local issue, the woes of the tenants of indigo planters in Bihar, which occasioned his first conspicuous entry onto the political stage in India. A simple agriculturist had talked to him at the Congress meeting at Lucknow in 1916 and insisted that Gandhi visit Bihar to see conditions for himself. At first Gandhi put him off, but the man was so persistent, waylaying Gandhi at Cawnpore and Calcutta and turning up at the *ashram* at Ahmedabad, that eventually he was persuaded to go to Bihar and visit the distant district of Champaran, near the border of Nepal, where the plight of the indigo tenants was said to be worst. Under the prevailing system, known as *tinkathia*, the tenants, were bound by law to plant three-twentieths of their land with indigo, but they were also subject to unlawful exactions and bullying by the landlords. Gandhi wanted to see the situation for himself and record the statements of those who claimed to have been ill-used. At an early stage he reached the conclusion that the remedy lay in ending the *tinkathia* system, and he also envisaged facing imprisonment in order to secure redress for the tenants—in other words, he was prepared, if necessary, to use some form of *satyagraha*.

Before setting out for Motihari, the headquarters of the Champaran district, he met the secretary of the Planters' Association and the Commissioner of the division. Both of them treated him as an undesirable outside agitator, and the Commissioner advised him to leave the division forthwith. This made Gandhi think that he might have to go to jail earlier than he had expected, and, sure enough, a day or two after he had reached Motihari he was served with an order to leave the district of Champaran on the ground that his presence there was likely to cause a breach of the peace. When he would not comply he was summoned to appear before a magistrate the next day to stand trial for disobeying a legal order.

Gandhi pleaded guilty and made a dignified and cogent statement explaining his reasons for coming to the district and for disobeying the order to leave.

The magistrate adjourned the case without passing judgment, and before the date of the next hearing he was instructed by the provincial government to inform Gandhi that the case against him had been withdrawn. At the same time the Collector of the district wrote to him saying that he was quite at liberty to conduct his proposed inquiry and could count on all the help he needed from local officials.

Gandhi took a very long time making his inquiry and in the meantime, with his usual enthusiasm, started primary schools, medical relief, and sanitary and cow-protection programs in some of the villages of Champaran. But, as he himself confesses, he and his co-workers built many castles in the air. After some time the Bihar Government gently suggested that his inquiry should be brought to an end, but expressed its willingness to appoint a committee of inquiry of which he should be a member. Gandhi agreed to serve; the committee presented a unanimous report; and the result was that legislation was passed abolishing the *tinkathia* system.

This remarkable triumph, achieved by Gandhi singlehandedly, caused a considerable stir in nationalist circles. His exploits in South Africa had been much admired, but South Africa was a long way off and very different from India, and since his return to India two years earlier not much notice had been taken of him and his *ashram* on the banks of the Sabarmati and his somewhat cranky ideas, nor had he himself sought to play a prominent part in Congress or national politics. But now in Champaran he had signally demonstrated what he could do. Quite unaided, relying entirely on himself—how rightly had Gokhale admired his self-reliance!—he had forced the mighty Bihar Government to apply remedies to long-neglected grievances. It had been a practical achievement brought about in quite a novel manner. The systematic on-the-spot study of the peasants' hardships, the resolute defiance of a foolish order, the transparent readiness to face imprisonment—it was all so different from the endless talk and high-sounding

resolutions of the stock Indian politicians. To many of the
younger nationalists, who disliked terrorism but wanted action,
Champaran came as a revelation. Here was a new type of leader
with unconventional but seemingly effective methods of his
own. These methods had brought results, it was said, in South
Africa; and now he had shown his readiness to apply them in
India with, apparently, every promise of success. Among those
who were impressed by Champaran and began to feel a far
stronger admiration for Gandhi than they had ever felt for any
other leader were two men who over the next thirty years were
to be his principal lieutenants, Jawaharlal Nehru and Vallabhbhai Patel.

Politicians in Gandhi's home region, Gujarat, were impressed
by his success at Champaran. He was invited to become president of the Gujarat Sabha (Association)—a sedate, mildly
political body that had hitherto contented itself with passing
resolutions and sending petitions to the Government. At about
the same time Vallabhbhai Patel was elected its secretary. The
son of a well-to-do peasant, Patel was at this time in his early
forties and a leading criminal lawyer and municipal councilor
at Ahmedabad. Before Champaran he had been indifferent to
Gandhi, and when Gandhi had visited the Gujarat club to
interest its members in a scheme for national schools, Patel had
continued playing bridge and not listened to a word Gandhi
had to say. But now he gladly cooperated with him in breathing
new life into the Gujarat Sabha and championing the rights of
the people.

In 1918 heavy rain caused widespread damage to crops in the
Kaira district. The Gujarat Sabha petitioned the Government
to remit the land revenue paid by the farmers. Under the
Revenue Rules farmers were entitled to remission if their
crops yielded less than 25 per cent of the normal. Government
officials granted remissions in a few villages, but throughout
most of the district they assessed the crop at nearly 50 per cent
of the normal and refused remissions. Vallabhbhai Patel and
others, after inspecting some of the crops themselves, felt that
an injustice was being done and requested Gandhi to intervene.
When petitions and agitation in the Bombay Legislative Coun-

cil proved vain, Gandhi advised the farmers to resort to *satya-graha*. Accordingly, about two hundred farmers pledged not to pay the land revenue and gladly to suffer the consequences of nonpayment, even if it meant forfeiting their land. Vallabhbhai Patel discarded his smart Western clothes and trudged around the villages in a shirt and *dhoti*, encouraging the peasants to stand firm and refuse payment. He was by now a willing disciple of Gandhi, for, hardheaded and matter-of-fact realist though he was, he had succumbed to the force and charm of Gandhi's personality and in *satyagraha* he thought he saw a really potent method of fighting the British-controlled government.

This was the first instance of organized *satyagraha* in India and, to begin with, it met with some success. There was quite a solid refusal to pay the land revenue. But the Government, after some slight initial hesitation, proceeded to take coercive measures against the defaulters. Their cattle, equipment, and standing crops were confiscated and in some cases sold. These measures were not without effect, for the resolution of some of the *satyagrahis* was broken when they saw their crops attached, and though quite a few stood by their pledge not to pay and to suffer the consequences, Gandhi himself recognized after about three months that the people were exhausted and began "casting about for some graceful way of terminating the struggle which would be acceptable to a *satyagrahi*."

The Government presented him with a way out. It too had grown tired or had become convinced that there was justice in the farmers' complaints and that some concessions were called for. In June orders were issued for land revenue to be collected only from those who could afford to pay and that in other cases it should be suspended. From the very start the *satyagrahis* had agreed that those who were in a position to pay should do so and that relief should be confined to the poorer farmers, but they wanted the relief to be conceded before any payment was made. Since this had now been done, it could reasonably be claimed that the objective of the *satyagraha* had been achieved, so the struggle was brought to an honorable and apparently victorious end.

Undoubtedly some concession had been wrung from the Government and the termination of the *satyagraha* was celebrated as a triumph. But Gandhi "could not enthuse over it, as it lacked the essentials of a complete triumph." A *satyagraha* compaign, he maintained, should, if really successful, "leave the *satyagrahis* stronger and more spirited than they are in the beginning." But by the end of this campaign the morale of the Kaira farmers had been broken and they were beginning to give way. Moreover, although the poor had been granted suspension, it was left to the Government officials to decide who was "poor" and the number who actually benefited was much smaller than Gandhi would have wished. He also noted that "an inborn gentleness and desire to do the opponent good," which should show themselves in every act of a *satyagrahi*, were, not surprisingly, gravely lacking in the peasant farmers of Kaira.

Nevertheless, despite these shortcomings, *satyagraha* had, to all appearances, been successful against the authority of a powerful government. Was not this the answer to those who were looking for a weapon with which to fight foreign rule in India? Vallabhbhai Patel thought so, and many others began to think the same way. Nor was Gandhi's own faith in *satyagraha* at all shaken, for although he was dissatisfied with the results in Kaira, he was far from discouraged. On the contrary, he thought that through the Kaira compaign *satyagraha* had taken firm root in the soil of Gujarat, and, more generally, that "the lesson was indelibly imprinted on the public mind that the salvation of the people depends upon themselves, upon their capacity for suffering and sacrifice." Finally, as he very rightly observed, the Kaira campaign "compelled the educated public workers to establish contact with the actual life of the peasants." Politics were being brought to the countryside. Here, and at Champaran, was the beginning of mass contact and a mass movement.

One other episode that occurred at this time deserves mention as it affords an early example of Gandhi's use (or misuse) of one of his favorite tactics—the self-imposed fast. Just before *satyagraha* was launched in Kaira a dispute arose between the

workers in the cotton mills at Ahmedabad and the mill
owners. Gandhi requested the owners, with whom he was on
friendly terms,* to refer the dispute to arbitration, but they
would not agree to this. Gandhi then advised the workers to
strike, warning them, however, that they must neither resort to
violence nor call off the strike once it had started, no matter how
long it might have to continue. The workers went on strike,
pledging themselves not to resume work until their terms were
accepted or the owners agreed to arbitration. For two weeks
they enthusiastically stood by their pledge, but after that they
began to falter and there were evident signs that the strike was
about to collapse. With failure staring him in the face, Gandhi
suddenly announced that unless the strikers rallied and continued the strike until a settlement was reached, he would not take
any food.

The effect was instantaneous. The strikers begged forgiveness
and promised to remain faithful to their pledge. But the fast,
although it was not directed against the mill owners, affected
them also, especially since they had enjoyed close relations
with Gandhi. Within three days they agreed to appoint an
arbitrator and the strike was called off.

Thus the strike, supplemented by the fast, was successful,
although, Gandhi conceded, the fast suffered from a grave
defect in that it was undertaken against the workers rather than
the owners, but inevitably put pressure on the owners—and
that, in Gandhi's view, amounted to coercion, and as a *satyagrahi* he knew that it was not right to apply coercion. Nevertheless, in spite of this grave defect, he had felt that his duty to
undertake the fast was clear.

In the local and limited operations which he had undertaken
since his return to India, Gandhi had enjoyed an unbroken run
of success. His reputation within the country was now firmly
established, and the time had come for him to enter national
politics and play a prominent part as an all-India leader. Yet,
paradoxically enough, just when he was about to give a revolu-

* They had contributed to his *ashram*.

tionary turn to national politics and deflect Congress from the constitutional path it had followed since its birth, he gave one last demonstration of loyalty to the British Empire.

In the spring of 1918, when World War I was at a critical stage, the Viceroy invited a number of Indian leaders, including Gandhi, to a war conference in Delhi. Gandhi objected to the fact that certain extremist leaders—such as B. G. Tilak and two fanatical Muslims who were then in jail, the Ali brothers—were not invited to the conference. But after prolonged discussion with the Viceroy, Gandhi finally agreed to accept the invitation. The Viceroy pointed out that if Gandhi believed that the Empire had been, on the whole, a power for good and that India had, on the whole, benefited by the British connection, then surely he must agree that it was the duty of every Indian citizen to help the Empire in its hour of need. The argument was familiar. Gandhi had himself used it, or something very like it, in the past; it appealed to him. He attended the conference and supported, in a single sentence—uttered, with the Viceroy's permission, in Hindustani instead of English—a resolution in favor of enlisting recruits for the armed forces. He himself then embarked on a recruiting campaign in the very district of Kaira where he had so recently been conducting a *satyagraha* campaign against the Government. But his support of the war effort was not disinterested, as he himself frankly admitted. It did not spring, as he claimed his support for the British in the Boer War had, simply from a sense of duty as a loyal British citizen. In a long letter to the Viceroy he explained very clearly why he had responded to the call for support and what the people of India expected from the Government:

> I recognise that in the hour of its danger we must give, as we have decided to give, ungrudging and unequivocal support to the Empire of which we aspire in the near future to be partners in the same sense as the Dominions overseas. But it is the simple truth that our response is due to the expectation that our goal will be reached all the more speedily. . . .
>
> I was present at the sessions of the last Congress, and I

was party to the Resolution that full Responsible Government should be granted to British India within a period to
be fixed definitely by a Parliamentary Statute. I admit that
it is a bold step to take, but I feel sure that nothing less
than a definite vision of Home Rule to be realised in the
shortest possible time will satisfy the Indian people. . . .

The Conference means for me, and I believe for many of
us, a definite step in the consecration of our lives to the
common cause, but ours is a peculiar position. We are
today outside the partnership. Ours is a consecration based
on hope of [a] better future. I should be untrue to you
and to my country if I did not clearly and unequivocally
tell you what that hope is. I do not bargain for its fulfil-
ment, but you should know that disappointment of hope
means disillusion. . . .

I write this, because I love the English nation, and I
wish to evoke in every Indian the loyalty of Englishmen.

There were not many Indians who revealed their real motives
so frankly as Gandhi. The British tended to regard Indian
demonstrations of loyalty and offers of assistance as evidence of
gratitude for the blessings of British rule, but Gandhi left the
Viceroy under no such illusion. The expectations so clearly expressed in this letter partly account for what was to follow.
While disclaiming the intention to bargain, Gandhi was, in
fact, hoping to strike a bargain with the British or, at least, to
saddle them with a moral obligation to grant India what educated India desired. But the British, while accepting Gandhi's
and India's help, struck no bargain and were resolved to interpret and discharge their moral obligation in their own way.

VIII ⌒

Jallianwala

Bagh

The 1914–18 war had an unsettling effect on India and at its close many parts of the country were in a state of ferment. British defeats had shaken confidence in the stability and permanence of the British Raj, and vague expectations of impending change had encouraged latent forces of disorder. There was widespread discontent because of the rise in prices, which was intensified by the rapacity of dealers and middlemen. The Muslim population had an additional reason for disaffection. The war with Turkey had always been unpopular with them, since the Sultan of Turkey was the Caliph, or supreme head, of the Muslim world, and when the Turkish armies were completely defeated in the autumn of 1918 rumors that the Turkish Empire would be dismembered and the caliphate abolished began to cause stirrings of Muslim fanaticism. In addition to this ground swell of dissatisfaction among the masses, there was a rising tide of nationalist feeling among the educated classes, whose hopes and ambitions had been aroused but by no means satisfied by the prospect of imminent political reforms.

Nearly a century earlier Macaulay had envisaged that the people of India, "having become instructed in European knowledge," might "in some future age demand European institutions." That age, and with it Indian nationalism, may be said to have dawned in 1885 when the Indian National Congress met for its first session at Bombay. Sponsored by a retired member of the Indian Civil Service and blessed by the Viceroy of the day, this body was not at first anti-British, although from the outset it saw itself as "the germ of a Native Parliament" and as constituting "an unanswerable reply to the assertion that India is still unfit for any form of representative institutions." Twenty years later the proclaimed goal of Congress had become "the attainment by the people of India of a system of government similar to that enjoyed by the self-governing members of the British Empire."

By 1905 moderate Indian nationalists who, like Gokhale, still felt, or at any rate expressed, basic loyalty to the British Empire and British Crown, predominated in Congress, but there had also grown up a small extremist wing which denounced in unmeasured terms the British Raj and all its works and encouraged terrorist activities such as the assassination of officials, both Indian and British. In the first decade of the twentieth century the extremists were active mainly in Bombay and Bengal, and they appealed to the literate but often unemployed or badly paid youth of the lower middle class. The most distinguished extremist leader was B. G. Tilak, who, like Gokhale, was from the province of Bombay.

The British authorities were not wholly unsympathetic to the aspirations of Indian nationalists. They granted that a purely foreign despotism, however benevolent in intention, must in due course give way to some form of native government, but they doubted, with good reason, whether it should take the form of English parliamentary government. Nevertheless, despite these doubts, steps were very cautiously taken to set India on a path leading toward parliamentary self-government on the English model, and by 1909, with the introduction of the Morley-Minto reforms, the threshold of representative parliamentary govern-

ment had been reached. In every province and at the Center *
the legislative councils (which had existed since 1861 and in
some provinces from an earlier date) now included elected
members and were no longer composed solely of officials and
nominated nonofficials. Furthermore, except at the Center, the
officials were now outnumbered by the nominated nonofficials
plus the elected members, and in the province of Bengal the
elected members were in a clear majority. Though the Government remained essentially autocratic, elected Indian representatives had at least been given a recognized right and opportunity
to discuss the operations of the Government and to voice their
views. For the first time Indians were also admitted to executive
office at the highest level with the appointment of an Indian to
the Viceroy's (Governor General's) Executive Council and to
every provincial executive Council.

The Morley-Minto reforms had been welcomed by Congress
and throughout India "with deep and general satisfaction."
Congress recognized them as a definite step toward their goal of
parliamentary self-government, as indeed they were. Yet Lord
Morley himself and other British spokesmen were careful to
disclaim any intention of establishing a parliamentary system in
India. They implied, without actually stating, that self-
government, when it came, might have to be autocratic in character, although they gave no hint how autocracy was to be
reconciled with the liberal spirit of British institutions that
Indians had been taught to admire.

The grounds for the British hesitation to introduce parliamentary government in India were well founded and were
admirably stated by A. J. (Lord) Balfour in the House of Com-
mons. Such a system, he said,

> is only suitable . . . when you are dealing with a popula-
> tion in the main homogeneous, in the main equal in every
> substantial and essential sense, in a community where the
> minority are prepared to accept the decisions of the major-

---

* The "Center" refers to the central government located in the
capital city (Calcutta and, later, Delhi) as distinct from the provincial governments located in the provinces.

ity, where they are all alike in the traditions in which they are brought up, in their general outlook upon the world and in their broad view of national aspirations.

These conditions did not exist in India. Its population was not only composed of diverse, distinct races, but was also deeply divided by caste and by differences of religion, culture, and tradition. Of these differences the most serious by far was the clash of Hinduism with Islam. The sharp opposition between these two creeds and cultures—tersely summed up in Jinnah's phrase, "The Hindus worship the cow, we eat it"—had not been softened over the years by natural ties of kinship, since inter-marriage between the two communities was prohibited by their own laws and customs. Although the two groups lived side by side, the strictness of religious institutions had kept even neighbors apart with the result that Hindus and Muslims constituted two distinct and often antagonistic communities. In a parliamentary system how were the separate interests of these two communities to be reconciled? The Hindus, who constituted over two-thirds of the population, could hardly be expected to surrender the rights of a majority, and yet the Muslims, who had been the ruling power in India before the arrival of the British, could not readily agree to permit the Hindus, by virtue of their numbers, to acquire a permanent monopoly of political power.

Muslim leaders were conscious of this inherent dilemma in the introduction of a parliamentary system in India, and partly for this reason they never joined Congress in large numbers, even though it was nominally a national body. As its goal of parliamentary self-government became more clearly defined, the Muslims were even less inclined to make common cause with it; still less disposed to participate in the activities of "extremist" nationalism which, being inspired largely by revivalist Hinduism, remained exclusively a Hindu movement. But the prospect that the British, in response to nationalist pressure, would grant reforms leading inevitably to parliamentary government spurred the Muslims to independent action, and in 1905 they formed a separate political organization of their own—the

All-India Muslim League.

By this time the principle of representation and, in practice if not in theory,* even the principle of election had already been conceded by the British in the constitution of the provincial legislative councils. The Muslim League could not turn back the clock, but they did succeed in getting one important safeguard of Muslim interests incorporated in the reforms of 1909, wherein provision was made for the separate representation of Muslims in the legislatures by representatives chosen only by Muslim electors. While this offered no ultimate solution to the problem of curbing the power of a permanent Hindu majority, it did at least insure that for the time being Muslims would be represented not by compromising candidates dependent on Hindu votes, but by wholehearted champions of Muslim interests. The Congress, not unnaturally, condemned this violation of democratic principle, which was calculated to keep the two communities apart rather than draw them together. But "separate electorates" had come to stay. For the remaining period of British rule they were regarded by the Muslims as an indispensable safeguard.

The Muslims had created their own separate political organization, but there were always some Muslims in the Congress ranks, and in the League itself and the population at large there were militant Muslim nationalists who, though aware of the danger of Hindu domination, were as eager as the members of Congress to be rid of the humiliation of foreign rule. The impact of the war intensified national feeling among all the educated classes of India, and especially among the Muslims, who resented being involved against their will in hostilities with Turkey, the major independent Muslim state at that time. So while year after year the Congress and the League passed resolutions affirming their loyalty to the British Crown and their determination to stand by the British Empire in its hour of

* A large number of seats on the councils were filled after 1892 on the recommendations of local bodies, chambers of commerce, universities, etc., but as the recommendations were invariably accepted, these seats were in practice filled by the persons chosen or "elected" by these bodies.

peril, the two organizations were drawn together by a common desire to wrest a larger measure of self-government from the British when the war was over. At the end of 1916, under the inspiration of the extremist Tilak, they reached agreement on a plan for an immediate advance toward partial self-government. One notable feature of this agreement, known as the Lucknow Pact, was the acceptance by Congress of "separate electorates." For their part the Muslims agreed to the principle of representative government, with the corollary of majority rule once the residual powers to be retained by the British were finally withdrawn.

Meanwhile the war was also affecting British opinion. The loyal support that had been forthcoming from the peoples of India plainly demanded some friendly, appreciative response, and a war in defense of freedom and democracy could hardly be reconciled with India's continued subjection to the autocratic rule of foreigners. Some further advance toward self-government was called for. Moreover, there was an obvious danger that unless some concession was made to national feeling, extreme demands would be put forward and would gain wide support. Accordingly, in August 1917 the British Government made a historic pronouncement, declaring the aim of British policy in India to be "the gradual development of self-governing institutions with a view to the progressive realisation of responsible government in India as an integral part of the British Empire." This aim was to be achieved "by successive stages," but the promise was made that substantial steps would be taken in this direction as soon as possible.

The die had been cast. Britain's proclaimed aim was now not only to bring India into the ranks of independent nations, as it long implicitly had been, but also to enable India to attain this status while enjoying parliamentary government on the English pattern, for this alone was what "responsible government" could mean—government responsible to the elected representatives of the people. Thus the goals of the British Government and of Congress were now unquestionably the same, and the difficulties of introducing parliamentary government visualized by Lord Morley and Mr. Balfour (and also by Muslim leaders) had for the moment been swept under the carpet.

The "substantial steps" that had been promised were revealed in the summer of 1918 when the proposed constitutional changes known as the Montagu-Chelmsford reforms were published. In the provinces a measure of responsible government was established by the introduction of a dual system of government or "dyarchy." While certain subjects were to continue to be controlled by the Governor and his Executive Council, others were to be "transferred" to the control of ministers responsible to the majority in an elected legislature. At the Center there was no provision for responsible government even of a partial character, but a drastic reform of the legislature was proposed to make it far more representative. In place of the existing Legislative Council, in which officials were in a small majority, there was to be a new legislature of two houses, in both of which the majority of members would be elected. Though it would be unable to control, it could at least discuss all activities of the central government and its creation would be a stepping stone toward responsible government at the Center at a later date.

The reforms were to be reviewed by a parliamentary commission at the end of ten years, and further periodic reviews were contemplated thereafter in accordance with the declared intention of achieving responsible government "by successive stages."

These proposals fell considerably short of the hopes of the more ardent nationalists. Congress, while admitting that they represented "an advance in some directions," declared them to be "disappointing and unsatisfactory" and passed a resolution demanding full responsible government in the provinces within six years and "in the whole of British India within a period not exceeding fifteen years." But this querulous attitude was not universal. A group of moderate Congressmen broke away and declared their "hearty support" of the proposals. Gandhi did not join this group; he supported the Congress resolution. Nevertheless, his reaction to the British proposals was by no means wholly unfavorable, and he proceeded with his recruiting campaign on behalf of the British Government. Even the main body of Congress does not seem to have contemplated outright rejection of the proposals, much less a violent breach with the Government, and at the close of the war a resolution was passed congratulating the King on its successful termination. The differences were, after all, not fundamental; they related not to the goal but to the timetable for reaching it. Congress, including Gandhi, wanted a guarantee of full responsible government by a fixed date, not one in the indefinite future. The British believed—and intended—that the "progressive realization" of responsible government would be a lengthy process extending over many years, but obviously there was a good chance that under steady pressure from Indian nationalist opinion the British might be induced to move more quickly. There was, therefore, no urgent need to resort to desperate courses.

On their own intrinsic merits the reforms would probably have been accepted, but events intervened to cause a fatal cleavage between Congress and the Government. The Government was partly to blame, for although it offered political reforms with one hand, it presented with the other a strong dose of repressive legislation. A committee headed by Mr. Justice Rowlatt, which had been appointed in 1917 to advise on legislation for dealing with criminal conspiracies in India, submitted its report in the summer of 1918. On the strength of its recommendations the Government, alarmed by terrorist activity and the prevailing unrest, planned to arm itself with additional powers and, in particular, to retain the powers of arbitrary arrest and internment which were due to lapse with the expiration of wartime legislation. There were strong protests from those representing all shades of nationalist opinion, but, in spite of this, orders were given for the necessary bills to be drafted.

Gandhi was seriously ill at this time. While still engaged on his recruiting campaign, he had had a bad attack of dysentery and it was while he was in bed that he learned that Germany had surrendered and that his duties as a recruiting sergeant were at an end. He was thankful to be relieved of this troublesome task, but his illness did not abate and at one point he thought he was at death's door. Only the ministrations of a quack from Maharashtra—"a crank like myself," Gandhi called him—who prescribed the application of ice to all parts of the body, gave him new hope and set him on the road to recovery. He was, however, still weak and ill when he found out about the proposed Rowlatt bills. Always more aroused by specific grievances than by broad general issues, Gandhi felt at once that the threatened curtailment of basic liberties should be resisted and would afford an opportunity for employing his favorite weapon, *satyagraha*. He told Vallabhbhai Patel that if he recovered his health he would be ready to do battle all alone.

For the time being he was too weak for this undertaking, but at his instance a body called the Satyagraha Sabha was formed. Members were enlisted who pledged themselves to disobey the Rowlatt bills and such other laws as might be selected. Pamphlets were issued, meetings held to protest against the bills, and agitation worked up in earnest, "recalling all the familiar features of the Kaira campaign," but this time the campaign was for the redress of an "all-India" grievance, not merely a local one. Gandhi's eagerness to be ready for the fray was so great that to rebuild his strength he broke his vow not to drink milk and began drinking goat's milk.

Meanwhile, in both private and public correspondence he begged the Viceroy not to proceed with the bills and warned him that he would resort to *satyagraha* if they became law. But the Government of India was not to be moved by either threats or pleadings. The bills were enacted; the only concession made was to limit their operation to three years.

Before the bills had actually become law, Gandhi, though still weak, paid a visit to Madras. It was during this visit that he became acquainted with C. Rajagopalachari, a rising lawyer destined to be one of the pillars of Congress in the south. They discussed, together and with others, the form which *satyagraha* should take. The projected new legislation could not be disobeyed or defied unless the Government provided the opportunity. In this case, should other laws be disobeyed and, if so, which ones? No firm conclusion was reached and Gandhi was still undecided as to what concrete step to take, when suddenly one night he had a flash of inspiration which he communicated to Rajagopalachari the next morning:

The idea came to me last night in a dream that we should call upon the country to observe a general *hartal*. Satyagraha is a process of self-purification, and ours is a sacred fight and it seems to me to be in the fitness of things that it should be commenced with an act of self-purification. Let all the people of India, therefore, suspend their business on that day and observe the day as one of fasting and prayer.

The observance of a *hartal* was a very ancient Hindu method of protesting against the actions of a ruler. The proposal, therefore, was acceptable to Rajagopalachari and to others. March 30, 1919, was fixed for the *hartal*, but was subsequently changed to April 6. Gandhi drafted a short appeal calling on the people to observe the day as one of national mourning, to suspend all business, and to hold public meetings of protest against the legislation. It was decided that disobedience of law—"civil disobedience," as it was termed—should take the form of breaches of the salt laws and the sale of proscribed literature. For the latter purpose "Hind Swaraj" and another harmless book of Gandhi's that had been needlessly proscribed were conveniently available.

The response to the call for a *hartal* was enthusiastic and far exceeded expectations, especially in the south, which may have been due in some degree to the unscrupulous mendacity with which the agitation against the bills had been conducted. Their provisions were represented as including the inspection of all couples before marriage and the prohibition of festive assemblies of more than two or three people.

Events were now set in motion that left a greater imprint on Indo-British relations than anything that had occurred since the Mutiny of 1857. Both sides temporarily lost their sense of balance, and even when tempers had cooled there remained a legacy of distrust and hostility that was never fully liquidated during the remaining period of British rule. The year 1919 witnessed the conversion of many moderate members of Congress from friendly critics to implacable opponents of the British Raj, among whom Gandhi himself may be counted. Within twenty months he had ceased to be "a staunch loyalist and cooperator" and had become uncompromisingly alienated and noncooperative. This revulsion of feeling was partly due to actual happenings within India during these months but still more to the superior, contemptuous attitude of some of the British toward Indians which these happenings so glaringly revealed. This attitude, tolerated in the nineteenth century, had become by the end of World War I an intolerable anachronism; it undermined the widespread Indian belief in basic British justice, good will, and benevolence. "We have been cherishing what we thought was a valuable diamond," said Vallabhbhai Patel, "but have found it to be a stone."

For the *hartal* and day of mourning on April 6 Gandhi went to Bombay. Muslims as well as Hindus joined processions and protest meetings in large numbers and Gandhi was even invited to deliver a speech in a mosque. Everything went peacefully. But in Delhi, where by mistake the *hartal* was observed on March 30, a huge procession clashed with the police and there were a number of casualties. In view of these disturbances Gandhi left Bombay for Delhi on the evening of April 7, intending to proceed from there to the Punjab. But en route he was served with an order forbidding him to enter the Punjab on the grounds that his presence there was likely to cause a disturbance of the peace. He protested that he was going to the Punjab not to foment unrest, but to allay it, which was, no doubt, true. But since he had been inciting people to break the law, however peacefully, the British authorities took a different view. When Gandhi refused to comply with the order voluntarily, he was taken off the train, escorted back to Bombay by a police officer, and then set free.

Some friends picked him up at the station and rushed him by car to pacify an excited crowd which, incensed by the news of his arrest, seemed likely to get out of hand. He begged the people to remain calm and peaceful, but in the shouting and hubbub that greeted his appearance he was unable to make himself heard. The crowd formed itself into a procession and threatened to break through a cordon of police that had been thrown across the road, whereupon it was charged by a body of mounted police and scattered in all directions.

Gandhi now drove straight to the office of the Commissioner of Police, a Mr. Griffith, to complain of the event he had just witnessed. A charge by mounted police whose horses were bound to trample on some of the people, Gandhi told Griffith, was quite unnecessary. Mr. Griffith's reply was somberly prophetic:

> You cannot judge of that. We police officers know better the effect of your teaching on the people. If we did not start with drastic measures the situation would pass out of our hands. I tell you the people are sure to go out of your control. Disobedience of law will quickly appeal to them; it is beyond them to understand the duty of keeping peaceful. I have no doubt about your intentions, but the people will not understand them. They will follow their natural instinct.

Gandhi replied that the people were not by nature violent but peaceful, and they argued about this for some time, until Mr. Griffith asked what Gandhi would do if he was really convinced that his teaching had been lost on the people. "I would suspend civil disobedience, if I was so convinced," he answered. Mr. Griffith assured him that he would be so convinced when he heard what had been happening in Ahmedabad and Amritsar. Gandhi said that he could not answer for Amritsar, as he had never been there, but he would be "deeply pained and surprised" if he found there were any disturbances in Ahmedabad.

Pain and surprise were in store for him, for there had indeed been serious disturbances there. A mob of millhands had run riot, killed a police sergeant, attempted to tear up the railway line, and set fire to a number of government buildings. On reaching Ahmedabad and learning of these disorders, Gandhi said that a rapier run through his body could hardly have pained him more. He went straight to the Commissioner, expressed unqualified regret for what had happened, and offered to cooperate in restoring peace. His offer was accepted and with the Commissioner's concurrence he held a public meeting in the grounds of his Sabarmati *ashram* at which he reproved the people for their acts of violence and tried to awaken in them a proper sense of contrition. It was intolerable to him that the millhands, with whom he had been so closely associated only a year earlier in connection with their strike, should have taken part in riots, and he felt himself to be "a sharer of their guilt." He announced that he would undertake a penitential fast for three days, advised the people to fast for one day, and suggested that any of them guilty of acts of violence should confess their guilt. At the same time he suggested to the Government that it should overlook the crimes that had been committed. Neither suggestion was adopted.

Prominent citizens of Ahmedabad now asked him to suspend *satyagraha*. He had already made up his mind to do so, and a day or two later, announcing its suspension, he confessed publicly that he had made a "Himalayan miscalculation" in calling upon the people to offer civil disobedience before they had learned the lesson of peace and nonviolence. This frank but unconventional admission of error earned him a good deal of ridicule, but Gandhi, a confirmed crank and eccentric, was used to ridicule and undeterred by it. He had no qualms whatever at appearing to be a fool if he believed that what he was doing was right.

The disturbances at Ahmedabad and other places in western India were insignificant compared with what had taken place in the Punjab. But the order barring him from entering that province was still in force and he did not think it would be right, as an individual, to offer civil disobedience by defying that order when feelings were running high and the atmosphere was far from peaceful. As for mass *satyagraha*, he was convinced that before it could be used again he must raise a corps of sincere *satyagrahis* who fully understood its implications and could explain them to the people. On his return to Bombay he called for volunteers, but the response was lukewarm and the people in general showed little interest in the peaceful side of *satyagraha*.

The means for teaching the public the inner meaning of *satyagraha* in a regular, systematic manner were presented to him, however, by the directors of the Bombay *Chronicle*, who invited him to assume charge of the paper. Before he could do so the paper was suppressed by the Government, whereupon the directors asked him to become editor of a weekly they controlled called *Young India*. Gandhi readily agreed, but he disliked the idea of training the public in *satyagraha* only through the English language and was therefore pleased when some friends also placed at his disposal a Gujarati monthly, the *Navajiwan*. It was converted into a weekly and arrangements made for both journals to be printed and published at Ahmedabad. Through these two organs Gandhi tried as best he could to "educate the reading public in *satyagraha*" and also aired his views on a variety of topics, as he had done in *Indian Opinion* in South Africa. He was occupied with reorganizing and editing these journals during the summer of 1919, which alleviated to some extent his frustration at being excluded from the Punjab at a time when, in his view, "lawless repression was in full career, and was manifesting itself in the Punjab in all its nakedness." He was sorely tempted to defy the ban on his entry into that province, but this would have been futile, and he wisely curbed his impatience, meanwhile bombarding the Viceroy with requests for permission to go there. Permission was not granted until October.

The outbreaks of violence in the Punjab in April 1919 acquired lasting significance from the manner in which they were suppressed. In themselves they were as ephemeral and as of little consequence as the contemporary outbreaks at Ahmedabad, but whereas the latter have been forgotten the disturbances in the Punjab, and in particular at Amritsar, have left an indelible mark on history.

Of all the peoples of India the sturdy inhabitants of the Punjab were the most prone to violence and the most loyal to the British. They provided the majority of the recruits for the Indian Army and during the war had responded magnificently to repeated calls for men and money. It may be that the British Governor, Sir Michael O'Dwyer, in his eagerness to assist the war effort, had overdriven and overstrained the province and that this contributed to the unrest at the beginning of 1919, and it is undoubtedly true that the Muslim rabble in the towns had been affected by anti-British propaganda regarding the dismemberment of Turkey and the abolition of the caliphate. With the prospect of imminent war with Muslim Afghanistan (which actually broke out in May), the latent hostility of sections of the Muslim population was naturally disquieting to the British authorities in the Punjab. The District Magistrate of Amritsar painted a gloomy picture:

> The soil is prepared for discontent by a number of causes. The poor are hit by high prices, the rich by a severe income tax assessment and the Excess Profits Act. Muhammadans are irritated about the fate of Turkey. From one cause or another the people are restless and ripe for the revolutionist.

Nevertheless, from the British point of view, the heart of the Punjab was sound; in the province at large there was no serious disaffection. The people maintained their traditional loyalty to the British regime, and there was certainly no thought of concerted rebellion to synchronize with an Afghan attack, as was later contended by the Punjab Government. This was, as was subsequently shown, an alarmist figment of their imagination, although it was perhaps partly responsible for the severity of the repressive measures they used.

Disturbances occurred in a number of cities of central Punjab, but it was those in Amritsar, the commercial capital of the province and the sacred city of the Sikhs, that attracted attention at the time and swayed the course of events afterward. Early in April, in anticipation of the general *hartal* scheduled for April 6, there were a number of ominous public meetings at which mob orators proclaimed the imminent collapse of the British Raj, and at a huge meeting on April 5 Hindus, Muslims, and Sikhs demonstrated their united hositility to the British by drinking water from the same vessels. The general temper of the populace so alarmed the District Magistrate that he asked for reinforcements for the single company of troops stationed at Amritsar. Meanwhile, he received orders from the Punjab Government to arrest and deport from the district the two principal agitators, Dr. Saif-ud-din Kitchlew, a Muslim lawyer, and Dr. Satyapal, a Hindu medical practitioner. Without waiting for the military reinforcements he had requested, he summoned them both to his bungalow on the morning of the tenth and had them arrested.

As news of the arrests spread through the city large crowds gathered and attempted to make their way across the railway into the Civil Lines, where the British officials lived, in the hope of discovering what had become of Dr. Kitchlew and Dr. Satyapal. The crowd was held up at the railway bridge by a military picket which had orders to prevent them, at any cost, from entering the Civil Lines. After some time the picket, unable to hold back the crowd any longer, opened fire. There were about twenty casualties.

The crowd rushed back into the city, set fire to government buildings, cut telegraph and telephone lines, and murderously assaulted any Europeans they could find. Three bank officials, unaware of the trouble, were ferreted out of their offices and beaten to death, after which their bodies were thrown into the street and burned. Two other officials were brutally murdered near the railway goods yard. A missionary, Miss Sherwood, was knocked off her bicycle on her way to school, beaten as she lay on the ground, and left for dead in the gutter. At the main police station in the heart of the city there was an armed reserve of seventy-five police, but, without leadership or instructions, it was unable to intervene effectively. The city was given over to the mob.

The civil authorities now formally abdicated and martial law was proclaimed. Brigadier General Dyer arrived from Jullundur on the evening of the eleventh to assume command. He issued orders forbidding all gatherings and processions, marched through the city with troops and armored cars, established pickets, and warned the people at nineteen places by beat of drum that gatherings in defiance of his orders would be fired on.

The populace of Amritsar was not particularly awed by the troops. They jeered at them as they marched through the city and, finding that no attempt was made to disperse gatherings in the streets, they tauntingly declared that the troops would never open fire.

On the afternoon of the thirteenth Dyer learned that in defiance of his orders a meeting was to be held at 4:30 P.M. in the Jallianwala Bagh. Although *"bagh"* means garden, the Jallianwala Bagh was at this time no more than a dusty, sunken courtyard surrounded by houses and low walls, with only a few narrow exits. At about 4:00 P.M. Dyer proceeded to the Bagh with a strong force of troops. On arriving at the entrance he found that a large crowd had already assembled and the meeting was in progress. Without warning, he ordered his troops to open fire. The crowd, hemmed in by the walls and houses and unable to disperse, surged to and fro, vainly seeking some way of escape. After more than sixteen hundred rounds had been fired Dyer withdrew, leaving three hundred seventy-nine dead and more than a thousand wounded.

This drastic remedy was effective. There was no more trouble; the hooligan element in the city was completely cowed and life quickly returned to normal. In the surrounding districts, where there had also been disturbances and martial law had been proclaimed, news of Jallianwala Bagh had an immediately sobering effect and within a few days throughout the Punjab it became unnecessary to fire another shot.

Dyer did not rest content with firing more than sixteen hundred rounds into an unarmed crowd. He was determined to make absolutely clear who was master and issued a series of humiliating orders, one of which required Indians to go on all fours if they wished to pass down the lane in which Miss Sherwood had been assaulted, with public flogging prescribed for those who disobeyed. In some other districts of the Punjab where martial law had been proclaimed similar humiliating orders were issued.

Dyer's action at Jallianwala Bagh—but not his subsequent "Crawling Order"—was approved by the Divisional Commander and by the Governor of the Punjab. The merchants and shopkeepers of Amritsar thanked him for rescuing the city from mob violence, and the Guardians of the Golden Temple showed their gratitude by investing him as a Sikh. There is no doubt that his strong-arm methods of dealing with disorder were warmly applauded by a considerable section of the Punjab population. But it raised an understandable outcry among the intelligentsia, particularly the Hindu intelligentsia. Was it to be expected that a civilized and "benign" government—for so the British Government in India was habitually termed—would mow down with rifle fire several hundred of its unarmed subjects? And was it "benign" for high government officials immediately to approve such drastic action before any inquiry had been held?

Some British officials, notably Sir Malcolm (Lord) Hailey, appreciated the gravity of the incident and realized that an inquiry should be ordered immediately. But the authorities moved slowly and it was not until late summer that a committee of inquiry was set up, composed of five Englishmen and three Indians and known after its chairman as the Hunter Committee.

Meanwhile, the greater the Indian outcry against Dyer, the more British public opinion rallied to his support. He was hailed as the savior of the Punjab and twenty thousand pounds was collected for him by his admirers. Amid these plaudits he cast aside his own original misgivings about the action he had taken and came to regard himself as a hero who almost single-handedly had quelled a widespread rebellion. In his evidence before the Hunter Committee he rashly claimed that he had aimed not merely at dispersing the crowd in Jallianwala Bagh but at making a wide impression and producing a moral effect throughout the Punjab. "We have little doubt," the Hunter Committee drily commented, "that he succeeded in creating a very wide impression and a great moral effect, but of a character quite opposite from the one he intended."

Although Dyer was censured by the Hunter Committee and subsequently relieved of his command, this could not remove the impression that a majority of the British public approved his massacre and humiliation of Indians. The whole episode was a tremendous shock to the Indians and proved to be a turning point in their attitude toward the British. For Gandhi it was an important factor in his conversion from a loyalist into a determined opponent of Government, for it afforded a striking illustration of the extent to which British rule had, in his words,

emasculated the people of India. In his eyes the massacre paled
into insignificance before the outrage of the "Crawling Order."
He was amazed that the Punjab, which had furnished the largest number of soldiers to the British Government during the
war, should have meekly submitted to such humiliations, and
he became convinced that British rule, which had brought such
degradation to the people, was an evil thing in itself, and not, as
he previously seems to have thought, "on the whole, a power
for good."

Even more far-reaching was the effect of the episode on
moderate Congressmen and nationalists, who were so outraged
that nearly all of them were ready to swing into line behind
Gandhi in the extreme course of action he was soon to advocate. Notable among those whose attitude was materially influenced by Jallianwala Bagh were Pandit Motilal Nehru, father of
the more ardent Jawaharlal, a moderate but influential Congressmen with a wide circle of English friends, and the poet,
Rabindranath Tagore, who although detached from politics was
sufficiently moved by the Punjab "atrocities" to renounce his
knighthood.

The Punjab disorders propelled Gandhi into the center of
Congress politics. Congress had boycotted the Hunter Committee because the Government had not named any Congress and
Muslim League representatives to it, and set up a parallel inquiry committee of its own. Gandhi, when he was finally permitted to visit the Punjab in October, was given a tumultuous
welcome and at once appointed a member of this committee.
He threw himself into its work with characteristic energy. The
main responsibility for direction rested with Motilal Nehru and
the Bengali leader, C. R. Das, but much of the actual inquiry
devolved on Gandhi and he was entrusted with the task of
drafting the report. The Congress leaders were impressed by
him and began to invite him to their inner conclaves.

The annual session of Congress was held at Amritsar in
December. Gandhi himself says that this marked his real entrance into Congress politics, and Jawaharlal Nehru describes
the Amritsar Congress as "the first Gandhi Congress." Although Tilak was present and took a prominent part in the

deliberations, "there could be no doubt about it that the majority of the delegates, and even more so the great crowds outside,.
looked to Gandhi for leadership. The slogan *Mahatma Gandhi
ki jai* * began to dominate the Indian political horizon."

Gandhi's belief in the efficacy of *satyagraha* and the temptation he was always under to resort to it were bound to
lead to a struggle with the Government, but, despite the Punjab
"atrocities," he does not seem to have wished or intended to
precipitate such a confrontation at this time. At the Amritsar
session he threw his growing influence on the side of modera-
tion. The Montagu-Chelmsford reforms, which had just received the Royal Assent, were the main subject for consideration. Tilak and C. R. Das, the two most prominent Congress
leaders, wished to reject them as wholly inadequate, but
Gandhi, supported by Jinnah, among others, pleaded warmly
for their acceptance, in spite of their defects. A compromise
resolution was adopted which, while condemning the reforms as
unsatisfactory and disappointing, expressed the hope that the
people would make use of the political opportunities that they
provided so as to secure the early establishment of full responsible government. The reforms were, in Gandhi's view, an
earnest attempt by the British people to do justice to India and
showed British character at its best, as General Dyer's inhuman-
ity showed it at its worst. Writing in *Young India* at this time
he said: "Our duty is not to subject [the reforms] to carping
criticism, but to settle down quietly to work so as to make them
a thorough success and thus anticipate the time for a full measure of responsibility."

Wise words, all too soon to be forgotten! However, for the
time being political reform was clearly not the issue which he
would select for a struggle with the Government. The issue
would be one of his own unorthodox choosing.

The confidence that leaders of Congress now had in Gandhi
was further demonstrated by their request that he undertake

* *Mahatma* means "great soul." This title, used by Tagore in a
letter to Gandhi in 1915, was in great vogue for a number of years,
but later went out of fashion. Gandhi himself expressed dislike of
it.

the revision of its constitution. The existing constitution and rules of business were Gokhale's legacy. They had served well enough when Congress was little more than a debating society which met once or twice a year, but they were inadequate if Congress were to be a countrywide political organization. Gandhi gladly accepted the task.

The reforms and the reorganization of Congress were proper subjects to engage the attention of a political leader. But simultaneously Gandhi's mind was running on quite different lines. "The immediate problem before us," he wrote in *Young India*, "is not how to run the Government of the country, but how to feed and clothe ourselves." His visit to the Punjab, where hand spinning had survived to a much greater extent than in Gujarat, fortified his belief that herein lay the sovereign remedy for India's poverty, and he gave typical expression to it: "The real reform that India needs is *swadeshi*.* . . . If every educated Indian will realise his primary duty, he will straightaway present the women of his household with a spinning wheel and provide facilities for learning the art of spinning."

Thus self-government and hand spinning became closely interwoven. Many desired self-government. Few cared for hand spinning. Nevertheless the ideal of universal hand spinning was capable of being put to political use, as Gandhi instinctively realized.

* Manufacture of essential goods within one's own country.

IX

The Khilafat Movement

and Noncooperation

If Gandhi had entertained any doubts about his ability to rouse the Indian masses, the experiences of 1919 swept them away. His call for a countrywide *hartal* had been a remarkable success, and thereafter wherever he went he was acclaimed and venerated. On his visit to the Punjab the crowds that greeted him were, in his own words, delirious with joy. Even a sober official estimate conceded that he

commanded among his countrymen all the traditional reverence with which the East envelopes a religious leader of acknowledged asceticism. . . . His readiness to take up the cudgels on behalf of any individual or class whom he regards as being oppressed has endeared him to the masses of his countrymen. In the case of the urban and rural population of many parts of the Bombay Presidency his influence is unquestioned, and he is regarded with a reverence for which "adoration" would hardly be too strong a word.

He was himself conscious, perhaps too conscious, of his popular appeal. "Rightly or wrongly," he told the Viceroy's private secretary in April 1919, "I seem to command, at the present moment, in an excessive degree, the respect and affection of the people all over India"; and a little later he asserted with a rather dangerous arrogance, "I am the one man who can today preserve the peace in India as no other man can."

Grave temptations beset all forms of power. Gandhi, with his power of appeal to the masses, was not immune to these temptations, and there were others besides himself who were aware of his power and saw how it might be exploited for political ends. So while he was advising his countrymen to settle down quietly and work to make the reforms a success, he was himself, in direct contradiction to this advice, being drawn insidiously into the leadership of a mass movement against the Government.

The issue which Gandhi chose for a breach with the Government was almost wholly irrelevant to any of India's real interests. He selected it partly from a commendable desire to promote Hindu-Muslim unity, but partly from a shrewd perception that it was an issue on which mass Muslim feeling could be aroused. The threatened dissolution of the Turkish Empire and abolition of the caliphate, though of no lasting significance to the Muslims of India, had become a focus for Muslim discontent, and a group of anti-British Muslims headed by the brothers Muhammad and Shaukat Ali, who had been interned during the war, were working up an agitation against Britain's "betrayal of Islam." This agitation, known as the Khilafat (caliphate) movement, had had Gandhi's sympathy from its inception, for it seemed to him to afford "such an opportunity of uniting the two communities as would not arise in a hundred years." He kept in close touch with the Khilafat Committee, which was guiding the movement, feeling that if he was to become a true friend of the Muslims he must help them as much as possible in securing a just settlement of the Khilafat question. He did not profess to go into its merits; he was satisfied that the Muslim demand did not offend any ethical principle—and that it had a mass appeal for the Muslims.

The British Government was deeply committed to releasing the Arabs from Turkish rule, thus curtailing the temporal powers of the Caliph (the Sultan of Turkey), and there was never any chance that it would back down on these commitments and accept the demands of the Khilafat Committee. But Gandhi was blind to these obvious facts and threw himself into the Khilafat movement with uncritical enthusiasm. His support was eagerly welcomed; with the backing of the Hindus there were the makings of a powerful agitation. In November 1919 the Khilafat leaders held a conference at Delhi to decide what should be done if their demands were rejected by the British Government. Gandhi attended. Various ways of expressing displeasure were proposed, such as nonparticipation in the peace celebrations and a boycott of British cloth. But Muslim extremists clamored for something that would produce an immediate effect on the British. At this point Gandhi introduced the idea of "noncooperation." Since resort to arms was impossible and undesirable, he said, the only true resistance to the Government was to cease to cooperate with it.

The idea was well received, but it was given no concrete shape at that time. Gandhi himself, having advocated noncooperation at Delhi, a month later at the Congress session at Amritsar pleaded earnestly for cooperation in making the reforms a success. He did so, he says, in the belief that the Government would not betray them on the Khilafat issue and so there would be no need for noncooperation. This ill-founded belief, if he really entertained it, was quickly dispelled. In January a Khilafat deputation, including Gandhi, saw the Viceroy and received a discouraging reply, and another deputation that had been sent to Europe was bluntly told that Turkey would not be allowed to hold sway over non-Turkish lands. There was clearly no prospect of a compromise, and Gandhi, though still claiming that he yielded to no one in his loyalty to the British connection, was by now busy working out with Muslim leaders the details of the projected "noncooperation" campaign. One of those who assisted him in drawing up the program was Maulana Abul Kalam Azad, destined later to be a prominent figure in Congress. Gandhi made it clear to the Muslims that if they chose to have him as their leader, they must observe the rule of nonviolence and submit to strict discipline. They could kick him out whenever they liked, but as long as he remained their leader he must be a dictator.

The Muslim leaders had no belief in nonviolence as an ethical principle, but they wanted Gandhi's support and the mass influence that he could command, and they were ready to put themselves in his hands and pledge themselves as a matter of tactics and expediency to the principles and policies that he advocated. For them the arrangement was an opportunistic alliance, while Gandhi believed that he was laying the foundations of Hindu-Muslim unity.

The Khilafat Committee fixed August 2 for the inauguration of the program. By this date it had not been accepted or even considered by Congress, but Gandhi, full of self-confidence, was running ahead of Congress and on August 1 sent a letter to the Viceroy announcing the withdrawal of his cooperation and surrendering the medals awarded to him by the British which, he said, he could not "wear with an easy conscience so long as my Mussulman countrymen have to labour under a wrong done to their religious sentiment." He charged the Imperial Government with having acted in the Khilafat matter "in an unscrupulous, immoral and unjust manner." Its attitude on the Punjab atrocities had been an additional cause of grave dissatisfaction.

On this very same day Tilak died in Bombay. "My strongest bulwark is gone!" Gandhi exclaimed on hearing the news, but it is very doubtful that Tilak would have supported him in the novel venture of noncooperation. In the last months of his life Tilak, the extremist and advocate of violence, had become more and more intent on taking advantage of the opportunities provided by the new reforms, while Gandhi, the apostle of nonviolence, carried away by the rising tide of national feeling, had become more and more indifferent to them.

A special session of Congress, held at Calcutta in September, decided—not without considerable opposition from prominent Congressmen, including Jinnah—to adopt the program of noncooperation to which Gandhi was already personally committed. For him its *raison d'être* was as a means of redressing the Khilafat and the Punjab wrongs. As usual he was concentrating on specific grievances rather than general issues. "But what about *swaraj?*" some speakers asked. "Surely the absence of *swaraj* is the biggest wrong of all?" Gandhi agreed to *swaraj* being included among the objectives of the movement, but, as far as he was concerned, it was an afterthought. The movement was started not as a struggle for independence, but in support of the Khilafat agitation.

As a first installment of his program of "progressive non-violent noncooperation" Gandhi proposed the return of decorations and honors awarded by the British, the withdrawal of children and students from Government schools and colleges (they were to be sent to "national schools" which existed only on paper), the boycott of law courts by lawyers and litigants (they were to submit cases to Congress arbitration), and the boycott of elections to the new legislative councils under the Montagu-Chelmsford reforms.

Most prominent Congress leaders of the older generation were opposed to the noncooperation program. They thought it impracticable—as certain items in it clearly were; they were apprehensive as to where subsequent installments might lead them; and C. R. Das, in particular, objected to the boycott of the new legislatures. But the younger members of Congress were behind Gandhi and his noncooperation resolution was accepted. The one veteran leader to support him was Motilal Nehru. Egged on by his ardent son and deeply impressed by Gandhi as a man, he had decided, after considerable thought, to back the new movement, although it meant giving up his lucrative legal practice. Jawaharlal has described his father's feelings: "The accumulated anger with which a series of events, culminating in the Punjab tragedy and its aftermath, filled him; the sense of utter wrong-doing and injustice, the bitterness of national humiliation, had to find some way out."

The next full session of Congress was held in December at Nagpur. Gandhi's mastery was now unquestioned, for the boycott of the elections to the new legislatures had been quite successful * and though the first installment of noncooperation, by its very nature, had not been a serious threat to the stability

* Of the six million people entitled to vote only about one-third went to the polls.

of the Government, the response to it by the literate classes had been a tremendous blow to the Government's prestige. With the election issue out of the way, C. R. Das and most of the other old stalwarts of Congress rallied to Gandhi's support. According to Jawaharlal, "the very success of the movement had convinced many a doubter and waverer." Jinnah, however, remained steadfast in his opposition to noncooperation.

The Nagpur session, besides confirming Gandhi's ascendancy and giving a fresh impetus to noncooperation, was memorable for its adoption of a new constitution for Congress based on recommendations put forward by Gandhi as requested by Congress at the Amritsar session. He regarded this constitution "with a certain measure of pride," and with good reason, for Congress was tranformed from little more than a decorous upper-middle-class debating society into a compact and effective political organization with a Working Committee of fifteen, an All-India Committee of three hundred and fifty, and provincial committees with roots reaching down to districts, towns, and even villages instead of being confined, as previously, to the more important cities. Gandhi was a believer in agitation— "We shall gain nothing without it," he had said—but he knew that successful agitation must rest on the foundation of a stable organization that would work consistently and continuously instead of intermittently as did the existing machinery of Congress. He gave Congress such an organization and also definite work programs. The over-all objective was now defined as the attainment of *swaraj*, within the British Empire if possible and outside it if necessary. The continued connection with Britain was thus no longer assumed to be axiomatic. This objective was to be achieved not "by constitutional means" and "a steady reform of the existing system of administration," as before, but "by all legitimate and peaceful means"—and this was interpreted to include deliberate breaking of the law. The immediate tasks to be undertaken, apart from the intensification of the noncooperation movement, were to expand Congress membership to ten million,* with special emphasis on rural

* This goal was not achieved. By 1939 membership was only about five million.

areas, and to collect ten million rupees for a Tilak Memorial Fund. Gandhi, however, also set Congress to work on other special programs of his own that required more sustained effort —the revival of hand spinning and the removal of untouchability. Though quite a few Congressmen looked on these programs as fads of Gandhi's, they were now woven into the fabric of Congress, for the Gandhian era in Congress politics had begun and Congress was being converted from a westernized into an essentially Indian institution. Jawaharlal Nehru described the effects:

> The whole look of the Congress changed. European clothes vanished and soon only *khadi* was to be seen; a new class of delegate, chiefly drawn from the lower middle-class, became the type of Congressman; the language used became increasingly Hindustani . . . and a new life and enthusiasm and earnestness became evident in Congress gatherings.

Thus Gandhi refashioned Congress and impressed on it the character it was to bear for the next generation, and by making it build up a solid, countrywide organization he conferred on it a benefit more lasting than he either imagined or wished. Years after independence, when Gandhi himself was dead and the prestige and popularity of Congress had long sinced waned, it still remained the only political party in the country with branches everywhere and thus was the only one able to fight elections in every constituency. No other political party could challenge its All-India supremacy.

The many Congressmen who fell under Gandhi's spell at this time felt that at last they had found the leader they needed. Here was a unique man, the embodiment of traditional Hindu virtues, who combined a capacity for organization and action with a saintly, ascetic way of life that commended itself widely to a population still addicted to the centuries'-old cult of the *sadhu* and *faqir*.* True, there were few of Gandhi's followers who gave unqualified allegiance to his doctrine of nonviolence, but it appealed to Hindu sentiment and, as Nehru put it, "with

* Hindu ascetic and holy man; Muslim ascetic.

our background and traditions it was the right policy for us."
The strongly moral, quasireligious element that Gandhi in-
jected into politics had a great attraction for the average Hindu;
even those without religious beliefs thought "the spiritualisation
of politics a fine idea." Some of Gandhi's admirers, however,
realized that with all his remarkable qualities he was a bit of a
crank. "Often we discussed his fads and peculiarities among
ourselves," Nehru records, "and said, half-humorously" —but
prophetically—"that when *swaraj* came these fads must not be
encouraged."

The new strength and vitality that Congress had acquired
was accompanied by a few losses. A group of able and eminent
moderates, who were ready to accept without cavil the
Montagu-Chelmsford reforms, had broken away at the end of
1918 and formed a new party, the National Liberal Federation.
Naturally they did not join in the boycott of the elections to the
new legislatures, and though they could not muster many
voters, their cooperation helped to provide Hindu members for
the legislative councils. A few other stalwarts fell away from
Congress after the Calcutta and Nagpur sessions had established Gandhi's ascendancy and accepted his policy of noncooperation, among them Jinnah, a fervent nationalist who in the
past few years had done much to bring the Muslim League
into line with Congress policies and had been acclaimed the
"Ambassador of Hindu-Muslim unity." Jinnah disapproved of
noncooperation. The constitutional way, he told Gandhi, is the
right way; your way is the wrong way. He also disapproved of
the move to turn Congress into a popular mass organization
and disliked the Hindu revivalist tone that Gandhi was giving
to it. As an apostle of Hindu-Muslim unity his instincts were
right. Unwittingly Gandhi, by "Hinduizing" the national
movement, was setting Congress on a course that could only
lead to disunity. This was not generally realized at the time and
not fully realized even by Jinnah himself, but he did complain
that Gandhi had caused split and division in almost every
institution he had approached. Gradually Jinnah drifted away
from Congress. Only many years later was the significance
of his departure appreciated.

At the beginning of 1921 Gandhi and Congress were on the crest of a wave. Thanks to Gandhi's espousal of the Khilafat movement, Hindus and Muslims were working together as never before, and if they had no common constructive aim, they were at least united in common antagonism to the British Raj. The Hindu-Muslim entente, regarded by the British as their greatest danger in India, had seemingly come about. The British authorities were perturbed, and an outbreak of unrest among the Sikh peasantry of the Punjab, ostensibly over a religious issue, gave them further grounds for uneasiness.

During this time Gandhi was touring the country extensively and wherever he went thousands of people assembled to hear him. At least this was the apparent purpose of their gatherings, but he himself complained: "I went to a place where everybody was busy shouting 'Mahatma Gandhi-ki-jai' and everyone was trying to fall at my feet but no one was willing to listen to me." People bowed down and touched his feet in such numbers that his ankles became quite sore and had to be rubbed with Vaseline.

Feeling the tide running in his favor and misled by his previous successes in South Africa and locally in India, he promised that if there was sufficient response to his program, a *swaraj* would be attained within a year. Noncooperation was extended to cover a boycott of foreign cloth and the picketing of liquor shops, and preparations were made for adding to it a new campaign of civil disobedience to be concentrated initially in the Bardoli * *taluk* of the Surat district of Bombay.

The boycott of foreign cloth aroused great enthusiasm, which was shared and stimulated by the Indian mill owners. On July 31, in commemoration of Tilak's death, a huge bonfire of such cloth was made in Bombay, reminiscent of the burning of registration certificates in Johannesburg, and the example was followed in other cities. Because of its connection with his beloved *khadi*, Gandhi took a particularly keen interest in the drive against foreign cloth. Believing that millions of his countrymen would be too poor to buy enough *khadi* to replace their dis-

* Bardoli was chosen because a number of Gandhi's associates in South Africa came from there.

carded garments, he advised people to be satisfied with a mere loin cloth, and to set an example he decided to discard his vest and cap and to content himself with only a loin cloth and *chaddar*, a sheet worn as a wrap when required. Thus there emerged the familiar figure of a "half-naked fakir," known throughout the world as Gandhi.

What was the *swaraj* that he had promised within a year? To most Congressmen it meant political independence, preferably under a democratic form of government. Gandhi himself was careful not to define it and when pressed took refuge in vague generalizations. He was more interested in moral principles and moral character than in political forms and constitutional issues. *Swaraj* for him connoted self-government not merely in the political sense, but in the moral sense of individual and national self-control, and he used the term indiscriminately in these two distinct senses. Politically, *swaraj* was for him a sort of "homespun" self-government, based on *panchayats* * and traditional Indian political forms. But the attainment of political *swaraj* was itself only an aspect or necessary consequence of the moral reform of Indian society, including the removal of untouchability.

Swaraj was to be won by nonviolent, peaceful, noncooperation. As before in South Africa but now to a much wider audience he expounded his doctrine:

> The religion of non-violence is not meant merely for the *rishis* † and saints. It is meant for the common people as well. Non-violence is the law of our species as violence is the law of the brute. The spirit lies dormant in the brute and he knows no law but that of physical might. The dignity of man requires obedience to a higher law—to the strength of the spirit.
>
> I have therefore ventured to place before India the ancient law of self-sacrifice. For *satyagraha* and its offshoots, non-cooperation and civil resistance, are nothing but new names for the law of suffering. . . .

* A village council of five persons.
† Seers.

I am not pleading for India to practise non-violence because it is weak. I want her to practise non-violence being conscious of her strength and power. . . . If India takes up the doctrine of the sword, she may gain momentary victory. Then India will cease to be the pride of my heart.

This high-flown doctrine had no appeal to the Muslim leaders of the Khilafat movement. As Gandhi well knew, they had adopted nonviolence not as a creed, but as a tactic, to be discarded at will, if violence appeared to offer a better prospect of success. Very soon the fanatical Ali brothers, forgetting their pledges to Gandhi, were inciting the people to violence and the Muslim troops to mutiny. Their repeated declarations that they were "Muslims first and everything else afterward" and that the Amir of Afghanistan should be helped if he invaded India, gave the Hindu population grounds for disquiet and Gandhi food for thought. Hindu-Muslim unity and the principle of nonviolence were both threatened.

Lord Reading, who had become Viceroy in April 1921, decided to prosecute the Ali brothers. Immediately there was a Muslim outcry that Gandhi himself was skillfully keeping on the right side of the law, leaving the Muslims to face trial and imprisonment. Gandhi, on the advice of others, had an interview with Lord Reading and after prolonged discussions agreed to persuade the Ali brothers to apologize and to renew their assurances of nonviolence, whereupon the proceedings against them were discontinued. But the brothers were disgruntled; for them Gandhian leadership had begun to lose its charm, and a few months later they were again urging Muslim soldiers to desert. This time they were tried, convicted, and imprisoned. Gandhi, though he publicly applauded their seditious speeches, was not arrested.

Meanwhile in August a ferocious uprising of the Moplahs, Muslim peasants of partly Arab descent living in the Malabar territory of Madras, broke the façade of Hindu-Muslim unity. Inflamed by the Khilafat agitation, they at first attacked the Government, but soon turned their fury on Hindu money-

lenders and landlords. Gandhi, incautiously minimizing the
reports of the disorders, spoke of the "brave God-fearing
Moplahs fighting for what they consider as religion, and in a
manner which they consider religious." As this holy war, which
Gandhi seemed to bless, included desecration of Hindu temples
and forcible conversions and savage massacres of Hindus, alarm
and dismay spread through the Hindu community, which
became less inclined than ever to share the Ali brothers' hopes
of an Afghan invasion. Gandhi's whole policy of alliance with
extremist Muslims on a religious issue began to seem of doubtful wisdom.

The noncooperation movement, however, had not yet spent
itself. Gandhi was busily enrolling volunteers in a National
Volunteer Corps which would come forward to defy specified
laws when he gave the signal. The climax, therefore, was still to
come. The Government of India, in the misplaced hope of
easing the prevailing tension, had agreed that the Prince of
Wales should pay a ceremonial visit to the country. Gandhi,
courteous as always, decreed that the Prince should not be
greeted with *hartals*, demonstrations, and other signs of disapproval. Nevertheless, his arrival at Bombay in November
provoked a hostile demonstration by noncooperators against
those who took part in welcoming him, largely Parsis, Christians, and Anglo-Indians. This ended in a gruesome riot, and
there were disorders at other places during the Prince's tour.
Gandhi, who had himself been an eyewitness to the fearful
excesses in Bombay, suspended preparations for civil disobedience in Bardoli and vehemently rebuked those who had broken
the pledge of nonviolence.

The *swaraj* that I have witnessed during the last two days
has stunk in my nostrils. Hindu-Muslim unity has been a
menace to the handful of Parsis, Christians and Jews. The
non-violence of the non-cooperators has been worse than
the violence of the cooperators. For, with non-violence on
our lips we have terrorised those who have differed from
us, and in so doing we have deceived our God. . . . I
invite every Hindu and Musalman citizen to retire to his

house, ask God for forgiveness, and to befriend the injured
communities from the very depth of his heart.

On the same day he announced that he would fast until the
Hindus and Muslims of Bombay made peace with the other
communities. Quiet was restored after two or three days and he
broke his fast, but he took a vow "to observe every Monday a
twenty-four-hour fast till *swaraj* is attained."

The preparations for civil disobedience had been suspended,
but the next month at its annual session Congress was in a very
bellicose mood. A resolution that nonviolence should be abandoned and that India should become a republic totally independent of Britain attracted a good deal of support. It was
rejected at Gandhi's instance, but, pressed by his followers to
make good his promise of *swaraj* within a year, he himself put
forward a resolution calling for "aggressive civil disobedience,"
and preparations for launching a no-tax campaign in Bardoli
were resumed.

Some Englishmen—notably Sir George (Lord) Lloyd,
Governor of Bombay—believed that Gandhi's preaching of
nonviolence was no more than a screen for plans for violent
revolution, and urged that he should be arrested immediately.
In the early part of 1921 individual Congressmen had been
arrested from time to time and sentenced under the ordinary
law, but it was not until the end of November that the Government struck hard and, declaring the National Volunteer Corps
an illegal organization, began to make mass arrests. During the
next two months about thirty thousand persons, including most
of the Congress leaders, were arrested and imprisoned. But the
Government still hesitated to touch Gandhi himself, and
indeed made a conciliatory move. He was told that the Viceroy
was prepared to call a conference of political leaders at which
considerable political concessions would be announced. But
nothing came of it as Gandhi, disregarding the advice of C. R.
Das, A. K. Azad, and others, insisted that the Ali brothers and
other Khilafat prisoners should be released first.

At last, on February 4, 1922, Gandhi took a step that left the
Government no room for further lenience. In a letter to Lord

Reading, he announced that he would personally inaugurate civil disobedience at Bardoli unless the Government showed a "complete change of heart" within a week. The Government replied firmly: "Mass civil disobedience is fraught with such danger to the State that it must be met with sternness and severity." Instructions were issued for his arrest on February 14.

An event now occurred that upset both Gandhi's and the Government's plans. At Chauri-Chaura, a village in the Gorakhpur district of the United Provinces, a mob of peasants led by Congress volunteers attacked and set fire to the police station and killed or burned to death twenty-two police constables. Gandhi's reaction to this outrage was immediate. He summoned a meeting of the Working Committee of Congress at Bardoli and, instead of inaugurating civil disobedience, had a resolution passed ordering its suspension. Noncooperators were forbidden to defy the law or to seek to get themselves arrested and were instructed to confine themselves to "constructive work" such as the promotion of hand spinning and temperance and the improvement of the lot of the depressed classes. The country, Gandhi said, must undergo a course of self-purification and penance before there could be any thought of resuming *satyagraha*. He imposed on himself a five-day fast.

The Government of India was relieved but puzzled, and put off Gandhi's arrest. Gandhi's followers were puzzled and resentful. Some of them began to question the soundness of his whole policy. But what could they do? Most of the prominent leaders were already in jail and there was almost no one still at liberty who could challenge his authority. Those in jail, according to Jawaharlal Nehru, learned of the suspension of civil disobedience with "amazement and consternation" and were angry at the halting of the struggle when it seemed to be meeting with such success. Later they realized that they had misjudged the situation, for the whole movement, as they subsequently admitted, "in spite of its apparent power and the widespread enthusiasm, was going to pieces. All organisation and discipline was disappearing; almost all our good men were in prison, and the masses had so far received little training to carry on by themselves." Gandhi was fully aware of all this. If a civil-disobedience campaign had been launched at this time, it would have achieved nothing and would have quickly degenerated into outbreaks of violence which the Government could have crushed with demoralizing severity. "We should have been leading not a non-violent struggle," Gandhi told Jawarhalal, "but essentially a violent struggle." The Chauri-Chaura episode afforded him a good reason for abandoning a campaign in which he had ceased to believe.

With the suspension of civil disobedience the noncooperation campaign also began to wilt and soon collapsed. Lawyers resumed their practice and school children their studies. Gandhi's promise of *swaraj* within a year remained signally unfulfilled. In March he was at last himself arrested and sentenced to six years' imprisonment. Contrary to the Government's apprehensions, there was no trouble.

Meanwhile interest in the Khilafat agitation was fast waning among the Muslims. Early in 1922 the Viceroy, to sooth Muslim feelings, had formally requested the British Government to revise the Treaty of Sèvres and accord Turkey more lenient treatment, and he astutely obtained permission from the Secretary of State to publish his dispatch.* Muslim confidence in the Government of India began to revive and the Hindu-Muslim alliance, resting on the shaky foundation of the Khilafat issue, began to crumble. The Moplahs had dealt it the first blow; the Turks, by abolishing the Khilafat themselves, gave it the final *coup-de-grâce*.

Gandhi had naïvely hoped to lay the foundations of Hindu-Muslim unity by supporting the Muslims over a religious issue. But this issue, of which he himself knew little and the Hindus in general cared less, represented no real interest of the Indian Muslims and had a sentimental appeal for them that was only transient. Therefore, support for the Khilafat agitation and its irresponsible leaders afforded no basis for a Hindu-Muslim alliance. Such an alliance could rest securely only on an adjustment of their conflicting interests—a problem which Gandhi,

* Mr. Montagu, the Secretary of State, gave this permission without consulting his Cabinet colleagues and was compelled to resign.

unlike Tilak, had thus far ignored and one which could not be solved in conjunction with extremist fanatics like the Ali brothers. Gandhi's instinct to seek Hindu-Muslim unity was a sound one, but his choice of men and methods was mistaken. The Khilafat agitation, by importing religious fanaticism into politics, had opened the door to communal frenzy.

Gandhi had also seriously underestimated the strength of the Government and the difficulty of organizing an effective agitation that would also remain nonviolent in a huge country like India with such a numerous and diverse population. India was very different from South Africa. Although his movement, largely because of Muslim support, had frightened the English and shaken their prestige, it had not remained nonviolent and had brought no tangible result. _Swaraj_ seemed as far off as ever.

Nevertheless Gandhi, although temporarily defeated, had created a new situation. He had gained a hold on the population greater than that of any former nationalist leader and had successfully organized a widespread resistance to British authority unparalleled since the Mutiny. In the process he had started, under Congress' leadership, a powerful national movement directed toward conflict rather than cooperation with the British Government and enjoying a large following among the town population throughout the country. Imprisonment, the principal deterrent at the disposal of Government, had been made to lose its terrors. "Jail," Jawaharlal Nehru told a magistrate, "has indeed become a heaven for us, a holy place of pilgrimage." Since the upheaval of 1857 British rule had rested on the tacit consent of the bulk of the population, but Gandhi had shown that among the literate classes such consent was no longer assured. A rent had been made in the mystic fabric of British authority.

Gandhi was tried on three charges of causing disaffection toward the existing government by articles that he had published in _"Young India."_ He pleaded guilty to the charges and said that he was ready to submit not to a light penalty but to the highest penalty. Preaching disaffection, he told the judge, had become almost a passion with him and it was, in his view, "a virtue to be disaffected towards a Government which in its totality had done more harm to India than any previous system." He did not attempt to disclaim responsibility for "the diabolical crimes at Chauri-Chaura." He should have known the consequences of his acts, and he did know them.

I knew I was playing with fire. I ran the risk and if I was set free I would still do the same. . . . I wanted to avoid violence. Non-violence is the first article of my faith. It is also the last article of my Creed. I had to make my choice. I had either to submit to a system which I consider has done an irreparable harm to my country, or incur the risk of the mad fury of my people bursting forth when they understood the truth from my lips.

Here was a frank statement. British rule in India was such an evil thing that to rid the country of it he was prepared to break the first article of his faith and run the risk of violence—and would do it again. He was not blind to the contradiction; he admitted it.

But why had he—until recently a cooperator with the British, who as late as December 1919 had pleaded for making the Montagu-Chelmsford reforms a success and only a little earlier had agreed with Lord Chelmsford that India had on the whole benefitted from the British connection—why had he within so short time come to take a diametrically opposite stand? The carefully prepared statement that he read to the court offered no very convincing explanation of this sudden change. He had, he said, reluctantly reached the conclusion that the British connection had rendered India more helpless, politically and economically, than she ever was before. The British had disarmed her, crushed her spirit of manliness, and ruined her cottage industry of spinning and weaving. But these ill effects of British rule were not new to him; he had been aware of them twelve years earlier when he wrote "Hind Swaraj." They may have been more forcibly impressed on him since his return to India—in particular, the events in the Punjab had opened his eyes to the helpless submissiveness of his countrymen before a British show of force. But he had urged the acceptance of the reforms several months after these events took place, and his later complaint that "the Punjab crime had been whitewashed" by the British was hardly justified, for the Hunter Committee had roundly condemned General Dyer and his military career had been abruptly terminated.*

The truth is that Gandhi's change of course and attitude between December 1919 and August 1920 cannot be wholly explained or justified in the light of cold reason. It was to some extent an emotional reaction. No doubt by his espousal of the Khilafat agitation and the suggestion of noncooperation to its leaders he had unthinkingly committed himself to action on their behalf if their demands were not met. He was, however, a man of sufficient strength of mind and moral courage to extricate himself from this commitment if he had wished to do so. But the wish was lacking. Still smarting under such indignities as the "Crawling Order," sensing the strong current of popular feeling that was still running against the Government, itching as always to use the weapon of *satyagraha*, and flattered by his previous successes, he was only too ready to honor his commitment to the Khilafatists and to assume leadership of the noncooperation movement that he had himself suggested to them.

The judge, Mr. C. N. Broomfield, sentenced Gandhi to six years' simple imprisonment—the same sentence that Tilak had received twelve years earlier for a similar offense. In awarding this sentence he said that he did not ignore the fact that in the eyes of millions of his countrymen Gandhi was a great patriot and a great leader and that even those who differed from him in politics looked upon him as a man of high ideals and of noble and even saintly life. And he concluded: "If the course of events in India should make it possible for the Government to reduce the period and release you, no one will be better pleased than I."

Gandhi was now publicly committed to the termination of British rule in India, even at the risk of violence, and for the

* Gandhi publicly declared that he did not desire vengeance or punishment, yet he demanded that the pensions of General Dyer and Sir Michael O'Dwyer should be canceled. In his eyes, apparently, the withholding of a pension was not a punishment.

rest of his life this remained his avowed object, as from his early childhood, when he had started to eat meat in order to be a match for Englishmen, it had probably been his inmost wish. But he still had faith in nonviolence—and some faith even in the British.

X

Partial
Eclipse

Gandhi's imprisonment marked the beginning of a period of about six years during which he remained, politically, in partial eclipse. His leadership of Congress had been dynamic. He had kindled enthusiasm and roused popular feeling as never before —but to what purpose? Noncooperation had brought not *swaraj*, but the Bardoli resolutions. Nonviolence had ended in violence, as had been widely predicted. Outside Congress many Indians of eminence had all along been severely critical of the Gandhian technique of mass defiance of authority, which they saw to be fraught with long-term danger to the country. Now that it had not proved successful, there were doubts and disenchantment within Congress also. A movement under the leadership of C. R. Das and Motilal Nehru was started to revoke the boycott of the legislatures and to take part in the general elections which were due at the end of 1923. The legislatures, it was contended, offered the best arena in which to fight and obstruct the Government, and by entering them Congressmen could "wreck the reforms from inside."

At first their proposal to reverse Gandhi's policy encountered considerable opposition, headed by C. Rajagopalachari, and early in 1923 C. R. Das, having failed to get his way in Congress, seceded with a group of followers to form temporarily a separate "Swaraj" Party with Motilal as secretary. During the year, however, the Swarajist views began to prevail, and at a special session of Congress in September a resolution was passed permitting Congressmen to enter the legislatures if they had no conscientious scruples against doing so. As was to be expected, these Congress or Swarajist candidates met with a good deal of success.

Gandhi did not approve of these developments, but from jail he could not and did not wish to attempt to control them. The only message he sent his followers was: "Peace, non-violence, suffering." He himself, incarcerated in the Yeravda jail near Poona, was "as happy as a bird" and felt that he was accomplishing just as much inside as outside the prison. He spent six hours a day reading—mostly books on religion—and four hours spinning and carding.

Suddenly on January 13, 1924, there was a curt Government announcement: "Mr. Gandhi was operated on for acute appendicitis last night." After some hours of intense anxiety it was reported that the operation had been successful, and by the beginning of February he was well on the way to recovery.

As soon as his illness became known there was vigorous agitation for his release. The Government decided to yield to it. With more than half of Congress now supporting entry into the legislatures and many Congressmen already elected, there was little likelihood of Gandhi effectively renewing "noncooperation" in the near future; indeed, it was reckoned that after his convalescence it would take him some time to regain leadership of the Congress from C. R. Das and Motilal Nehru. So on February 5 he was unconditionally released and shortly afterward was moved for convalescence to Juhu, a seaside resort near Bombay.

Within a few weeks he resumed editorial charge of his two weeklies, *Young India* and *Navajiwan*, whose circulation had declined greatly in his absence, and soon a copious stream of

articles began to flow from his pen. During the next few years
of partial eclipse it was partly through his articles in these
weeklies that he retained his hold over the public.

From his point of view the situation in India had sadly deteriorated during his two years of imprisonment. There was disunity in the Congress and disunity in the country. "Our noncooperation," he wrote in *Young India*, "has taken the form of
non-cooperation in practice with each other instead of with the
Government." The spurious Hindu-Muslim concord of Khilafat
days had given way to an antagonism more pronounced than
ever before. The Moplah rebellion of 1921 had been followed
by savage Hindu-Muslim riots in Multan in September 1922,
and by 1924 there was no longer any pretense of Hindu-Muslim
unity. Throughout the country divisions of caste and creed were
becoming sharper. In the south, Brahmins were set against non-
Brahmins. In the Punjab, militant Sikh nationalism was raising
its head. Among the downtrodden "Untouchables" there were
stirrings of opposition to the caste Hindus. How was *swaraj*
possible in a society so lacking in cohesion?

These fundamental problems of unity troubled Gandhi even
more than the squabbles within Congress, but it was to the
latter that he first had to turn his attention. C. R. Das and
Motilal Nehru visited him at Juhu and tried to get his blessing
for their policy of entry into the legislatures. The outcome of
much polite discussion was an agreement to differ. Gandhi declined to help them actively in a course of action in which he
did not believe, but he would not seek to oppose a *fait
accompli*. The Swarajists, having been permitted by Congress to
enter the legislatures, should not now be called upon by the
"no-changers"* to withdraw nor be made the target of hostile
propaganda. He advised the "no-changers" to observe strict
neutrality and, instead of worrying about what the Swarajists
were doing, to devote themselves to the constructive program of
promoting *khaddar* and Hindu-Muslim unity.

What support was there now in Congress for Gandhi's program and principles? C. R. Das and Motilal had a large follow-

* The name applied to those in Congress who opposed the
Swarajists.

ing of their own, and perhaps even commanded a majority. Recognizing that his word was no longer law, Gandhi deliberately decided to clear the air and, at the risk of defeat, to put his authority to the test. In June, therefore, he framed and laid before a meeting of the All-India Congress Committee a number of resolutions designed to reveal Congressional support for two elements that he considered vital in his program—*khaddar* and nonviolence. One resolution proposed that office holders in Congress should be required to spin at least half an hour a day and to send in a prescribed quantity of self-spun yarn every month, in default of which they should be deemed to have vacated their office. Another resolution condemned a recent terrorist outrage in Bengal, in which a European named Day had been mistakenly murdered by a young Bengali, Gopinath Saha, who thought he was killing the Commissioner of Police; and, further, it emphatically declared that "all such acts are inconsistent with the Congress creed and its resolution of non-violent non-cooperation." These resolutions provoked a storm; at one stage all the Swarajists walked out of the meeting, and the final outcome was far from being a victory for Gandhi. The first resolution was passed only after an amendment which rendered it innocuous by withdrawing the penalty clause, and the Gopinath resolution was passed by a margin of only eight votes. Such a narrow majority for a principle that was so vital to Gandhi was in his opinion equivalent to an outright defeat. He broke down and wept in public, and a few days later, writing in *Young India,* declared himself "defeated and humbled."

Yet in spite of the defeat and the clear evidence that, for the time being at least, he could not dominate Congress, at the annual session at Belgaum in December 1924 he allowed himself to be elected president for the ensuing year. Previously, as Jawaharlal remarked, he had been the permanent superpresident, but he was now content with a humbler office. At Belgaum noncooperation was formally suspended except for the refusal to wear foreign cloth, and it was also formally resolved that work in connection with the central and provincial legislatures should be carried out by the Swaraj Party as an integral part of Congress. Thus the Swarajists were triumphant. It was believed that their Bengali leader, C. R. Das, and some of his lieutenants, notably the Bengali Subhas Chandra Bose, had no more faith in nonviolence than they had in spinning and secretely sympathized with Bengali terrorists, which explained the narrow majority for Gandhi's Gopinath Saha resolution.

The Viceroy of the day, Lord Reading, has given a picture of Gandhi's position at this time which, though unflattering and somewhat uncharitable, contains some elements of truth:

> Gandhi is now attached to the tail of Das and Nehru, although they try their utmost to make him and his supporters think that he is one of the heads, if not *the* head. It is pathetic to observe the rapid decline in the power of Gandhi and the frantic attempts he is now making to cling to his position as leader at the expense of practically every principle he has hitherto advocated. . . . I have always believed in his sincerity and devotion to high ideals, but I have always doubted the wisdom of his political leaderships and have felt that personal vanity still played far too important a part in his mental equipment. . . . Apparently he has still faith in the spinning wheel, although he should be aware that the vast majority of all those obtained during his great missionary period have lain idle in the corner, if they have not been broken up since he was incarcerated.

Gandhi's influence and popularity, permanent and unchanging among the masses, waxed and waned in Congress and among the intelligentsia of India, and it was on the wane at this time. The Swarajists, not Gandhi, were in daily conflict with the Government in the central and provincial assemblies, castigating its many supposed iniquities and opposing its bills and motions, and it was they who got the headlines in the newspapers and attracted public attention. Gandhi's program of spinning and doing away with untouchability was believed in by few and excited ridicule among many. "Spin and weave," asked Tagore; "Is this the gospel of a new creative age?" Even Gandhi's devoted disciple, Jawaharlal, felt disappointed. Spinning and social reform, excellent in themselves, hardly seemed the pathway to *swaraj*.

Hindu-Muslim unity was the other item in Gandhi's program. At the time he was released from jail it seemed to him to be the only problem in the country demanding immediate solution, and during the summer of 1924 he devoted most of one issue of *Young India* to a discussion of "Hindu-Muslim tension—Its Cause and Cure." He found that he was being blamed in some quarters for the increase in Muslim aggressiveness. His critics said, "You asked the Hindus to make common cause with the Muslims in the Khilafat question. That resulted in unifying and awakening the Muslims and now that Khilafat is over, the awakened Muslims have proclaimed a kind of Holy War against us Hindus." There was truth in this criticism, but Gandhi was unrepentant. He was never ready to admit that his alliance with Muslim fanatics over the Khilafat question had been unwise, and he evaded his critics by putting the discussion on a broader plane: "The awakening of the masses was a necessary part of their training. It is a tremendous gain. I would do nothing to put the people to sleep again." How could Gandhi, who had such an appeal for the masses and such a deep sympathy for them, wish to put them to sleep again? It would have been an impossible contradiction. But he does not seem to have perceived that the awakening of the masses was unlikely to be compatible with nonviolence or communal harmony.

The debate in *Young India* on communal tension was scarcely ended when a wave of Hindu-Muslim riots swept across India, culminating in a shocking outbreak in Kohat in the North-West Frontier Province in September, when a hundred fifty-five people were killed or injured and the entire Hindu population fled from the town. Gandhi, after mature deliberation, imposed on himself a twenty-one-day fast "as a penance and prayer." "It seems," he said, "as if God had been dethroned. Let us reinstate Him in our hearts." The fast, which was undertaken in the Delhi house of the Khilafat leader, Muhammad Ali, assumed something of the character of a religious rite. When it was finally broken, there were recitations from the Koran and the Upanishads, and the Christian hymn "When I Survey the Wondrous Cross" was sung.

Meanwhile a "unity conference," presided over by Motilal Nehru, was held in Delhi, but beyond generating good feeling among those who attended, it achieved nothing. A few months later Gandhi called an all-parties conference, which appointed a subcommittee to outline the terms for an agreement between Hindus and Muslims. This also ended in failure; the subcommittee reported that agreement on any of the really important points at issue was impossible. Gandhi publicly confessed that he had been "found wanting as a physician prescribing a cure for this malady," as neither Hindus nor Muslims were ready to accept his cure. Fast and conference alike were ineffective.

Inevitably this failure was accompanied by a strengthening of communal parties, and public figures who had hithero been counted as nationalists began to drift toward them. The Muslim League, moribund during the Khilafat period, revived and at a meeting in Lahore under the chairmanship of former Congressman Jinnah began staking Muslim claims against the day of British withdrawal from India. Simultaneously the Hindu Mahasabha, an essentially communal organization, began to assume prominence, and a number of Hindu Congressmen gravitated toward it—a movement that was encouraged by a split in the ranks of the Swarajists after the death of their leader, C. R. Das in 1925. Differences arose among them over the question of accepting office and a group calling themselves the Responsivists, who were eager to accept office and enjoy its fruits, broke away and began to collaborate closely with the Hindu Mahasabha. In the elections of 1926, in which communal issues figured, they succeeded with Hindu Mahasabha support in routing the Swarajists.

Participation in the work of the legislatures by the Swarajists, Responsivists, and, from the very start, the Liberals—all of them offshoots of Congress—saved the Montagu-Chelmsford reforms from being a complete failure as a training for parliamentary government. The Central Assembly in Delhi attracted some of the best Indian talent, and over the years many keen Indian nationalists developed an affection for parliamentary institutions and skill in working within them. A sound parliamentary tradition was established which was to be of immense value to India after independence had been attained. But Gandhi cared for none of these things; he admitted that he had no aptitude for them, and he did not believe in parliamentary government—he had denounced it in "Hind Swaraj." The British program for importing the whole apparatus of Westminster into India was but another "unholy attempt to impose British methods and institutions on India." To preserve Congress unity he had acquiesced in the Swarajists entering the legislatures, but he never thought any good would come of it. *Swaraj* was not to be won, in his opinion, by following the route laid down by the English Government and participating in the work of English-modeled legislatures. In truth, in so far as *swaraj* connoted the moral reform of Indian society, and above all the ending of untouchability, it was not to be attained by these methods.

So while the Swarajists squabbled among themselves and fought wordy battles with government officials in the legislatures, Gandhi concentrated on his own "constructive program." "Go throughout your districts," he admonished Congressmen, "and spread the message of *khaddar*, the message of Hindu-Muslim unity, the message of anti-untouchability." He himself undertook extensive tours during 1925, preaching this gospel everywhere, with particular emphasis in the north on Hindu-Muslim unity and in the south on the removal of untouchability. "So long as untouchability disfigures Hinduism," he affirmed, "so long do I hold attainment of *swaraj* to be an utter impossibility. Supposing it was a gift descending from Downing Street to India, that gift would be a curse upon the land, if we do not get rid of this curse of untouchability."

The campaign against untouchability was not very popular, but by his persistence Gandhi did succeed in awakening the conscience of the Hindu community to this blot on Hindu society. Sometimes when he found Untouchables cordoned off in a corner by themselves at meetings he was to address, he would deliberately go and take his stand among them and address the meeting from their midst, incurring pollution for all to see by coming in actual physical contact with them.

His faith in *khaddar* remained unabated despite ridicule and some discouragement. "No one is listening to you," he was advised, "so why not stop talking of *khaddar?*" "But why should I stop reciting my favourite *mantra?*"* he asked in reply. *"Khaddar* and *khaddar* alone is the only passport to the hearts of villagers." He maintained that there was nothing better than the spinning wheel for industrializing rural India. Moreover, spinning was something that everyone could do without much effort, it could bring everyone together—rich and poor, villager and town dweller—and make them feel akin, and the effort to popularize it and dispose of the yarn produced afforded excellent scope for nonviolent political workers to develop their skill as organizers.

In September 1925 he was able to persuade Congress to establish an All-India Spinners Association with a branch in every district, which was to be part of the Congress organization but with independent existence and powers. Here was something for Congress workers to get their teeth into. Here was a means of training and keeping employed an elite corps of political workers who would be available for leading a new nonviolent campaign of civil disobedience when the right time came for it, as come it would. This political objective was never absent from Gandhi's mind. While in jail he had pondered on the need for training and organization, and when he was released he consciously applied himself to the task of meeting this need.

The *khaddar* program required both funds and a market for the *khaddar* that was produced. The boycott of foreign cloth— the one item of the noncooperation program that had not been suspended—and the elevation of *khaddar* into a symbol of patriotism (the wearing of *khaddar* was made compulsory for Congressmen in 1926) were expected to create the necessary market. Regarding funds, the appeal that Gandhi had for all classes of Hindu society as a holy man and and ascetic enabled him to raise funds from both princes and peasants, and his bonfires of foreign cloth, his support of *swadeshi* in all forms, and his indifference to socialist doctrines endeared him to Indian capitalists and manufacturers. Funds began to flow in.

---

* Religious formula or incantation.

During 1926 no less than nine hundred thousand rupees were distributed through the All-India Spinners Association to about fifty thousand spinners, weavers, and carders.

At the end of 1925 Gandhi resolved to withdraw for a year from active participation in politics and to remain at Sabarmati concentrating on the affairs of his *ashram* there and on the work of the All-India Spinners Association. His tours of the country were suspended, but he kept himself in the public eye by his articles in *Young India* and by the installments of his autobiography which began to appear in that journal and which evoked in turn a flood of questions from correspondents. The need for him to give his personal attention to the Satyagraha Ashram had been brought home to him by the misbehavior of some of the boys and girls there. As before when confronted with similar occurrences at the Phoenix settlement in South Africa, he undertook a seven-day fast in order to bring the delinquents to a proper sense of repentance. He gave a detailed account of this fast in *Young India*.*

During this year of withdrawal and throughout most of 1927 politics were at a low ebb and Gandhi, as he well knew, lost nothing by keeping out of them. Communal riots, on the other hand, were in full force. There were no fewer than thirty-five of them in 1926 and the year closed with the assassination in Delhi of a well-known Hindu proselytizer, Swami Shraddhanand, by a Muslim fanatic. For the time being Gandhi had ceased to meddle in Hindu-Muslim quarrels because he was convinced that his meddling could only do harm at that juncture. He also kept aloof from the struggle that was in progress between the Swarajists and Responsivists. He referred to it as a purely domestic quarrel.

This period of political inactivity and partial eclipse may be compared to the years in South Africa that he spent quietly at Tolstoy Farm between successive waves of *satyagraha*. He knew that the time was not ripe for renewing civil disobedience. "I would start it today," he had declared in 1925, "if I thought that the fire and fervour are there in the people. But alas! they are not." Yet he was certain—more so, probably, than he had

---

* See "Note on Fasting," p. 293.

ever been in South Africa—that the time for its renewal would come, and against that day he was methodically preparing his corps of workers devoted to the ideal of nonviolence.

The lull in politics was broken at the end of 1927. Gandhi, who after his year of withdrawal had resumed his tours and was traveling around India addressing meetings and collecting money, was invited by the Viceroy, Lord Irwin, to come and see him. Lord Irwin, who had succeeded Lord Reading in April 1926, was known to be a deeply religious man—a Christian who really believed in Christianity—and during his first year of office had impressed all India by the manifest sincerity of his appeals for a cessation of communal strife. Gandhi therefore did not hesitate to accept his invitation and went from Mangalore in the far south to Delhi to meet him. They had quite a long, good-humored conversation. Lord Irwin thought that Gandhi was "singularly remote from practical politics," but he was able to extract from Gandhi's rambling discourse a fairly clear idea of his basic political position. The English, in Gandhi's view, had "no moral claim to be judges of Indian progress." What they ought to do, therefore, was "to recognize that India should be accorded Dominion Status, and then to meet Indians and discuss the precise methods . . . by which this could be accomplished."

Lord Irwin's main object in meeting with Gandhi was to give him, as he gave to other political leaders, an advance copy of a statement that was about to be made by the Secretary of State regarding the appointment of the Simon Commission. The Act of 1919 which introduced the Montagu-Chelmsford reforms had provided that their progress should be reviewed after an interval of ten years. Almost from the start Indians had been pressing for a review and for further significant steps toward self-government before ten years were up, and as soon as the Swarajists entered the legislatures they demanded that a round-table conference be summoned immediately to work out a constitution conferring full dominion status on India. At first the British Government declined to alter its timetable, but in 1927 the Conservative Secretary of State, Lord Birkenhead, decided to appoint a commission forthwith so as to insure that it would not fall to a Labor Government to choose its members. In making his own choice he restricted himself, with Lord Irwin's full concurrence, to Members of Parliament, thus automatically excluding all Indians. Sir John Simon, an eminent lawyer and liberal politician, was selected as chairman and two peers and four commoners were chosen to serve as members—"a terribly weak team,"* according to the editor of *The Times.*

The announcement of the composition of the commission evoked a howl of rage from all political parties in India. What could be more wounding to Indian pride than an inquisition into India's fitness for self-government by a body composed entirely of foreigners? Lord Irwin was at pains to emphasize that Indians would be fully associated with assessing the commission's report when it became available and that the British Government had intended no deliberate affront to Indian honor and pride. But it *was* an affront, even if not intended. There was a concerted move to boycott the commission in which almost all political parties joined, including a section of the Muslim League under Jinnah. Sir John Simon and his colleagues were greeted on their arrival at Bombay by crowds bearing banners inscribed "Simon Go Back," and at Delhi and elsewhere there were "black flag" demonstrations. On the commission's second visit to India in October 1928 the boycott, instead of weakening, gathered strength. There were numerous clashes between the police and hostile demonstrators. In one of these scuffles at Lahore a veteran but ailing Congressman, Lala Lajpat Rai, was inadvertently struck across the chest by a police officer and his death a few days later was widely believed to have been hastened by the shock. Despite the boycott, however, the commission was able to do its job and received the cooperation of almost all the provincial legislatures, though not of the Central Assembly.

The advent of the Simon Commission put new life into Congress. It had been losing ground to communal organizations, but the opportunity to renew the fight with the Government revived enthusiasm. Jawaharlal Nehru, just home from a

* It included Major Clement Attlee, whose great ability was subsequently demonstrated.

tour of Europe and as ardent and extreme as ever, was at hand
to stoke the fires. At the Madras session in December 1927,
when the decision to boycott the commission was made, he
secured the passage of a resolution declaring complete independence rather than dominion status to be the goal of the
Indian people. The difference between the two was more
nominal than real, but independence implied a complete break
with the past, which is what he felt India needed. The resolution was passed almost unanimously, but does not seem to have
been taken very seriously.

Gandhi was present at the Madras session but took no active
part in its proceedings and did not attend the meetings of the
Working Committee of which he was a member. He was still
remaining aloof from politics, holding himself to be morally
under constraint until the period of his six-year sentence of
imprisonment expired He felt little real interest in the Simon
Commission and the proposed procedure for constitutional reform, but it may be presumed that he approved the boycott. He
disliked the independence resolution but did not oppose it. He
wanted to be free from the British yoke, but continued to be in
favor of the British connection. "Personally I do not crave for
'independence,' which I do not understand," he wrote in
Young India.

Congress was not content with the merely negative policy of
boycott. The rejection of the all-British Simon Commission
made it necessary for Indians themselves to put forward some
constructive alternative. Accordingly at the Madras session
Congress, besides deciding on the boycott, also passed a resolution proposing that an all-parties conference be convened to
draw up a constitution for India. There was a good response
from other parties, with the Liberals, the Hindu Mahasabha,
and the section of the Muslim League headed by Jinnah all
agreeing to cooperate. Since the other parties regarded dominion status as the goal, whereas Congress had just opted for
complete independence, the conference steered clear of dissen-
sion over this issue by defining the basis of the constitution as
"full responsible government." A committee, with Motilal
Nehru as president and the eminent Liberal Sir Tej Bahadur

Sapru as one of its members, was appointed "to determine the principles" of the constitution.

Its report, known as the Nehru Report, was published in August 1928. It was a genuine attempt to reach the greatest measure of agreement on the political issue and at the same time to face squarely the Hindu-Muslim problem. The attainment of dominion status was declared to be the next immediate goal; no party would be satisfied with less, nor would those who wanted more be affected in the long run by accepting this immediate objective. To solve communal dissensions which "cast their shadow over all political work," the committee proposed that Sind (which was predominantly Muslim) should be detached from Bombay and formed into a separate province and that the North-West Frontier Province (also predominantly Muslim) should acquire the same constitutional status and autonomy as other provinces. These were concessions to Muslim opinion. On the other hand, separate electorates, to which Muslims had pinned their faith since 1912 and which Tilak had accepted in 1916, were to be discarded, and reservation of seats for Muslims at the Center and in provinces in which they were a minority was to be allowed only for ten years. The committee referred approvingly to the possibility that the constitution might be of a federal character. This accorded with Muslim wishes, but the committee's tentative suggestion of a federation was put forward mainly with a view to accommodating the princely states within the constitutional structure and was hardly definite enough to satisfy the Muslims.

Gandhi, who spent most of 1928 at his *ashram*, played no part in the committee's work nor did he attend the meeting of the All-Parties Conference at which its report was considered. But he hailed its acceptance by the conference as a "brilliant victory," and also gave it his own blessing:

> I venture to suggest that the report satisfies all reasonable aspirations and is quite capable of standing on its own merits. All that is needed to put the finishing touch to the work of the Nehru Committee is a little forbearance, a little mutual respect, a little mutual trust, a little give and

take, and confidence not in our little selves but in the great
nation of which each one of us is a humble member.

It now rested with the principal political parties, including
Congress itself, to act in accordance with Gandhi's advice.

While the Nehru Committee was engaged on its exercise, a
small pilot civil-disobedience campaign was being conducted in
Bardoli, the *taluk* in which civil disobedience had been projected in 1922. A revision of the land-revenue settlement had
fallen due and the settlement officer had recommended an
enhancement of 25 per cent. Despite criticism of this proposal
by the Settlement Commissioner, the Bombay Government
ordered an enhancement of 22 per cent and directed that col-
lections at the new rates should begin in February 1928. The
enhancement was severe and the peasants, feeling that they had
a genuine grievance, were not inclined to accept it. They were
ready to pay at the old rates, but not at the new. Vallabhbhai
Patel took up their cause and, with the approval of Gandhi,
advised them to pay nothing at all until the enhancement had
been canceled. Under his leadership a regular no-tax campaign
was launched and was conducted with such efficiency that the
Bombay Government, which had at first made light of the
matter, soon found itself up against passive resistance by the
whole *taluk*. The peasants' cattle and lands were confiscated,
but buyers could not be found for them and by July only a sixth
of the revenue had been collected. Ordinary methods of coercion having proved of little avail, the Bombay Government
proposed to move in troops and seize the whole cotton crop.
But at this point Lord Irwin and the Government of India
intervened. They refused to countenance the dragooning of a
whole section of the population by military force and directed
the Bombay Government to come to terms with Patel by offering a special inquiry into the revenue enhancement on condition that the resistance movement was abandoned and payment
of land revenue resumed. On this basis a compromise was soon
reached. The two-man inquiry committee reported that the
proposed enhancement of the revenue was excessive and that
the peasants' objections to it were not unreasonable, with the

result that a much reduced enhancement was agreed to. Patel's capable leadership and Gandhi's technique had enabled the peasants to win their case.

This *satyagraha* campaign was of limited scope—it was not *satyagraha* for *swaraj* but only for a specific local object. Its success, however, heartened both Gandhi and the Congress. It was an encouraging small-scale dress rehearsal for *satyagraha* on a national scale. "Bardoli has shown the way," Gandhi wrote, "if the sanction to be employed against the British Government is to be non-violent."

The annual session of congress was held at Calcutta in December 1928 and marked Gandhi's re-entry into active politics. The expiration in March of his six-year sentence gave him moral freedom of action just at a time when he was needed to play a positive role instead of a purely passive one as at Madras a year earlier. Consideration of the Nehru Report was the main item on the agenda and it provoked a sharp division of opinion with the two Nehrus, father and son, on opposite sides. Gandhi had already commended it and both he and its principal author, Motilal, wanted it to be accepted without controversy. But Jawaharlal, Subhas Chandra Bose, and other younger Congressmen would not be reconciled to its moderate demand for a government "in no event lower than that of any self-governing Dominion," and called for unqualified independence and a complete break with Britain. Gandhi was, as usual, determined somehow to bridge the divisions and enable Congress to present a united front. He produced a compromise resolution, giving Britain to the end of 1929* to accept the Nehru Report, failing which Congress would revive nonviolent noncooperation. In issuing this ultimatum in order to resolve the differences within Congress, Gandhi became committed to another potential head-on collision with the Government. In 1919 and 1920 he had himself taken the lead in noncooperation and dragged Congress after him. It was now the extremists of Congress who were pushing him into it.

Congress accepted the Nehru Report with difficulty, but the

* Gandhi originally suggested 1930 but was compelled by Jawaharlal and the extremists to change it to 1929.

Muslims would not accept it at all. The Ali brothers had long since parted with Gandhi and were denouncing him for trying to establish a Hindu dictatorship. But even the section of the Muslim League led by Jinnah, which had joined in the boycott of the Simon Commission and attended the All-Parties Conference, rejected the Nehru Report, and soon the two wings of the League were reunited and were unanimously demanding separate electorates, reservation of seats, and a federal system with wide autonomy for the constituent states. These demands had been conceded in the Nehru Report only partially or not at all, and no modifications were agreed to in response to Jinnah's strong pressure when, for the last time, the All-Parties Conference met at Calcutta concurrently with the Congress session. To Jinnah, the ex-Congressman and nationalist who had worked so hard for Hindu-Muslim unity, this was a bitter disappointment, and he spoke of it as "the parting of the ways." Thus, contrary to the intentions of its authors, the effect of the Nehru Report was to widen the breach between Hindus and Muslims, with the latter now solidly ranged in opposition to Congress. Only a handful of them remained in its ranks and they, however patriotic and high-minded, represented only themselves.

In the past Gandhi had repeatedly advised the Hindus that they, as the majority community, should show a spirit of generosity and give the Muslims a feeling of confidence and security by granting them the concessions they wanted. He had espoused the Khilafat cause, though it served no Hindu interest, to show his sympathy for the Muslims, and he claimed that he let no opportunity slip of fostering Hindu-Muslim unity. Yet it does not appear that at this time he made any attempt to get the Nehru Report modified so as to meet Jinnah halfway and reassure the Muslims, or that he even grasped the importance of doing so. A chance was missed and Gandhi must share responsibility with others for missing it.

Lord Birkenhead had predicted that Hindus and Muslims would be unable to agree on a constitution and present a united demand. His prediction was justified. It rested with the British to devise political changes that all would accept.

XI ∽

Civil

Disobedience

The all-white Simon Commission had been a first-class blunder. Lord Irwin, who had been largely responsible for it, recognized the need to make amends—some gesture to heal the wound to Indian pride, dispel distrust of British intentions, and bring Congress back to a mood of cooperation. He had no reason to hope that the proposals to be put forward by the Simon Commission would prove a salve; they were more likely to be a further irritant. If there was to be conciliation, the initiative would have to come from him.

Fortunately at this juncture a Labor Government took office in England. The new Prime Minister, Ramsay MacDonald, and the new Secretary of State, Wedgwood Benn, were both sympathetic to Lord Irwin's views, and during a visit to England in the summer of 1929 he had no difficulty in obtaining their approval of a plan for regaining Indian confidence. The Conservative leader, Baldwin—a personal friend, was also informally consulted and gave his assent.

Lord Irwin's plan was twofold. In the first place he proposed that as soon as the Simon Commission had reported, members of the British Parliament and Indians representative of all sections of opinion, including representatives of the princely states, should meet together at a round-table conference to consider proposals for constitutional advance in order to reach the greatest possible measure of agreement before final proposals were placed before Parliament. He hoped that by involving Indians fully and on equal terms in the constitutional deliberations the wound caused by the all-white Simon Commission would be healed.

Secondly he proposed to make it crystal clear that dominion status and nothing less was the accepted goal of India's constitutional progress. Several Indians had told him that such an unambiguous declaration would do much to clear away the miasma of suspicion, and Motilal himself was reported to have told the editor of *The Times* that what India wanted was an assurance that dominion status was on the way. The Labor Government was quite willing to commit itself to this objective.

The twofold announcement was made on October 31, after the Viceroy had returned to India, and created an immediately favorable impression. Lord Irwin had wanted, in his own phrase, "to bring to the body politic of India the touch that carries with it healing and health." It looked as though he had succeeded. A number of Indian leaders of different parties, advised in advance of the impending announcement, had assembled in Delhi. Gandhi was among them. He had spent most of the year touring India and Burma to collect money for *khadi*, but he had kept in close touch with political developments and was now on hand to give his views. Most of the assembled leaders were disposed to accept unconditionally what was offered and to promise wholehearted cooperation in the work of the projected conference, and Gandhi himself was not inclined to reject the offer. He could wait, he said, for dominion status, "if today there is a real change of heart, a real desire on the part of the British people to see India a free and self-respecting nation." Only Jawaharlal was suspicious and openly opposed to any settlement by negotiation.

The upshot was a compromise. After a day's deliberation the

assembled leaders issued a statement, known as the Delhi Manifesto, accepting the invitation to the Round-Table Conference but suggesting that Congress should have the largest representation and that, to induce a "calmer atmosphere," all political prisoners should be released. The statement concluded: "We understand, however, that the Conference is to meet not to discuss when Dominion Status is to be established, but to frame a scheme of Dominion Constitution for India. We hope that we are not mistaken in thus interpreting the import and the implications of this weighty pronouncement of the Viceroy."

This interpretation was certainly not justified. Nevertheless, for the moment, hopes ran high. Gandhi, who had been informed that Lord Irwin would agree, albeit reluctantly, to the release of political prisoners, publicly expressed his belief in Irwin's sincerity and said that the manifesto was an attempt to respond in the same spirit. It seemed as though the political situation in India had been transformed at a stroke and that the more sober elements in Congress, including Gandhi, were again confident of British intentions and genuinely desired to cooperate.

But Lord Irwin's good intentions and statesmanlike views did not accord with the prevailing temper of the British governing classes. The announcement, which had been welcomed in India, caused an outcry in Great Britain. Baldwin, although he had assented to it, found that his party was not behind him on this issue and felt compelled to disassociate the Conservatives from the declaration about dominion status. Prominent Liberals, among them ex-Viceroy Lord Reading, were also highly critical, and the former Conservative Secretary of State, Lord Birkenhead, complained bitterly that the Simon Commission had been short-circuited and that the Viceroy had merely encouraged Indians to make further and more extravagant demands.

This British reaction played into the hands of the Congress extremists. Jawaharlal was able to argue, plausibly enough, that the Viceroy's "ingeniously worded announcement, which could mean much or very little," had been shown to mean in fact very little and certainly could not be accepted as sufficient answer to Congress' ultimatum of the previous year. As for the change of heart for which Gandhi was looking, the utterances of Lord Reading and Lord Birkenhead furnished no evidence of it.

So the hopes of an understanding began to fade. Nevertheless Lord Irwin's sincerity and good will—all the more appreciated because of the criticism he had incurred in England—were so respected that one last-minute effort was made to effect a reconciliation between the Government and the Congress before the latter met for its annual session, which was to be held at Lahore at the end of December. At the instance primarily of the Liberal leader Sir Tej Bahadur Sapru and the Speaker and former Congressman Vithalbhai Patel,* the Viceroy was persuaded to meet a mixed bag of leaders consisting of Gandhi, Motilal, Vithalbhai Patel, Sapru, and Jinnah. Sapru was as usual full of optimism and believed that Gandhi would make no unreasonable demands. The Viceroy thought otherwise.

The meeting was fixed for December 23. On returning that morning to Delhi from a tour in the south, Lord Irwin narrowly escaped being blown up by a bomb which tore a hole in the railway line near the New Delhi Station just after his carriage had passed over the spot. The meeting, therefore, began with expressions of concern and horror at this attempted assassination. When it got down to business Gandhi proved to be in an intractable mood. Contrary to his own theories of how to treat an opponent, he questioned the sincerity of British intentions toward India and demanded—as the Viceroy expected—an assurance that the sole function of the Round-Table Conference would be to frame a dominion-status constitution to be put into effect immediately. The Viceroy was not able to give such an assurance, and so the meeting ended infructuously. Most of those present, including Vithalbhai Patel, got the impression that Gandhi and Motilal had no intention of reaching an agreement. It seems probable that they had already succumbed to the extremists and decided to face a head-on collision with the Government.

From Delhi Gandhi proceeded to Lahore for the annual ses-

* A brother of Vallabhbhai Patel.

sion of Congress. It had been the general wish that he should be president, but he declined, preferring to remain an informal "superpresident," and at his urging Jawaharlal was elected. The choice was eminently suited to the occasion and was an indication that Gandhi had already decided on open war. At Lahore, Congress proclaimed independence, not dominion status, to be the immediate objective, declared that nothing was to be gained by attending the Round-Table Conference, called on Congressmen in the central and provincial legislatures to resign their seats, and authorized the launching of civil disobedience in such form as its leaders might determine. At the first flush of dawn of January 1, 1930, the flag of independence was unfurled on the banks of the River Ravi.

There was intense opposition to these resolutions from some of the older members of Congress who implored Gandhi, even at this late hour, to accept the olive branch that Lord Irwin had proffered. But Gandhi was deaf to their arguments and entreaties. He had thrown in his lot with the more youthful element, led by Jawaharlal and Subhas Chandra Bose, and with his support the resolutions were passed. "I have but followed the Inner Voices," he wrote to a friend in explanation. These voices are not susceptible of analysis; but there were rational grounds for his conduct. A year earlier at Calcutta, under pressure from the extremists and in order to prevent a split in Congress, he had committed himself to delivering an ultimatum to the British Government, and now this had caught up with him. The Viceroy's announcement had offered an honorable way of escape, and he had toyed with the idea of taking it. But after a short period of indecision he concluded—not without good reason—that however sympathetic toward Indian aspirations Lord Irwin personally might be, there had been no real change of heart in Britain and that therefore the Viceroy's offer should be rejected. This left him with no alternative but to carry out the Calcutta threat and embark on a nonviolent struggle with the Government. Once again, as in Khilafat days, he was bound by an earlier committment that he had half thought he would never have to honor. But whereas on the earlier occasion he had himself spontaneously taken the lead in proposing noncooperation, at Calcutta he had been pushed into delivering an ultimatum by the pressure of the extremist wing of Congress.

Did he regret the compulsion he was now under to launch a campaign of civil disobedience? There is no reason to suppose so. After all, organizing political agitation in the form of non-violent *satyagraha* was his métier. It was in this that he excelled and had found his vocation. In Africa and later in India it had occupied the best years of his life, and since his release from jail in 1924 he had been quietly making preparations—training an elite in the *ashram*, enlisting workers in the *khadi* movement, strengthening the Congress organization—against the day when a renewal of *satyagraha* might become necessary. Now at last the time seemed to him to be ripe for it and the country in a mood for it.

Some elements of the population were in the mood for a good deal more, and this may have been a factor persuading Gandhi to run the "tremendous risks" of civil disobedience. The explosion of a bomb under the Viceroy's train was not an isolated incident. In April 1929 bombs had been thrown in the Central Assembly chamber in Delhi and a few months earlier a young English police officer named Saunders, believed to have been indirectly responsible for Lajpat Rai's death, had been murdered in Lahore. A spirit of violence was abroad, discreetly fanned by some sections of Congress. Aware of this temper, Gandhi probably hoped that civil disobedience would serve to divert national feeling from violent to nonviolent channels.

The members of the All-India Congress Committee had been authorized to determine the form that civil disobedience should take, but they delegated to "Gandhi and those working with him" the power to lead and control the campaign. He had not yet made up his mind what form to give it, nor was he altogether confident of obtaining sufficient mass support to achieve success. Subhas Chandra Bose was critical of the lack of clear strategy and advance planning, but Gandhi had a great belief in improvisation in these matters. A righteous struggle, he had written a few years earlier, has no need of preparation; "he who creates it and conducts it is God." However, something had to be done; he decided that to test the public temper January 21 should be celebrated as Independence Day and that people all over the country should be invited to take the Independence Pledge. This consisted of a long indictment of British rule, which was said to have "ruined India economically, politically, culturally and spiritually," and a solemn resolve to carry out the instructions of Congress for the purpose of establishing *purna swaraj*. British authorities felt that the response to this invitation was only moderately enthusiastic, but Gandhi and the Congress were fully satisfied. According to Jawaharlal, the great gatherings of the people peacefully taking the pledge "revealed, as in a flash, the earnest and enthusiastic mood of the country."

Gandhi now surprised his colleagues by suddenly producing "eleven points," the acceptance of which by the Viceroy he apparently felt would be equivalent to granting independence. They were a miscellaneous assortment of demands, some quite impracticable, but shrewdly chosen. There was something in them to appeal to almost every section of the population— reduction of the land revenue and abolition of the salt tax for the peasants and poorer classes; imposition of a protective tariff on foreign cloth and reservation of coastal traffic to Indian shipping for the commercial classes; an amnesty for political prisoners and abolition of the secret police for the politicians; and "prohibition" for the orthodox. Gandhi's colleagues did not take these demands very seriously. What they wanted was a plan of campaign, not a program of social and political reform, and Gandhi still gave no hint of what form the campaign was to take.

At last, in the second half of February, some glimmerings of his intentions began to be discerned. "Salt," Jawaharlal records, "suddenly became a mysterious word, a word of power. The Salt Tax was to be attacked, the salt laws were to be broken. We were bewildered and could not fit in a national struggle with common salt." But they soon overcame their bewilderment and applauded their leader's decision.

Gandhi's choice of the salt laws for defiance was characteristically original, but it was hardly the stroke of genius it has been called. The manufacture of salt had long been a Government monopoly in India and its private manufacture and the posses-

sion of salt not derived from Government sources were prohibited. A light tax was included in the price at which salt was sold
to the public, and when this tax had been raised a few years
earlier there had been a good deal of political controversy which
was still fresh in the public mind. The salt tax was therefore a
topical grievance, at least in political circles, and to an outside
world ignorant of the facts a tax on salt, one of the necessities
of life, could be plausibly represented as British exploitation of
impoverished Indians. Its publicity value was therefore considerable. Moreover, in every province there were some places
where, because of the presence of natural salt, violation of the
salt laws was quite easy. On the other hand the salt tax was so
slight that it was not felt as a burden, and agitation against it
had little popular appeal among the masses. Furthermore, the
places where salt could be collected or manufactured, although
widely scattered throughout the country, were limited in extent,
and the salt that could be readily produced was unpalatable.
The number of persons, therefore, who could defy the salt laws
was restricted, and the production of small quantities of rather
inedible salt was likely to lose its charm quickly.

On a wider view, it is clear that as a method of subverting
British authority in India—the aim of some of Gandhi's lieutenants—defiance of the salt laws was bound to be ineffective;
indeed, British officials in India were rather pleased to learn
that civil disobedience was to take such an innocuous form.
Gandhi's own avowed aim, however, was different. He sought
to convert the British so that they would grant India independence of their own accord, and this conversion was to be
brought about by Indian *satyagrahis* voluntarily submitting to
the pains and penalties resulting from violating the law. Yet
even for the achievement of this aim the choice of the salt laws
for defiance was not particularly felicitous. The spectacle of a
few thousand *satyagrahis* courting fines or a few weeks' imprisonment for petty infringements of the salt laws was hardly likely
to convert the British. It was more calculated to excite their
ridicule than their compassion.

Having decided the form that civil disobedience should take,
on March 2 Gandhi sent the Viceroy a long letter announcing

that unless his eleven points were accepted he would set out from his *ashram* on March 11 with the intention of breaking the salt laws. To emphasize that he had no ill feeling against individual Englishmen, the letter was delivered by a Quaker disciple, Reginald Reynolds. It afforded no basis for negotiation and the Viceroy replied coldly that he regretted Gandhi's decision to violate the law and endanger the public peace. All was now set for the struggle.

Gandhi had a better appreciation than in 1921 of the risks he was running in launching a civil-disobedience movement and of the small prospects of its success. He realized that to overturn, convert, or even make a significant impression on the British Government in India was a tremendous task, and he made no incautious promise of *swaraj* within a year. Moreover, though he still believed, quite rightly, that the people as a whole were nonviolent, he knew now that there were violent elements in the population that might well get out of hand, and he had decided, much to the relief of some of his lieutenants, that he would not suspend the movement, as after Chauri-Chaura, if there were sporadic outbreaks of violence.

Even though the prospects of success were not good, Congress was much better equipped for a struggle with the Government than it had been nine years earlier. Its organization had been strengthened; it now had disciplined workers in every district, enjoyed the financial backing of Indian commercial magnates from whom funds could be drawn for subsidizing "volunteers," and had developed publicity channels through which it could win sympathy and support for its cause both in India and in foreign countries, particularly the United States. Above all, Gandhi's influence among the Hindu masses was at its height. His constant tours throughout the country, the unceasing stream of articles in *Young India,* and the skillful emphasis on the ascetic and saintly features of his character had earned him the veneration and affection of millions. There were many for whom his word was law.

Against these advantages was to be set one very great disadvantage—Congress no longer enjoyed the support of the Muslims. That nightmare of the British, a Hindu-Muslim combination, which in Khilafat days had caused them such deep alarm, had vanished never to return. The Muslims were hostile or aloof, and Gandhi's old ally, Muhammad Ali, declared bluntly: "We refuse to join Mr. Gandhi, because his movement is not a movement for the complete independence of India but for making the seventy millions of Indian Musulmans dependents of the Hindu Mahasabha." It is significant that during the ensuing struggle the gravest situation that confronted the Government was in the one province where, exceptionally and contrary to expectations, Muslims joined the movement in large numbers.

On March 12, a day later than he had indicated to the Viceroy, Gandhi, accompanied by seventy-nine chosen followers set out from his *ashram* to march two hundred forty miles to the sea at Dandi. His route passed through Gujarat, and since Gandhi was a prophet not without honor in his own country, wherever he halted people flocked to see him and ask his blessings. Elsewhere in India the march aroused rather less interest than had been expected. Nevertheless, it created a deep impression. Lord Irwin expressed astonishment at Gandhi's will power, and the spectacle of this old man, staff in hand, with his motley band of followers, tramping along the dusty roads of India to defy peacefully the mighty British Empire attracted the attention and sympathy of millions all over the world. Years later, recalling his many memories of Gandhi, Jawaharlal said that the dominant picture in his mind was of the march to Dandi: "He was the pilgrim in the quest of truth, quiet, peaceful, determined and fearless, who would continue that quiet pilgrimage regardless of consequences."

Gandhi had expected, perhaps hoped, that one of the first consequences would be his own arrest. But the Government of India, which he had recently described as "a perfect personification of violence"—he had no experience of Nazi or Communist regimes—now gave its own exhibition of nonviolent noncooperation and allowed him to complete his march unmolested. On April 6 he reached Dandi and ceremoniously broke the law by collecting some salt from the seashore. The Government continued not to cooperate by taking no notice of this trivial though much advertised offense.

The Government's noncooperative attitude somewhat upset the Congress program. Gandhi had decreed that so long as he was in charge of the movement, it should be restricted to defiance of the salt laws by those who accepted nonviolence not merely as a policy, but as a creed, and that only after he was arrested would persons other than true believers in nonviolence be encouraged to take part in the program and its scope be extended to other forms of civil disobedience. Despite these restrictions, once Gandhi had given the signal at Dandi, there was a general rush to break the salt laws wherever possible. Another activity authorized by Gandhi was the picketing of shops that sold liquor and foreign cloth. This program, not being subject to the same natural limitations as defiance of the salt laws, was organized with tremendous enthusiasm and considerable success in nearly every town in India. Gandhi's restrictions precluded, for the time being, the development of a really dangerous mass movement, but the response to his limited program was much greater than either he or the Government had expected, and it demonstrated beyond question that in urban areas he had the sympathy, if not the active support, of most of the Hindu population. A feature of the movement was that a large number of educated women, with Gandhi's encouragement, broke their seclusion to take an active part in it. Their emergence constituted a social revolution. They were skillfully employed to embarrass the police and provoke incidents that would arouse antipolice feelings.

Gandhi's limited program had evoked an outburst of national feeling that surprised the Government but caused it no great inconvenience. It was content to confiscate contraband salt and to prosecute some of Gandhi's principal lieutenants—Jawaharlal was arrested and sentenced to six months' imprisonment under the Salt Act—but it made no mass arrests and Gandhi himself was allowed to remain at liberty. So long as the movement was confined to defiance of the salt laws and the picketing of liquor and foreign-cloth shops, it was felt that it could be fairly easily contained and would soon die down from sheer ennui.

Events soon occurred to upset these optimistic calculations.

On the night of April 19 a band of nearly a hundred trained men who belonged to a terrorist organization known as the Hindustan Republican Association made a daring raid on the police armories at Chittagong in east Bengal. The guards were overpowered and killed and the whole gang escaped unscathed into the jungle with a considerable quantity of arms and ammunition. News of this spectacular exploit startled and alarmed all of India, and it was roundly condemned by Gandhi. Its remarkable success seemed to bode ill for the future.

A few days later, at the other end of the country—the North-West Frontier Province—there were developments of an even more serious nature. An influential frontier Muslim, Abdul Ghaffar Khan, known as the "Frontier Gandhi," had in recent years headed a movement in the province for political and social reform and had organized a group of volunteers, popularly known as Red Shirts from the color of their distinctive dress. In spite of the color they were not Communists, nor were they formally members of Congress. But Abdul Ghaffar Khan was Gandhi's most celebrated, and most improbable, convert to the doctrine of nonviolence, and with some of his followers had attended the Congress session at Lahore. He was regarded by the provincial authorities as a potential source of trouble, but when the Viceroy visited this predominantly Muslim province early in April, it appeared to be quite tranquil, and it does not appear that Abdul Ghaffar and his Red Shirts actually started civil disobedience. However this may be, on April 23 the local authorities arrested him and some leading Congressmen in Peshawar, thereby provoking an outburst of mob violence for which they were wholly unprepared. Troops and armored cars were sent for, but in the narrow streets of the city the latter could not operate effectively. When the troops opened fire, killing and wounding a number of people, the populace became further inflamed. Reinforcements were summoned, and then a very grave incident occurred. Two platoons of a battalion of the Garhwal Rifles refused to enter the city on the ground that it was not part of their duty to shoot "unarmed brethren." It seemed that the very foundations of British rule were rocking. Other troops were ordered to relieve the Garhwali battalion

Gandhi as a young lawyer in
South Africa, 1913.

Gandhi and his wife,
Kasturbai, in 1921.

Gandhi in 1923, when he was sentenced to six years' imprisonment by the British for sedition.

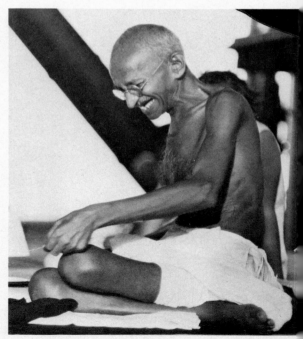

Gandhi at the spinning wheel.

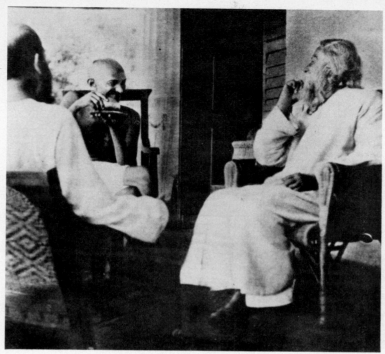

Gandhi with Indian poet Rabindranath Tagore in 1931.

Gandhi on his way to one of the series of meetings in 1931 with the British Viceroy, Lord Irwin, that resulted in the Gandhi-Irwin Pact.

Gandhi, in London to attend the Round-Table Conference in 1931, outside 10 Downing Street.

Kasturbai in 1932.

Gandhi with Mrs. Sarojini Naidu and Rajkumari Amrit Kaur *(behind)* on his way to visit the British Viceroy, Lord Linlithgow, in 1939, a few days after he had ended his "fast unto death" at Rajkot.

Gandhi with Vallabhbhai Patel, a close political associate in the Congress party and later Deputy Prime Minister.

Gandhi and Jawaharlal Nehru at a meeting of the All-India Congress, 1946.

Jawaharlal Nehru and Muhammad Ali Jinnah, leader of the Muslim League.

Gandhi gives his blessing
after addressing a crowd in
Bombay in 1946.

Gandhi with Lord and Lady Mountbatten outside the
viceregal palace in New Delhi, 1947.

Gandhi lies in state after his assassination in January 1948.

Gandhi's few personal possessions at the time of his death.

but, although they remained loyal, for over a week the Government was unable to regain control of the city. Meanwhile, the rest of the province was set ablaze and the flames soon spread to the tribal areas beyond the border. Martial law had to be proclaimed and military operations undertaken against hostile tribesmen, and it was many months before the disturbances in this Muslim area were finally quelled.

Gandhi was not responsible for events in Chittagong and Peshawar, nor could he control them, but they caused the Government of India to review their policy regarding him. Would the civil-disobedience movement die down if he remained at liberty? Half the provincial governments seemed to think it would; at any rate, they were in favor of taking no action against him. The salt campaign had lost its novelty and was, in their view, already proving a failure, and unless Gandhi gave the movement some fresh turn, it would gradually lose its momentum. The views of the Bombay Government, in whose territory Gandhi was operating, were very different. It believed that he was already planning mass raids on Government salt depots and that if he remained at large more and more people would join him, public confidence in the Government would be undermined, and it would become impossible to check the spread of civil disobedience. These views proved decisive. Very early on the morning of May 5 Gandhi was arrested while sleeping peacefully under a mango tree in his camp near Dandi. His followers were allowed to sing a few hymns before he was hurried away to the Yeravda jail. He was not charged with any offense, but simply detained at Government's pleasure under an ancient regulation of 1827.

With Gandhi's arrest the struggle entered a more intense phase. The boycott of foreign cloth and liquor shops was extended to a general and very effective boycott of all British goods and firms. Mass raids were made on salt depots, as contemplated by Gandhi himself, and beaten off by the police with some inevitable brutality. Breaches of forest laws were authorized, and plans were made not to pay land revenue and taxes in selected areas. The Working Committee of Congress called upon Indian troops and police not to act against their fellow countrymen and encouraged the social boycott of Indians who supported the British. Furthermore, participation in all these activities was no longer confined, nominally at least, to believers in nonviolence as an article of faith; all those who were willing to observe it in practice were invited to join in the struggle. It is not clear whether Gandhi himself would have approved all these measures, particularly the social boycott, but it is a tribute to his influence that the movement continued to be essentially nonviolent. Though there were a number of terrorist outrages in addition to the one at Chittagong, and one or two outbreaks of mob violence besides that in Peshawar, the principle of nonviolence was usually observed and throughout most of the country Englishmen went about their ordinary avocations without fear of assault or molestation.

The Government of India had so far handled the situation with great, perhaps excessive, restraint in the not ill-founded belief that enthusiasm would flag and the movement subside of its own accord. But now, at the urging of the military authorities who were disturbed by events in the Frontier Province and by attempts to tamper with the loyalty of the army, it adopted sterner measures. Arrests were made on a large scale; the press was muzzled; a number of ordinances were issued to combat every form of Congress activity; and finally, in June, the All-India Congress Committee and the Working Committee were declared unlawful associations and provincial governments were authorized to take similar action against local Congress committees. The organizers of the movement at all levels could now be quickly removed from the scene. Motilal, who on his son's imprisonment in April had succeeded him as President of Congress, was arrested along with the Secretary of the Working Committee on June 30, and the arrest of many other provincial and district leaders deprived the movement of steady and sustained direction. These measures enabled the Government gradually to master the situation. Despite a catastrophic fall in world agricultural prices that caused land revenue to press more heavily on the peasantry, attempts to foment nonpayment of land revenue and rent in Gujarat and the United Provinces were successfully countered and most of rural India remained calm and tranquil. By the end of 1930 civil disobedience was not yet dead—in particular, the boycott of foreign cloth was still very effective—but it had ceased to be a menace to British authority and had clearly failed in its objectives. It had not overthrown the Government nor caused it to yield on a single point, and it had not achieved Gandhi's professed aim of "converting" the British. It had, however, made some impression on them and especially on Lord Irwin.

XII ❧

The Gandhi-Irwin Pact

The civil-disobedience movement did not deflect the British from their purpose. Their policy of advancing India stage by stage along the road to full self-government remained unaltered, and while they quelled the disturbances in India they proceeded with preparations for the proposed Round-Table Conference.

Yet without the participation of Congress the conference was hardly likely to be a success. At the beginning of 1930 Lord Irwin may have half believed that by launching civil disobedience Congress would discredit itself and lose supporters to more moderate parties, but the events of the next few months soon compelled him to revise this opinion. Civil disobedience, far from discrediting Congress, had enable it to strengthen its hold on the country and had demonstrated that it enjoyed a far wider measure of public support than Lord Irwin and his advisers had supposed. Gandhi's assertion that it ruled the hearts of the masses may have been an overstatement, but Congress certainly commanded the sympathy of the great majority of politically conscious Hindus. Without at least the grudging cooperation of Congress there could be little hope of further constitutional progress.

Lord Irwin's first duty had been to contain the civil-disobedience movement, but he was aware of the need for a settlement that would enable Congress to share in the deliberations of the Round-Table Conference. When therefore in July the Liberal leaders, Sir Tej Bahadur Sapru and M. R. Jayakar, sought permission to negotiate with Gandhi and Motilal on the strength of statements alleged to have been made by them to George Slocombe, an English journalist, he readily gave his blessing to their endeavors.

Slocombe had been allowed to interview Gandhi in jail in the middle of May and had reported that Gandhi would be ready for a settlement if the Round-Table Conference was empowered to frame a constitution giving India "the substance of independence" and if four of his eleven points, including the repeal of the salt tax, were conceded. Later, in June, Slocombe had talks with Motilal, who told him that negotiations were possible on the basis of full responsible government subject to adjustments for the period of transfer of power. It seemed that both of them were thinking in terms of just such a settlement as should have been possible in the preceding autumn immediately after the Viceroy's announcement.

On their first meeting with Gandhi in Yeravda jail the Liberal leaders elicited what appeared to be an encouraging response. He wrote a note to the two Nehrus, who by this time were both in jail in Naini, suggesting that "the conference be restricted to a discussion of the safeguards that may be necessary in connection with self-government during the period of transition." This seemed a promising beginning, but the favorable impression was partly negated when Gandhi added, "Jawaharlal's must be the final voice." On reaching Naini, Sapru and Jayakar found that Motilal, under the baleful influence of his son, was already regretting the statement he had made to Slocombe. Jawaharlal had made it clear all along that he did not want peace by negotiation, and with his the "final voice" there was little hope of compromise. Undismayed, however, by the Nehrus' attitude, the Liberal leaders persuaded the

Viceroy to have them both temporarily transferred to Yeravda jail so that there could be a joint discussion with Gandhi. But by this time Gandhi's own attitude had stiffened and he put forward demands which made further discussion impossible.

With the failure of these negotiations the Government of India and the British Government had no option but to go ahead with the Round-Table Conference without the participation of Congress. Fifty-eight delegates from British India, representing all political parties and interests except Congress, and sixteen delegates from the princely states assembled in London in November to confer with representatives of the three British political parties. It was a distinguished array of Indian talent, yet it was not truly representative of India as Gandhi and most of the Congress leaders were still in jail.

By the time the conference opened, the report of the Simon Commission, published in the preceding summer, had for all practical purposes been brushed aside. Its timid proposals for provincial autonomy subject to safeguards, but with no provisions at all for political advance at the center were out of date, and although it envisaged a federal constitution as an ultimate objective, it made no mention of dominion status. Lord Irwin was very conscious of this weakness. However, thanks to his efforts, the report had really been superseded. The Round-Table Conference was what mattered. At its opening session all the Indian delegates with one accord voiced the desire for dominion status, meaning thereby full responsible government both in the provinces and at the Center, and a status in the eyes of the world equal to that of other dominions such as Canada and Australia. This unanimity included the representatives of the princes, and it was they who gave a turn to the discussions which made this first session significant and fruitful. One of the problems posed by the progress of India toward self-government was how the autocratically governed states, whose rulers' relations to the Crown were governed by treaty, should be integrated with British India, where the British governed directly but where democratic institutions had already been implanted. The Montagu-Chelmsford report had adumbrated "a sisterhood of States . . . presenting the external semblance of some form of federation," and subsequently the idea of a federal system for India had been widely accepted, although little had been done to explore its implications. At the Round-Table Conference the princes caused a mild sensation by not only agreeing in principle that India should be united on a federal basis, but by expressing their readiness to consider joining such a federation immediately, provided it was self-governing or at least set well on the road to self-government.

The princes' attitude created a common Indian front and took the wind out of the sails of the British diehards. It also appeared to smooth the path to a united self-governing India, for the princes' participation in a federal government was expected to reassure the minorities, particularly the Muslims, who dreaded a central government completely dominated by Congress politicians. Dominion status, acceptance of which as a goal had aroused such a storm in political circles in Britain earlier, was suddenly seen to be not fifty years distant but almost within reach. The first session of the conference closed in January 1931 with a statement by Prime Minister Ramsay MacDonald in which he made it clear that in addition to full responsible government in the provinces, the central executive would be made responsible to a federal legislature subject only to certain statutory safeguards for a transitional period, and, he concluded, "in such safeguards . . . it will be the primary concern of His Majesty's Government to see that the reserved powers are so framed and exercised as not to prejudice the advance of India to full responsibility for her own government." This was surely some evidence of the "real change of heart" that Gandhi wanted, and was almost equivalent to the assurance desired by Motilal that dominion status was on the way.

Two days before this statement was made by the British Prime Minister, Lord Irwin appealed to Gandhi, during a speech to the Central Legislature in Delhi, to change his course and cooperate in the further work of the Round-Table Conference in view of the encouraging progress already made. He recognized, he said, "the spiritual force" impelling Gandhi, but looked to Gandhi to recognize the sincere desire of those responsible for government in India to serve the best interests of the country. Their ultimate purposes, he concluded, differed very little.

These generous sentiments were followed a few days later by a practical gesture of conciliation. On January 25 Gandhi and his principal colleagues were released unconditionally and the notification declaring the Congress Working Committee an unlawful association was withdrawn. "I am content," said Lord Irwin, "to trust those who will be affected by our decision to act in the same spirit as inspired it."

A man of Gandhi's temperament and principle could not but respond affirmatively to Lord Irwin's magnanimity, and he sensed that public opinion in India and in the world at large would expect him to do so. The Viceroy and the British Government had together turned the tables on the Congress leaders and compelled them to reconsider their attitude—an offer of self-government with safeguards for a transitional period had been accompanied by an evident desire to let bygones be bygones and hold out the hand of friendship. In the circumstances what more was to be gained from civil disobedience? Gandhi was aware that many people in India would be asking themselves this question and giving the answer, "Nothing."

His first reaction was, however, cautious and noncommittal: "I have come out of jail with an absolutely open mind, unfettered by enmity and unbiased in argument and prepared to study the situation from every point of view and discuss the Premier's statement with Tej Bahadur Sapru and other delegates on their return." A few days later he went a little farther and said that he was hankering after peace, if it could be had with honor, and would leave no stone unturned to attain it. On February 1 Congress leaders met at Allahabad. Although they decided against formal suspension of civil disobedience, they issued private instructions that no new campaign should be started.

At this critical juncture Gandhi was deprived of his most valued counselor when Motilal Nehru, who had been released from jail because of his health in the previous September, died on February 6. In the delicate negotiations that now had to be undertaken with the Government there was for the time being no one to whom Gandhi could turn for advice with the same confidence that he had felt in Motilal. Left to his own resources, his opening approach to the Viceroy was ungracious and petty-minded. Instead of responding constructively to Lord Irwin's overtures he wrote to him demanding an impartial inquiry into excesses alleged to have been committed by the police in dealing with civil disobedience, and said that without this he would not be able to cooperate.

The Viceroy firmly rejected this demand, knowing that a general investigation of the conduct of the police would be fatal to their morale. There had, of course, been some excesses. On the other hand, the nonviolent *satyagrahis* had in many instances deliberately provoked the police into action which could later be proclaimed oppressive. There was nothing to be gained by raking over the past, and the Viceroy urged Gandhi to forget it and to consider the future.

There was no immediate response; Gandhi seems to have been in a state of indecision and, in his own words, "missed the guidance of the Inner Voice." Once again the Liberal leaders intervened, this time effectively. Three of them, Sapru, Jayakar, and Srinivasa Sastri,* visited Gandhi. At their urging, he wrote rather charmingly to the Viceroy asking for an interview, saying that "without personal contact and heart to heart talk" he would not be able to advise his Congress colleagues properly. The Viceroy, who had also been approached by the Liberal leaders, consented to see him.

Lord Irwin's release of the Congress leaders and his conciliatory policy toward them, although fully in harmony with the views of the Labor Government in England, had inevitably provoked angry criticism. The granting of an interview to Gandhi was for Winston Churchill the last straw and drew from him a celebrated diatribe. He was alarmed at "the nauseating and humiliating spectacle of this one time Inner Temple lawyer, now seditious fakir, striding half-naked up the steps of the Viceroy's palace there to parley on equal terms with the representative of the King-Emperor." Churchill was still

* Sastri seems to have been the member of the trio mainly instrumental in bringing about the talks.

wholly unreconciled to ending British rule in India. With unerring prevision he foresaw the consequences: "The loss of India would be final and fatal to us. It could not fail to be part of a process that would reduce us to the scale of a minor power." It followed, in his view, that Britain must retain the essentials of power in India indefinitely, and on this premise he rightly opposed negotiations with a "seditious fakir."

Lord Irwin and the British Government were acting on a different set of premises. They accepted that British rule would end in the not too distant future; they recognized that, in accordance with the Declaration of 1917, India was being steadily advanced toward self-government and that the goal was already in sight, perhaps the last stage of the journey had been reached. On these premises they were justified in going to great lengths to win the confidence and cooperation of Congress, even when it was in open revolt against them. The aspirations of Congress did not differ in essentials from their own avowed aims; it enjoyed the sympathy of a very large section of Indian opinion; and it was likely to inherit a great measure of the power that the British were committed to surrender.

Many Englishmen in India recognized the wisdom of Lord Irwin's decision to negotiate with Gandhi, but the majority were critical. Why pander to Congress when Congress had been defeated? Why start talks with Gandhi when civil disobedience was petering out? Those sections of the Indian people which were opposed to Congress, notably the Muslims, were no less critical and denounced the betrayal of the loyal to the disloyal. In general, however, Indians—including most Congress sympathizers and many Congress members—welcomed the prospect of compromise. Youthful extremists might still thirst for battle, but the majority of Congress workers were weary of the struggle, and the public at large was heartily sick of it. After ten months, enthusiasm and funds were drying up; prison had lost its novelty and attraction; demonstrations, picketing, and ritual infractions of the law had ceased to be exciting and become a bore. Civil disobedience was being killed by ennui, as many shrewd administrators had foreseen. And now that dominion status was really on the way, as revealed by the Round-Table

Conference, what was the point of continuing it? What more could it achieve?

This was the background of public opinion to the Gandhi-Irwin negotiations, and to some extent it explains their outcome. Gandhi was aware of the public mood. More responsive to every tremor of popular feeling than his lieutenants, he sensed the widespread desire for a settlement, and this reinforced his own "hankering after peace." He approached the talks in a conciliatory frame of mind.

Circumstances were favorable to a settlement, but the personalities of the principal actors played a big part in bringing it about. Gandhi had already met Lord Irwin two or three times and was disposed to trust him. In his letter asking for an interview he had said that he "would like to meet not so much the Viceroy as the man in you," and in reply to Sastri's assurance that he would be conquered by the Viceroy's personality he had said, "I wish to be conquered." He came away from the first day's talks convinced of Lord Irwin's sincerity, and there is no doubt that thereafter he fully trusted him and became convinced that there really had been "a change of heart." The talks were conducted, in his own words, "in a friendly manner and with much sweetness."

Lord Irwin on his side realized that in handling Gandhi it was no good "appealing to his head unless you have first got an entry into his heart." He resolved to gain that entry by genuine sympathy and "understanding of his hopes, suspicions and disappointments" as well as by some play on what Sastri had described as Gandhi's most dominant quality—"vanity, unconscious but no less real." One facet of this vanity was a liking for the sound of his own voice. Lord Irwin and his principal assistant in the negotiations, Sir Herbert Emerson, the Home Secretary, humored him by surrendering themselves for hours to his diffuse and often irrelevant monologues. Gandhi was captivated. He had started with a prejudice against Emerson, whom he had heard was "such a hard man and so unkind to the poor people," but contrary to his expectations this powerfully built rocklike man, with his blunt, forthright speech and manner—the antithesis of Gandhi himself—made a complete conquest of him.

Gandhi perceived that the smile that gleamed occasionally from his rugged face was one of genuine benevolence, and he was willing to listen with infinite patience to all Gandhi had to say.

Lord Irwin was impressed by the sheer force of Gandhi's personality and his judgment of him, although not uncritical, was more sympathetic than Lord Reading's:

> I came to have no doubt whatever that, if Mr. Gandhi gave me his word on any point, that word was absolutely secure, and that I could trust it implicitly. On the other hand, I found what had always been my impression being confirmed, namely, that though intentionally he was completely sincere, yet in some matters he was the victim of unconscious self-deception. The tendency to this showed itself in the importance he attached to different matters, and the weight that he seemed prepared to give to different kinds of evidence.

The talks lasted, with breaks and near breakdowns, from February 17 until the early hours of March 5, when final agreement on all points was reached. "If there is any victory," Gandhi declared, "I should say it belongs to both." But to all appearances the Viceroy decidedly had the best of the bargain. He made only minor concessions, whereas those made by Gandhi were substantial, reflecting the fact that, because the Congress rank and file was weary of civil disobedience, the Viceroy was negotiating from a position of strength, Gandhi from one of weakness.

It was on Gandhi's original demand for an inquiry into police excesses that the negotiations almost foundered. In the course of the discussions Gandhi renewed the demand, but Lord Irwin refused to consider it and ultimately Gandhi was persuaded to abandon it. Lord Irwin pointed out very frankly that even if there had been excesses, he could not afford to weaken police morale by inquiries into their conduct, since there was a possibility that civil disobedience would be renewed. Gandhi accepted the reasoning and gave way. "You do not deny," he said, "that I have an equitable claim but you advance unanswerable reasons from the point of view of government why you cannot meet it."

The main outlines of the settlement were simple. Gandhi agreed that civil disobedience in all its forms (defiance of law, nonpayment of land revenue and taxes, tampering with the loyalty of government servants) should be discontinued, and that Congress should participate in future sessions of the Round-Table Conference on the understanding that its work would be to draw up a federal constitution on the basis of self-government with safeguards "in the interests of India." Gandhi's acceptance of the constitutional position was obtained with remarkable ease—he did not even press for the safeguards to be qualified as "transitional" or for mention to be made of the right of India to secede. The fact is that he himself had always been ready to accept transitional safeguards and had been pushed by others into making more extreme demands. The proviso "in the interests of India" seemed to him to compensate for the omission of "transitional" and while Jawaharlal was furious at the jettisoning of the demand for independence, he was quite content: "If we can reach an agreement on these lines, I shall be satisfied that I have got *purna swaraj* or complete independence, and India will have got it in what to me is the highest form in which it can be attained, namely in association with Great Britain."

In return for cooperation in the Round-Table Conference and discontinuance of civil disobedience the Viceroy agreed to withdraw all the ordinances that had been enacted to combat it and all notifications declaring associations unlawful; to release all civil-disobedience prisoners (other than soldiers and police) convicted of offenses not involving violence or incitement to violence; to remit fines that had not already been paid; to restore movable and immovable property seized for nonpayment of taxes, if not already sold to third parties; to withdraw additional police quartered at the expense of the inhabitants in areas of disturbance; and to consider favorably the reinstatement of government servants and village officials who had resigned, if their vacant posts had not been permanently filled.

The Viceroy declined to make any substantial change in the

salt laws and Gandhi had to be content with a paltry concession
of little practical significance. The residents of villages immediately adjoining areas where salt could be collected or made were
to be permitted to collect or make salt for their own consumption or sale within their villages but not for sale elsewhere.

Over peaceful picketing there was some hard bargaining. It
had long been the policy of Congress to encourage the boycott
of *all* foreign cloth—one of the main planks in Gandhi's "constructive program." But during the civil-disobedience movement a boycott had also been directed against all British goods,
admittedly for political ends. Gandhi conceded that this boycott "was conceived essentially as a weapon of punishment" and
had to be suspended now that Congress was proposing to cooperate with the British Government, but he set great store by
picketing to discourage the use of non-Indian goods, particularly
foreign cloth, and the consumption of intoxicating liquor and
drugs. The Viceroy agreed to such picketing provided it was
unaggressive and did not involve "coercion, intimidation, restraint, hostile demonstration, obstruction to the public, or any
offence under the ordinary law." Thus the proviso was worded
in such a way that the Viceroy conceded little.

The settlement was an armistice, not a final peace; an opportunity to give cooperation a trial, not a resolve to enter into a
permanent partnership. Congress was embarking on cooperation deliberately, but only provisionally, and although at this
time Gandhi genuinely hoped to make the provisional truce a
lasting peace, the younger elements in the Congress leadership
did not share his hope.

The Working Committee of Congress endorsed the settlement, but most of its members, and particularly Jawaharlal
Nehru,* were not content with it and felt that Gandhi had
surrendered far too much. In the country at large it was welcomed with immense relief and adoring crowds thronged
Gandhi wherever he went. Perhaps they had a better realization
of his achievement than his colleagues in the Working Committee, for although he had gained few material concessions in

* In subsequent pages "Nehru" always refers to Jawaharlal
Nehru.

his talks with the Viceroy—not a single one of his eleven points had been conceded and in the constitutional field he had merely accepted what the British now offered—the talks themselves and the statement issued by the Government of India on their conclusion had elevated him and, through him, Congress to a new status vis à vis the British authorities. For the first time for nearly a century, since the far-off days when the East India Company was still consolidating its power against independent Indian potentates, an Indian had been allowed to negotiate an agreement with the highest British authority in India on something like terms of equality. He had also been tacitly recognized as the spokesman for the people of India, or at least the Hindu portion of them. In objecting to Gandhi negotiating on equal terms with the King-Emperor's representative, Churchill had highlighted the real measure of Gandhi's success.

Gandhi would have liked to claim that Congress was the intermediary between the Government and the people, but neither Lord Irwin nor the Government of India would accept this claim for undoubtedly Congress did not speak for some sections of the people, *e.g.*, the Muslims. They had, however, in effect acknowledged that constitutional progress without the cooperation of Congress was difficult if not impossible, and this enhanced Congress' prestige.

Aside from these intangible gains in prestige it could be claimed that the British had advanced farther and faster along the path to Indian self-government than they had intended two years earlier and that this was due, in part at least, to civil disobedience and the strength of the national feeling that it evoked and demonstrated.

On the day following the settlement both sides began to implement it. The Government withdrew all the relevant ordinances and notifications and on the same day all Congress committees were instructed to cease defiance of the law and abide by the terms of the pact. By March 23, all but two thousand of the 18,800 persons in prison for civil disobedience had been released. Lord Irwin expressed complete confidence that Gandhi would honor the spirit of the agreement, and at a public meeting Gandhi said, "Our word should be our bond, and it is a bond I implore you to respect."

But a shadow now fell across the path. The settlement had to be formally ratified at a plenary session of Congress which was to be held at Karachi in the last week of March. Just before this meeting a Punjabi terrorist named Bhagat Singh—who along with two others had fatally shot Saunders, the young English police officer in Lahore—was due to be executed. Since he and his companions had been guilty of a crime of violence, they did not fall within the scope of the settlement, but Gandhi had separately discussed their cases with the Viceroy and appealed to him as "a great Christian" to commute the sentences. Petitions for mercy poured in from all parts of the country and expectations rose high that, following the Gandhi-Irwin Pact, the Viceroy would defer to popular sentiment and save these young men who had committed murder out of patriotism.

In handling this delicate matter Lord Irwin and Gandhi both showed their strength of mind and integrity. They could have saved themselves embarrassment by postponing the executions till after the Congress session, but they agreed that this should not be done, and each in his own way resisted other strong temptations. The Viceroy, by commuting the sentences, could have eliminated all risk that Congress would not ratify the pact and could have left India—his term of office was about to expire—amid unprecedented popular applause. But he did not do so. He refused to allow his judgment in such matters to be influenced by political considerations. Gandhi, for his part, finding his strong plea for mercy rejected, might have given way to popular clamor and out of spite, allowed Congress to reject the pact. The executions came as a shock to the whole country, and so keen was the disappointment at Gandhi's failure to obtain a reprieve that he and Vallabhbhai Patel (who had succeeded Motilal as President of Congress) were greeted at Karachi with shouts of "Gandhi go back" and "Down with Gandhism." Gandhi himself described the executions as a grave blunder which endangered the settlement, and finding Congress in an angry mood, with all the young firebrands eager to reject the pact and loudly complaining that it was not being honored by the provincial governments, he could have just swum with the tide. But his better feelings and better judgment prevailed. Congress, he said, should endorse the settlement, notwithstanding the great provocation. "We must not put ourselves in the wrong by being angry. Let us recognize that commutation of the sentences was no part of the truce." His influence over Congress was at its highest at this time and he exerted it with consummate skill. To soothe outraged sentiments he drafted a resolution applauding the sacrifice of Bhagat Singh and his companions and deploring their execution, though also expressing disapproval of violence. To prevent a split over the ratification of the pact, he induced Jawaharlal to move the resolution approving it. In his heart Jawaharlal was strongly opposed to the pact; it was a confession of failure and unpopular with the left wing. But as a member of the Working Committee he had already assented to it and he was deeply loyal to Gandhi, so he could not easily refuse to move its approval. With Jawaharlal sponsoring it, the younger members fell into line and the opposition collapsed. Congress, while reaffirming *purna swaraj* as the goal, ratified the pact and agreed to send representatives to the Round-Table Conference. Gandhi's desire for cooperation, inspired largely by his faith in Lord Irwin, had at last prevailed over the intransigence of the extremists.

It is permissible to regard the civil-disobedience movement of 1930 and the Gandhi-Irwin Pact as the peak of Gandhi's political career. During the rest of his life there were to be some glorious episodes, but politically it is an almost unrelieved record of misjudgment and failure. Civil disobedience in 1930 also failed in its avowed objects, as neither independence nor the eleven points was secured. But as an example of disciplined mass pressure it was a most remarkable success, for coincident with it, and surely partly as a result of it, early in 1931 the British Government set India on the last lap of the road to independence, from which there could be no turning back.

XIII ❧

The Round-Table

Conference and

Poona Pact

Bhagat Singh's execution had endangered the Gandhi-Irwin Pact; it also provoked a communal riot. In mourning for the dead, Hindus in Cawnpore proclaimed a *hartal* and attempted to enforce it on Muslim shopkeepers. This resulted in one of the worst outbreaks of communal violence in Indian history. One year of civil disobedience, far from uniting the two communities, had widened the breach between them. Muslims everywhere, except in the Frontier Province, had openly shown their contempt for the movement and their pleasure at the discomfiture of those participating in it, and this attitude was resented by the Hindus. The tension thus created between the two communities was the background to the rioting in Cawnpore. News of it came through as the Congress delegates assembled at Karachi; it provided a grim commentary on their talk of independence.

At Karachi, Gandhi had been authorized to represent Congress at the Round-Table Conference. At first there were plans for other Congress delegates to accompany him and act under his leadership, but later, after much debate, it was decided that he should go alone. He himself very much wanted to attend as the representative not only of Congress but, as he liked to imagine, of the whole of India. There was some personal vanity behind this desire, but it was also prompted by a worthier motive. He had given his word to Lord Irwin to honor the settlement, and Congress' participation in further sessions of the Round-Table Conference was one of its terms. He did not wish to break his word.

There were, however, obstacles to his attendance, one of which was the Hindu-Muslim discord so forcibly demonstrated by events in Cawnpore. Was there any use taking part in constitutional discussions while the communal question remained unsolved? It seemed to Gandhi to be useless, but the efforts that he now made to solve this question were, once again, quite ineffectual, largely because he failed to live up to his own precepts. He himself, he said, was prepared to concede to the Muslims everything they wanted, and he advised the Hindus, as the majority community, to surrender all rights and privileges. "Let them say to the Musalmans, 'Have a big a share of the spoils as you want, we will be content to serve you.'" That the Muslims wanted separate electorates was made plain to Gandhi at an All-India Muslim conference he attended immediately after the Congress session at Karachi. But instead of urging Congress to accept this demand, he announced that it must be made unanimously before he could cultivate Hindu opinion on it, knowing full well that unanimity was impossible since the small number of Muslims who were members of Congress were opposed to separate electorates. This disingenuousness did not facilitate a Hindu-Muslim settlement or endear him to the Muslims.

Having failed to settle the communal question, he suggested to the Working Committee that, in the circumstances, it might be better if he did not attend the Round-Table Conference. But he really wanted to go, and when his suggestion was overruled by the committee he did not press the matter.

The other major obstacles to his attendance were the disputes that had arisen with the Government over the implementation of the Gandhi-Irwin Pact and the interpretation of some of its clauses. Gandhi's own earnest desire to fulfill it in both letter and spirit was manifest, but those elements in Congress with whom it was unpopular were eager to find pretexts for denouncing it. Again and again he urged them not to give in to their desire for a breakdown of the pact and a renewal of the fight, but to abide by it, whatever the Government might do, and to try their best to turn the provisional settlement into a permanent one. To smooth over the differences he ran from one place to another, interviewing the Viceroy, governors of provinces, and other high officials, but he got very little change out of them. The Government, confident that it had broken the back of civil disobedience, was giving nothing away; and Lord Willingdon, who had succeeded Lord Irwin as Viceroy, was less willing than his predecessor to grant Gandhi long personal interviews.

Petty though many of these disputes were, there seemed to be no end to them, and in the middle of August the Working Committee decided that in view of what they considered to be breaches of the settlement the Congress should decline to be represented at the Round-Table Conference. Gandhi, however, was still eager to go and still more eager, perhaps, that the settlement should not break down. He wrote to the Viceroy asking whether the Government would regard the settlement as void if Congress did not participate in the conference, and on receiving what appeared to be an affirmative reply, he hastened to Simla for further discussions. The Government was still conceding very little, but they conceded just enough to enable him to decide to attend the conference and thus preserve the settlement. Right up to the last minute it was uncertain whether he would go, and a special train had to be arranged to take him to Bombay in time to catch the boat that was carrying the Round-Table delegates to London.

"I must go to London with God as my guide," he had said; and with this guidance he fully expected to return empty-

handed. Such little hope as he may have had of wringing concessions from the British Government must have dwindled
almost to zero by the time he reached England, for when he
landed on September 12, the Labor Party was already out of
office and a national government headed by Ramsay MacDonald but of predominantly conservative complexion was in
power. From the Congress point of view this was decidedly a
change for the worse, for there was bound to be a more rigid
insistence by the British on transitional safeguards, whereas the
aim of Congress was to eliminate them altogether.

At the first session of the conference it had been agreed that,
at a minimum, defense and external relations should be the
responsibility of the Governor-General (Viceroy) during the
period of transition, and both the Muslims and the Liberals
firmly adhered to this decision. But at Karachi Congress had
resolved on just the opposite and although it had included a
proviso stating that its delegation at the conference should be
"free to accept such adjustments as may be demonstrably necessary 'in the interests of India,'" it had decreed that the delegation should work for *purna swaraj* "so as to give the nation
control over the defence forces, foreign affairs, finance and fiscal
and economic policy."

It was the responsibility of the Federal Structure Committee
—one of the two main committees of the conference of which
Gandhi was a member—to consider these issues. While fre-
quently expressing his desire for agreement ("I will count no
sacrifice too great, if by chance I can pull through an honour-
able settlement"), Gandhi took his stand on the substantive
portion of the Karachi resolution—his "mandate," as he called
it—and paid little heed to the proviso, which made agreement
very difficult: "I am here very respectfully to claim, on behalf of
the Congress, complete control over the army, over the defence
forces and over external affairs."

He admitted that complete Indian control of the army was a
"dream" that could not be immediately realized, but he did
not explain or discuss how, in the meantime, a compromise was
to be reached between control of the army and defense by the
Governor-General and control by Indian politicians and an

Indian parliament. Such matters were really beyond his range, and in any case he probably felt that any compromise he might be able to achieve with a predominantly Conservative Government would be too suspect to be acceptable to Congress extremists. If a Labor Government had still been in office, an attempt to negotiate a compromise over these matters might have been worth while. In the changed circumstances it was not.

Thus Gandhi's participation in the work of the Federal Structure Committee was fruitless. He failed, as he had foreseen, to get the British to grant any of Congress' claims, and he made no serious attempt to reach a compromise. It is unlikely, however, that he thought that this failure inevitably meant a renewal of civil disobedience in India. He was still committed to trying to achieve *swaraj* by argument and negotiation and to turning the provisional settlement into a permanent one. And he made it clear to the conference that he still believed in India's special relationship with the British and that the Congress demand for independence was not, in his opinion, incompatible with it:

> I do not want to break the bond between Britain and India, but I want to transform it. . . . I have aspired—I still aspire—to be a citizen, not in the Empire, but in a Commonwealth; in a partnership if possible—if God wills it an indissoluble partnership—but not a partnership superimposed upon one nation by another.

The other main committee of which Gandhi was a member and to which he devoted a good deal of time was the Minorities Committee. For a week he presided over a series of informal meetings, but at the end he had to report "with deep sorrow and deeper humiliation . . . utter failure to secure an agreed solution to the Communal question." He himself had not improved the chances of agreement, for at the very outset of the conference he had aroused the antagonism of the minorities by claiming that he represented over 85 per cent of the population of India, including the Muslims and the Depressed Classes

(Untouchables), and by hinting that the other delegates were not representative at all, as they had not been chosen by the people but nominated by the Government. This was a fatal attitude and had far-reaching and disastrous consequences. Dr. Ambedkar, leader of the Depressed Classes, refused to accept Gandhi's claim to speak for them, and it was unthinkable that the Muslims should accept a *bania* as their spokesman. Yet such was Gandhi's vanity that he seems to have thought that they might do so. Only a few months earlier he had said to a gathering of Muslims: "Brethren, I am a *bania* and there is no limit to my greed. It has always been my dream and heart's desire to speak not only for twenty-one *crores* but for thirty *crores* of Indians. . . . My heart is confident that God will grant me that position when I may speak for the whole of India." This confidence was unjustified and did great harm.

Discussions in the Minorities Committee broke down over the question of separate electorates. All the minorities except the Sikhs joined the Muslims in demanding them. As far as the Muslims were concerned, this was an old demand, but it was a new one for the Depressed Classes. Gandhi would not concede this point, although in the case of the Muslims Tilak had been prepared to concede it in 1916. In the absence of agreement the British Government announced that after a stated interval it would issue a communal award of its own. No other course was possible.

The second session of the conference closed on December 1 with a statement by Prime Minister Ramsay MacDonald reiterating the British Government's policy:

The great idea of an all-India Federation still holds the field. The principle of a responsible Federal Government, subject to certain reservations and safeguards through a transition period, remains unchanged. And we are all agreed that the Governors' Provinces of the future are to be responsibly governed units, enjoying the greatest possible measure of freedom from outside interference and dictation in carrying out their own policies in their own sphere.

Gandhi's closing remarks were ambiguous. He said that he thought he and the Prime Minister had probably "come to the parting of the ways," but he did not rule out the possibility of further cooperation:

> Whether I have the good fortune to tender my coopera-
> tion or not does not depend on me. It largely depends on
> you. But it may not even depend on you. It depends on
> many circumstances over which neither you nor we may
> have any control whatsoever.

He rightly surmised that he was already powerless to control the course of events in India.

The delegates to the Round-Table Conference did not have a high opinion of Gandhi as a practical statesman, although many of them were charmed and impressed by his personality, as was a considerable section of the general public. During this visit to England he attended numerous gatherings of intelligent, well-meaning people—a high proportion of them cranks—who listened with reverence, if not rapture, to his rambling but often original and humorous moralizings, for he had by this time attained the status of a world-teacher, whose casual utterances were invested with significance and profundity. In keeping with this character he was careful to adhere to his unusual but much advertised diet and to preserve his bizarre appearance. Throughout the visit he stuck to his loincloth—"the dress of my principals, the people of India," he rather charmingly explained—and he wore it when he went to Buckingham Palace to meet the King, who "had enough on for both of us," and to the cotton mills of Lancashire to meet the workers who had suffered from the boycott of foreign cloth in India. The general British public viewed him with good-humored tolerance not unmixed with faint derision, but a small number fell down and worshiped him. Being a celebrity, he met a number of others of the same class, among them Lloyd George, Bernard Shaw, and Charlie Chaplin—whom he had never heard of—and, on his return journey, Romain Rolland, who had already written a book about him, and Mussolini.

On his way home he sent a cable from Port Said to the India

Office saying that he would do all in his power for peace, a gesture prompted partly by the knowledge that during his absence the situation in India had deteriorated and that several of his lieutenants were again spoiling for a fight. In Bengal there had been a fresh wave of terrorism in which three officials had been murdered and others seriously injured. In the Frontier Province Abdul Ghaffar Khan was establishing "Red Shirt" camps and calling on Congress to denounce the Gandhi-Irwin Pact and resume the fight for freedom. In the United Provinces the Congress Provincial Committee was fomenting agrarian unrest. The peasants had been hard hit by the catastrophic fall in agricultural prices and claimed, not without justice, that they could not pay the full rent to their landlords, which meant that the landlords in turn would not be able to pay the full land revenue due to the Government. After a good deal of delay the Government of the United Provinces granted some remissions of rent and land revenue, but the Provincial Congress Committee, of which Jawaharlal was a member, thought this was inadequate and, near the end of the year, asked the peasants to withhold payment altogether until they obtained better terms.

The Government struck back hard. A comprehensive ordinance was issued to deal with the agitation and Jawaharlal was arrested under its provisons on December 26 and later sentenced to two years' imprisonment. Abdul Ghaffar Khan and other leaders in the Frontier Province had been arrested a few days earlier. Thus when Gandhi landed at Bombay on December 28 war had already been declared. Many in Congress had striven to avoid a rift until his return in the hope that he would somehow bring peace, and Gandhi himself appears to have drafted a resolution for the Working Committee that would have enabled the truce to be continued. He had no wish to revive civil disobedience; he knew it could achieve nothing, although he probably hoped to use it as a threat in order to extract concessions from the Government while at the same time keeping his own extremists happy. But he had been overtaken by events. There was no longer scope for such maneuvers.

He sought an interview with the Viceroy, but was rebuffed. Lord Willingdon was not going to be drawn into lengthy bargaining and give Congress time to mount a fresh civil-disobedience campaign. Convinced that no matter what Gandhi might wish, others were bent on a renewal of the conflict, the Viceroy was not only ready to meet the challenge but confident of defeating it. He told Gandhi that he could not see him to discuss events in the United Provinces, Bengal, and the Frontier Province. The path of negotiation, which Gandhi had said he would not abandon while there was a single ray of hope, was blocked.

A resolution was now passed by the Working Committee tentatively sketching out a plan for the renewal of civil disobedience, but before it could be put into effect the Government struck again. Gandhi and the Congress President, Vallabhbhai Patel, were arrested on January 4; the Congress and all its branches were declared illegal organizations; its principal leaders all over the country were imprisoned; and its funds and property were confiscated. It was a fight to the finish, as Gandhi promised it would be if negotiations failed; and the finish, when it finally came over two years later, was total surrender by Congress.

The movement had been crushed long before this final surrender, and Gandhi had turned his attention elsewhere. Its back was really broken in the first few months of 1932. The Congress rank and file dutifully courted imprisonment and went to jail in fairly large numbers—at the highest, in April 1932, civil-disobedience prisoners numbered about 35,500—but they were without direction, without funds, and without enthusiasm; even Jawaharlal admits that they "entered unwillingly to battle." They were helpless before the Government's well-organized measures of repression. Within a year the Government felt it was safe to release most of the prisoners, who returned quietly to their homes without attempting to court imprisonment again.

Gandhi, along with Vallabhbhai Patel, was sent to Yeravda jail. He lost interest in the struggle going on outside, which he knew to be futile, and as usual when not engrossed in political agitation his mind turned to his "constructive program," one item of which was the uplift of the Untouchables, or Harijans,*

* Children of God.

as now, at his suggestion, they began to be called. He had been greatly perturbed at the Round-Table Conference by Dr. Ambedkar's demand for separate electorates for them, since this would isolate them more than ever from the main body of Hindus, and, in his opinion, bring them no benefits. He wanted to end their degradation as "outcasts," but he felt this goal would be hampered by separating them statutorily from the Hindu fold, and that separation would also "vivisect and disrupt" Hinduism.

In March he wrote, from jail, a letter to the Secretary of State, Sir Samuel Hoare, warning him of his strong feelings in this matter: "You will perhaps recollect that at the end of my speech at the Round Table Conference, when the minorities' claim was presented, I had said that I should resist with my life the grant of separate electorate to the Depressed Classes. This was not said in the heat of the moment or by way of rhetoric. It was meant to be a serious statement." The Secretary of State acknowledged the letter and said that Gandhi's views would be taken into consideration, but the communal award that the British Government announced in August disregarded his wishes. The continuation of separate electorates for the Muslims was to be expected, but there was a new feature in that a number of seats were reserved for the Depressed Classes and they were to be filled by the members of these classes voting separately. When the award was made public, Gandhi intimated that beginning on September 20 he would undertake "a perpetual fast unto death" which would only be broken if the British Government revised its scheme for a separate electorate for the Depressed Classes. In a statement dated September 15 he explained to the public that the fast was intended above all "to sting Hindu conscience into right religious action" and "was resolved upon in the name of God, for His work, and as I believe in all humility, at His call. Friends have urged me to postpone the date for giving the public a chance to organise itself. I am sorry it is not open to me to change even the hour."

The Government of India offered to release him from jail as soon as the fast began—he was being detained, as before, under

Regulation 25 of 1827—but he told them that his fast would have to continue, even if he was released, and that he preferred to remain in jail. Thereupon he was given facilities for private interviews within the jail and was allowed unrestricted correspondence. He wrote to the poet Tagore asking for his blessing. Tagore, who had mocked at Gandhi's *khadi* program, had more respect for his efforts on behalf of the Untouchables and sent him the following telegram:

> It is worth sacrificing precious life for the sake of India's unity and her social integrity. Our sorrowing hearts will follow your sublime penance with reverence and love.

On the day before the fast was to begin, Hindu, Congress, and Depressed Class leaders met in Bombay and resolved that Gandhi's life must be saved at all cost and the blot of untouchability removed. At first Dr. Ambedkar, the Depressed Class leader, was not inclined to be accommodating and bluntly described the fast as a "political stunt." However, at Sir Tej Bahadur Sapru's suggestion a compromise formula was evolved in which it was proposed that the number of seats reserved for Depressed Classes in the provincial legislatures should be doubled but that they should be filled by a system of primary and secondary elections, with the principle of separate electorates applied only at the primary stage. The Depressed Class voters would first elect a panel of four candidates for each seat from whom final selection would be made by the general body of all Hindu voters. A deputation hurried to Yeravda jail to present this formula to Gandhi, and after a few days' discussion complete agreement was reached. Next the British Government had to be persuaded to modify its communal award in accordance with this agreement, which was called the Poona Pact. The Government consented, and on September 26, after prayers and a hymn and in the presence of a large audience, Gandhi broke his fast by accepting a glass of orange juice from Kasturbai.

The outside world was mystified by this curious drama. It could understand neither the reasons for the fast nor for its termination—it could not comprehend how life and death could hang on a small modification of an electoral formula. Within India itself ardent nationalists were disgusted that attention had been diverted from the national struggle to a quite different and subsidiary issue. Jawaharlal has described his own reaction, which was shared by a number of others:

> I felt annoyed with him for choosing a side-issue for his final sacrifice—just a question of electorate. What would be the result on our freedom movement? Would not the larger issues fade into the background for the time being? . . . And was not his act a recognition, and in part an acceptance, of the Communal Award and the general scheme of things as sponsored by the Government? Was this consistent with Non-Cooperation and Civil Disobedience? After so much sacrifice and brave endeavour was our movement to tail off into something insignificant? I felt angry with him at his religious and sentimental approach to a political question, and his frequent references to God in connection with it. He even seemed to suggest that God had indicated the very date of the fast. What a terrible example to set!

But Jawaharlal's love and loyalty soon overcame these angry feelings and enabled him to conclude that however impossible it was to justify from his own point of view, Gandhi's action might be right after all.

There was, in fact, a great deal to recommend it from a practical angle. Civil disobedience was already moribund; Gandhi, incarcerated in Yeravda jail, was as powerless as others to breathe fresh life into it. But the communal award offered an opportunity to promote another cause, one hardly less dear to him than the freedom of India—the removal of untouchability. Although the fast, as he subsequently explained, was precipitated by the grant of separate electorates to the Untouchables, its real object was "undoubtedly the removal of untouchability root and branch," and there was incorporated in the Poona Pact a resolution, drafted by himself, calling for "an early removal of all social disabilities imposed by custom upon the so-called untouchable classes, including the bar in respect of admission to

temples." He darkly hinted that if the caste Hindus neglected
to fulfill the conditions of the pact he would have to fast again
to sting them into action.

In the wave of crusading enthusiasm that followed the fast,
Untouchables were not only touched but embraced; in many
places temples and wells were opened to them; a society known
as Servants of the Untouchables was formed; an Abolition of
Untouchability Week was declared; money poured in; and
there was agitation for Gandhi's release so that he could personally direct the anti-untouchability campaign. The wave of
enthusiasm passed, but it was not without permanent effects.
Orthodox Hinduism was shaken.

The Government would not release Gandhi, but in November it granted to him all the facilities that had been allowed
temporarily during his fast on the understanding that they
would be used for work for the Untouchables. He started a new
weekly, called *Harijan,* and began propagating his views on
untouchability and answering his numerous critics. To those
who complained that he was neglecting the national struggle for
freedom, he replied that since he was in prison he was precluded from guiding civil disobedience in any shape or form
and was therefore concentrating on the work that he was still
able to do. Many Congress workers followed his example and
joined the Harijan cause, finding it safer than civil disobedience.

Gandhi was soon dissatisfied with the progress of this new
movement and in May 1933 announced that he would undertake a twenty-one-day fast. It was not directed in any way
against the Government, but was "a heart prayer for purification of myself and my associates for greater vigilance and
watchfulness" in connection with the Harijan cause. A general
remonstrance against this self-imposed penance elicited the
reply that "this fast it not of my will. It is God's peremptory
command." Obviously there was no arguing with God.

On the first day of the fast the Government released him
unconditionally and the Acting President of Congress, M. S.
Aney, at Gandhi's urging, suspended civil disobedience for six
weeks. By this time the movement was at a very low ebb and its

suspension, on the ground that during the fast the country would be in "a state of terrible suspense," made little practical difference. But this public confession of the failure of civil disobedience was a severe blow to some Congress stalwarts, and Vithalbhai Patel and Subhas Chandra Bose, who were abroad at this time, issued a manifesto declaring that Gandhi had failed as a political leader and that the time had come for Congress to be reorganized "on a new principle, with a new method, for which a new leader is essential." The manifesto made little impression. Gandhi now had such an emotional hold over the country that his replacement was impossible.

He had every intention of surviving his twenty-one-day fast, and did so with ease. It was terminated with the usual ritual of prayers, a hymn, and a glass of orange juice. What was he to do now? The suspension of civil disobedience was extended for another six weeks, but after that either the movement would have to be ended for good or he himself, now that he was out of jail, would have to take part in it again. He called an informal conference of leading Congressmen at Poona and received permission to ask for an interview with the Viceroy. He wanted to make peace with the Government, if he could do so without too much humiliation, and "to take up the thread at the point where I was interrupted on my return from England." But the Viceroy refused to see him unless civil disobedience was definitely abandoned. Peace efforts having failed, it was decided to continue the struggle in another form. Congress organizations were dissolved and mass civil disobedience was formally ended —in actuality it had already ended—but all those willing and able to offer individual civil disobedience on their own responsibility without assistance from Congress organizations were invited to do so. Gandhi felt that he himself should take the lead in offering individual civil disobedience and set out on August 1 to preach civil resistance to the Gujarat peasants. He was immediately arrested, served with an order to remain within the Poona city limits, and, on refusing to comply, was sentenced to one year's imprisonment and confined once more in Yeravda jail.

He was now a convict, not a mere detainee, and as such the

Government, although allowing him some restricted facilities
for carrying on Harijan work, would not permit him the wide
privileges he had enjoyed previously. There followed a most
undignified episode. Gandhi declined to eat unless his privileges
were restored in full. The Government refused to yield to this
hunger strike. But after only one week's fasting his condition
suddenly deteriorated, and he seemed to lose all will to live and
to be preparing for death. The Government, not wishing to
have his corpse on their hands, released him unconditionally—
just in time.

Once more Gandhi was in a quandary. If he went to jail
again, the same question of his privileges for Harijan work
would arise and presumably the same round would be repeated.
He felt that he ought not to be a party to such an undignified
cat-and-mouse game. The problem was solved when he decided
to abstain from political activity during the remaining ten and
a half months of his one-year sentence and devote himself to
Harijan work. He welcomed the prospect: "Whether inside or
outside prison Harijan service will be always after my heart and
will be the breath of life for me more precious than daily
bread." In November he set out on a long Harjian tour, during
which he traveled twelve thousand five hundred miles and collected eight hundred thousand rupees. Meanwhile, individual
civil disobedience dragged on in a desultory fashion. It was
wholly ineffective and attracted little attention.

In January 1934 Gandhi was still on tour collecting funds and
preaching against untouchability, which he believed to be on its
last legs, when there was a devastating earthquake in Bihar. He
saw the finger of God in this natural calamity; it was, he declared, a punishment for the sin of untouchability. Tagore and
Jawaharlal were shocked by this view which, being completely
"opposed to the scientific outlook," seemed to them to be quite
out of date. But it did not seem so to the mass of the Indian
people. Gandhi argued that since the laws of God were unknown there was nothing to disprove the connection he instinctively felt to exist between the earthquake and untouchability.
Congressman Dr. Rajendra Prasad was highly praised for his
organization of relief work in the stricken areas, and Gandhi

visited the province in March. The distraction caused by this disaster may have delayed slightly the final termination of civil disobedience, but the end was now at hand. Many Congressmen felt that the farce should not be prolonged, and some were turning their thoughts to a renewal of parliamentary activity and a revival of the Swaraj Party. Sensing the mood, Gandhi discovered farfetched moral reasons for the failure of the movement and for the need to bring it to an end. He felt that

> the masses have not yet received the message of *satyagraha* owing to its adulteration in the process of transmission. It has become clear to me that spiritual instruments suffer in their potency when their use is taught through non-spiritual media. . . . The indifferent civil resistance of many . . . has not touched the hearts of the rulers.

Even the change from mass to individual civil disobedience had not solved the problem, and he reached the conclusion that "*satyagraha* needs to be confined to one qualified person at a time" and that for the time being that one person should be himself.

In May 1934 the Government allowed the All-India Congress Committee to meet at Patna to endorse Gandhi's extraordinary conclusion. Civil disobedience was withdrawn totally and unconditionally except in the case of Gandhi himself, to whom it was left open to practice it when he thought it necessary. The Government withdrew the ban on Congress in June.

It was an inglorious end to a movement that had made some impact in its first phase, but which from 1932 onward certainly did not "touch the hearts of the rulers" and achieved nothing at all. Gandhi had not wanted it to be started again in 1932, but he could not easily reconcile himself to the humiliation of calling it off without obtaining any concession at all from the Government, and so it had lingered on without guidance or purpose while he concentrated on his campaign against untouchability.

Gandhi now gave Congressmen some advice regarding their future conduct and program. He told them that they must learn the art and beauty of self-denial and voluntary poverty. They must engage themselves in nation-building activities, the spread of *khaddar* through personal hand-spinning and hand-weaving, the spread of communal unity of hearts by irreproachable personal conduct towards one another in every walk of life, the banishing of untouchability in every shape or form in one's own person, the spread of total abstinence from intoxicating drinks and drugs by personal contact with individual addicts and generally by cultivating personal purity.

A few months later he himself resigned from Congress. "Outwardly," says Jawaharlal, "it marked the end of a great chapter in Congress and Indian history."

XIV ∽

Congress Ministries
and the Defeat of the
Left Wing

Following his own advice to Congressmen, Gandhi proclaimed his determination to devote himself unremittingly to his "constructive program" when he resigned from Congress. We enter now another period of recession in his political activity. *Satyagraha* was over and done with for the time being, and finding himself out of sympathy with both of the diverse trends of thought that now began to influence Congress, he preferred to remain in the background politically.

One of these trends was toward resumption of parliamentary activity and was prompted in part by the prospects of real political power that the new constitutional reforms seemed to offer. While Gandhi and most of the Congress leaders were in jail, a third session of the Round-Table Conference had been held, and in March 1933 the proposals formulated by the British Government as a result of the discussions were published as a

White Paper, and subsequently cast into the form of a bill which received the Royal Assent in August 1935.

In its main features the new constitution followed the outline given by Ramsay MacDonald at the end of the second session of the Round-Table Conference. In the provinces, ministers responsible to the legislature were to have almost complete authority over the wide range of provincial subjects, the governors retaining only certain special and emergency powers. At the Center, provision was made in Part II of the Act for a federal government for the whole of India, including the princely states. Ministers responsible to the federal legislature were to be in charge of all subjects except defense and external affairs, which were to continue to be the responsibility of the Governor-General (Viceroy). The federation could not, however, come into being until a specific number of the princely states had formally "acceded" to it. It was envisaged, therefore, that the other parts of the Act would come into operation some time before Part II and the inauguration of the federation.

The new constitution did not satisfy Indian aspirations. Nevertheless, it marked a considerable advance. Virtual self-government on the parliamentary model was established in the provinces, and although at the Center the withholding of defense and external affairs from elected ministers was unacceptable to Congressmen, the arrangement was admittedly transitional. The British looked on these reforms as the last milestone on the road to full self-government—as they proved to be.

With the publication of the White Paper and the failure of civil disobedience, moderate Congressmen began to think that the reforms, however inadequate, might after all offer scope for more fruitful political activity than trying to get arrested. They realized that the ministers commanding a majority in the provincial legislatures would enjoy real power and that if Congress stood aloof, this power, with all the patronage and prestige that would go with it, would be usurped by other political parties. Early in 1934 a group of influential Congressmen proposed that Congress should participate in new elections for the existing Legislative Assembly and should later, in two or three years, contest elections under the new constitution.

Gandhi had no great interest in parliamentary activity; it was not his line, and parliaments did not seem to him to be the place for his "constructive program" and ideas of social reform. Yet he recognized that "in the present circumstances of the country and in the absence of any general scheme of civil resistance, a parliamentary party within the Congress is a necessary part of any programme that may be framed by the Congress." Although he disagreed with the parliamentarians on many points, he was ready to let them go their own way; indeed he himself moved a resolution in favor of council entry at a Congress meeting in May 1934.

The other trend in Congress was represented by a younger, more radical group, who besides being violently anti-imperialist were thinking vaguely along socialist lines. In 1934 they formed the Congress Socialist Party as a wing of Congress. Jawaharlal, while remaining outside the organized socialist movement, believed "scientific" socialism to be the key to the solution of India's problems and hoped that Congress would become a socialist organization. Subhas Chandra Bose also professed socialist leanings. But the majority of the Working Committee was not favorably inclined toward socialism, and neither was Gandhi. He welcomed, he said, the formation of a socialist group and had no wish to interfere with the free expression of other socialist ideas, but he had "fundamental differences" with them on their program, and if their ideas gained ascendancy in Congress, he would not be able to remain in it.

Gandhi's lack of full sympathy with either of these active groups was matched by his feeling that Congress had no real faith in his own principles and program. In a long statement explaining his resignation he recorded his impression

that a very large body of Congress intelligentsia were tired of my methods and views and the programme based upon them, that I was a hindrance rather than a help to the natural growth of Congress, that instead of remaining the most democratic and representative organisation, it was dominated by my personality, that in it there was no free play of reason.

He also pointed out that whereas he put the spinning wheel and *khadi* in the forefront, hand spinning by the Congress intelligentsia had all but disappeared and most of them had no faith in it. Above all, nonviolence, which was his fundamental creed, was still considered to be a mere matter of policy by the majority of Congressmen.

Gandhi's retirement from Congress was formally registered at a session at Bombay in October 1934. He now threw himself with redoubled zeal into "constructive" activities and at his instance several resolutions designed to forward them were passed at the Bombay session. One of these barred anyone who did not habitually wear hand-spun and hand-woven *khaddar* from membership on a Congress committee. Another authorized the formation of an All-India Village Industries Association as part of the activities of Congress. Its function was to promote traditional village industries other than hand spinning and hand weaving.

Gandhi's retirement and his concentration on the "constructive program" did not signify a complete withdrawal from politics and political leadership. He continued to be in close contact with the foremost Congressmen and was always "available for consultation"—no major decision was, in fact, made without his advice. He remained the power behind the scenes, a kind of "permanent superpresident," ready, should necessity arise, to assume open and direct leadership but divorced from the day-to-day work of the Congress organization.

Moreover, though he had retired from Congress, he had not retired from public life and he continued to keep himself very much in the public eye. He toured the country to promote his "constructive program," he gave frequent interviews to the press, and he wrote increasingly for *Harijan*, generally avoiding controversial political issues and choosing for discussion such topics as *khadi*, village industries, untouchability, sanitation, prohibition, and self-control versus birth control. He regarded all this activity as complementary rather than antagonistic to the political program; it was "service to the people" and, as he was instinctively aware, also a means of retaining his power over them.

During the next few years Gandhi, as unofficial superpresident, skillfully held the balance between the diverse forces in
Congress. He allowed both the parliamentarians and the socialists free rein without appearing to commit himself fully to
either of them. This attitude was in accordance with that of the
majority of Congressmen who belonged to neither group; they
were rather scared of socialism, but dubious about parliamentary activity, which seemed to imply too much cooperation with
the Government. In practice, Gandhi put his weight behind the
moderate constitutional elements at crucial moments, thereby
giving them effective dominance, and yet he continued to
humor the socialist group. In three successive years, on his advice, a leftist was made president—Jawaharlal in 1936 and 1937
and Subhas Chandra Bose in 1938. In 1936 Vallabhbhai Patel,
an ardent nationalist but by no means a socialist, whose name
had been proposed, was persuaded by Gandhi to withdraw in
Jawaharlal's favor, and as president Jawaharlal appointed a
number of socialists as members of the Working Committee.
In this way the defection of the left wing was avoided. But
while the leftists were given plenty of opportunity to let off
steam, the Congress organization remained in the grip of solid
conservatives like Patel.

Gandhi's headquarters were no longer at Sabarmati. The
ashram there, disorganized during the civil-disobedience campaign by Gandhi's imprisonment and that of many of its residents, was dissolved in 1933 and the land and buildings given to
the Servants of the Untouchables Society. In September 1933
he settled at Wardha, a small town in the very center of India;
but, he said, "my mind is living in villages. They are calling me
to bury myself in them," and in 1936 he moved to a nearby
village called Segaon (later renamed Sevagram, which means
"village of service") and lived in a one-room hut. Many other
huts soon sprang up to house the motley collection of disciples
and co-workers—"the menagerie," Vallabhbhai Patel called it—
that gathered round the Master to share his labors and follow
his simple style of living. Segaon became the center for Gandhian experiments in rural economics and village uplift, and
the All-India Village Industries Association established its

headquarters in another larger village close by.

Gandhi, like many others, was appalled by the poverty of Indian villages. It was being aggravated, he felt, by the development of modern industry. Not only cotton mills, but rice mills, flour mills, oil mills, and sugar factories were causing the decay of traditional village industries and creating widespread rural unemployment. This was particularly brought home to him during his Harijan tour, as it was the landless lower castes in the villages who were most affected. His remedy was simple. There must be a revival of village industries and handicrafts so that villages could meet their own needs by their own labor instead of being robbed of employment and earnings by the encroachments of modern industry. He sought, therefore, to promote not only hand spinning, hand weaving, and handicrafts of all kinds, but also hand pounding of rice, hand grinding of corn, oil pressing in the traditional village *ghani*,* and production of village-made *gur* instead of factory sugar.

This program was an attempt to swim against the tide. Rural poverty could not be cured nor the advance of industrialization halted by bolstering a primitive village economy. Gandhi claimed that *swaraj* would be won when he had succeeded in ridding the villages of their poverty. *Swaraj* was won, but the poverty of the villages remained. His program, although continued by "constructive workers" for many years after his death, brought about no perceptible improvement. It was, however, at least an earnest attempt to grapple with an intractable problem that most politicians were content to ignore. It was partly through his influence and example that over the next thirty years "rural reconstruction" became fashionable, and if his own program failed, those of successive governments, British and Indian, did little better.

Nutrition, sanitation, and education were subjects that had interested him from his earliest days in South Africa, and he tried to use his experience for the benefit of the villages of India. He wrote incessantly on these and kindred topics in *Harijan,* which became a sort of guide to rural reconstruction. As a "practised cook" he expounded methods of preparing food

* A primitive oil press worked by a bullock.

so that its nutritive value would not be destroyed. He advocated the addition of green leaves to the diet of villages to counteract its deficiency in vitamins and called upon Indian scientists to be ready to starve themselves "in order to find an ideal diet for their poor countrymen." He expatiated at length on the disposal of night soil:

> Faeces must be buried. This is a most difficult question owing to the erroneous training of villagers. . . . [They] still obstinately refuse to throw earth on their own evacuations. "Surely this is *bhangi's* * work; and it is sinful to look at faeces, more so to throw earth on them," they say. They have been taught to believe so. . . . But I know that if we have faith in our mission, if we have patience enough to persist in the daily work of morning scavenging and, above all, if we don't get irritated against the villagers, their prejudice will disappear as mist before the rays of the sun.

His proposals on education were presented to a conference of educationists which he held at Wardha in October 1937. The conference endorsed his view that during the first seven years of schooling "the process of education should centre round some form of manual and productive work, and that all the other abilities to be developed or training to be given should, as far as possible, be integrally related to the central handicraft chosen with due regard to the environment of the child." This system of "basic education," which Gandhi hoped would be self-supporting through sale of the children's products, was closely related to his ideas about village life and the value of spinning, weaving, and similar manual work. It became known in Congress circles as the "Wardha scheme" or, more lightheartedly, as "Gandhi's latest fad." It was never very popular, because the villagers who thirsted for education wanted their children to become paid clerks rather than hand spinners, and "basic education" schools did not help them realize this ambition.

As part of his program of rural reconstruction Gandhi delivered constant exhortations against the evils of untouchability and of drink and drugs. The preaching against untouchability

* Scavenger—in India, always an Untouchable.

encountered a good deal of opposition from orthodox Hindus. Feelings ran so high that in 1934 a bomb was thrown at a car in which Gandhi was believed to be riding, and this event occasioned one of his numerous fasts. The preaching was not without effect, but his own impression, recorded as early as 1934, that untouchability was on its last legs, was erroneous.

While Gandhi busied himself with social reform and village uplift, there was continuous debate within Congress on its position in regard to the new constitution. Congress had completely rejected it at the Congress session at Bombay in 1934 and had passed a resolution calling for a Constituent Assembly to draw up a constitution for the country. But whatever resolutions Congress might pass, the constitution framed by the British was going to become effective, and Congress, by participating in the elections to the old Legislative Assembly at the end of 1934, was already half committed to a return to constitutionalism. At a session at Lucknow in April 1936, the new constitution was again roundly condemned—Jawaharlal described it as "a Charter of Slavery." Nevertheless, it was decided to contest the elections under it, and in August an Election Manifesto was issued.

What course was to be followed after the elections were over? The Election Manifesto had stated that the purpose of sending representatives to the legislatures was "not to cooperate in any way with the Act, but to combat it and seek to end it." Would accepting office and running the government in provinces where, after the elections, Congress might have a majority be consistent with "not cooperating with the Act in any way"? Jawaharlal and the left wing were certain that it would not and that Congressmen should on no account take office. They contemplated organizing another mass struggle in order to make possible the convening of a Constituent Assembly. But it was argued by the right-wing parliamentary group that the really objectionable portion of the constitution was that which dealt with the administration at the Center and that acceptance of office in the provinces would not be inconsistent with the general policy of "combating the Act and seeking to end it."

There was such keen division of opinion that neither at

Lucknow nor at a subsequent Congress session held at Faizpur in December 1936 could any firm conclusion be reached on this question, and it was left to be decided by the All-India Congress Committee after the elections were over. By March 1937 the election results were known. In six out of eleven provinces Congress had secured an absolute majority and in three others it was the largest single party. This electoral success whetted the appetite of Congressmen for power and swung opinion in favor of accepting office.

Gandhi, although ostensibly in retirement, had been quietly backing this point of view all along, and when the All-India Congress Committee met he was available to lend his decisive influence to its deliberations. From Congress' point of view, the only really objectionable feature of the part of the constitution relating to the government of the provinces was the governors' power to interfere with the ministers in special circumstances, *e.g.*, to prevent a grave menace to the peace or tranquillity of the province and for the protection of minorities. At Gandhi's suggestion, the All-India Congress Committee authorized the formation of Congress ministries in the provinces, provided that "the leader of the Congress Party in the legislature is satisfied and able to state publicly that the Governor will not use his special powers of interference or set aside the advice of Ministers in regard to their constitutional activities."

This formula, which Gandhi put forward with good intentions but without having read the relevant sections of the Act, assumed that the governors could on their own authority divest themselves of statutory responsibilities that the Act had placed upon them—which was, of course, impossible. But the Congress wanted to take office and the British authorities wanted them to do so, and so after three months of negotiation, during which Gandhi, even though not a member of Congress, acted as its spokesman—or, in his own words, as "mediator between the Congress and Government"—a gentleman's agreement was reached. Congress gave assurances that Congress ministers would act constitutionally, and the Viceroy (Lord Linlithgow) and the provincial governors gave assurances that they were anxious "not merely not to provoke conflicts with their ministries but to leave nothing undone to avoid or resolve such conflicts." These assurances fell considerably short of what the All-India Congress Committee had demanded, but on this basis the Congress agreed to take office and in July Congress ministries were formed in six provinces (Bombay, Madras, United Provinces, Bihar, Central Provinces, and Orissa), and shortly afterward in the North-West Frontier Province.

Gandhi had played a major part in this decision both by his support of the right-wing parliamentarians against the left-wing socialists in Congress and by his subsequent guidance of the negotiations with the Viceroy. He had a far sounder appreciation than the extremists of the merits and potentialities of the new constitution. It was widely condemned "as wholly unsatisfactory for achieving India's freedom," but he saw in it "an attempt, however limited and feeble, to replace the rule of the sword by the rule of the majority," and he expressed the view that if the Congress worked it to achieve the goal of independence, "it would avoid bloody revolution and a mass civil disobedience movement." It also appeared to offer some scope for his own "constructive program." Thus he had backed down somewhat from his earlier complete rejection of English-style parliamentary institutions.

The Congress ministries remained in office until just after the outbreak of World War II, a period of a little over two years. In spite of Gandhi's continued avowals that they had not entered upon office to work the Act in the manner expected by the framers, in actual practice they soon settled down to do just that, and the British were on the whole very pleased with the experiment of provincial self-government. There was, however, one feature of its working in the Congress provinces that they disliked. The Congress ministries, which included none of the top Congress leaders, far from being autonomous, were kept under strict control by the central Congress organization on the principle, enunciated by Jawaharlal, that they were "responsible to Congress and only through it to the electorate." This control was exercised by the Working Committee through a subcommittee consisting of Vallabhbhai Patel, Dr. Rajendra Prasad, and Maulana Abul Kalam Azad. But behind this triumvirate and the Working Committee there stood Gandhi, holding no office in Congress and not even a primary member of it, but still a dominating influence. On all important matters relating to the Congress ministries, especially those involving differences with the British authorities, he was consulted, and his name and authority helped to reconcile the ministries to a control that some of them found irksome. It is clear that, having permitted Congress ministries to take office, he was anxious to give the experiment a fair trial, and he used his influence fairly consistently to promote compromises over differences that arose with the British—the most serious was the matter of releasing political prisoners—and to avoid an open breach that would necessitate the ministries' resignation.

He also came out strongly in support of measures taken by Congress ministries for the maintenance of law and order. When in October 1937 there was an outcry against the Congress Premier of Madras, C. Rajagopalachari, for ordering a prosecution for seditious speeches—quite in the style of the old imperialist regime—he countered the critics: "Civil liberty is not criminal liberty. . . . It seems to be assumed by some persons that in these [Congress] provinces, at least, individuals can say and do what they like. But so far as I know the Congress mind, it will not tolerate any such licence." A year later the All-India Congress Committee passed a strong resolution drafted by Gandhi himself warning the public "that civil liberty does not cover acts of, or incitements to, violence or promulgation of palpable falsehoods" and that measures taken by the Congress governments for the defense of life and property would be supported.

Gandhi's articles in *Harijan* during this period have been described as "the instrument of instructions" to Congress ministries. It is true that whatever he said or wrote was treated with the utmost respect, but many of the Congress ministers were fully aware that much of what he preached could not be put into practice. His writings in *Harijan* were not "directives"; they were exhortations which, if the Congress ministries had remained in office, would have been progressively disregarded as time passed.

Once the Congress ministries were installed in office, the real
center of interest, in the light of history, shifts from the provinces to the Center and to the reactions of the princes, the
Muslims and Congress itself to the prospect of the introduction
of the federal part of the constitution. Gandhi's influence on
these reactions was more significant for the future than his influence over the Congress ministries.

The princes, who had caused such a stir at the Round-Table
Conference by declaring their willingness to enter an All-India
federation, very soon began to have second thoughts about it,
and the original hopes that a sufficient number of them would
signify their "accession" to enable the federal part of the constitution to be introduced soon after the provincial part were not
realized. One of several reasons for their disenchantment was
the changed attitude of Congress toward them. The demand
for responsible government in the princely states and for the
ending of autocracy had always attracted Congress sympathy,
but it had been Congress policy to avoid direct intervention in
state affairs, and at the Round-Table Conference Gandhi had
claimed that this position was not only a sound one but a
"service to the Princes." He had also expressed the view that
"any attempt on the part of Congress at interference can only
damage the cause of the people in the States. . . . I have not
lost hope that the Princes will become real trustees of their
people. I do not seek to destroy their status." Beginning in
1937, however, Congress adopted a more aggressive policy,
for which its left-wing members had long been pressing. While
Congress as an organization still only offered "moral support
and sympathy" to the people of the states in their struggle for
freedom, individual Congressmen were to be permitted—and
this meant encouraged—"to render further assistance in their
personal capacities." By the beginning of 1939 Gandhi had performed a complete about-face and was declaring that the rulers
must accept full responsible government or face the total extinction of their states and that "whenever the Congress thinks
it can usefully intervene, it must intervene."

It was much easier to mount a program of agitation against
the states from the neighboring provinces of British India now

that Congress ministries formed the governments in seven provinces, and, with the prospect of federation, it was also more
worth while. If autocratic rule in the states were replaced by
popular rule, Congress would be able to secure a numerical
majority in the Central Assembly and thereby control the proposed federal government, but if states' respresentatives continued to be nominated by the rulers, the combination of these
nominees and the representatives of minorities would out-
number Congress members.

This shift in Congress policy was immediately followed by
agitation in a number of states, in some of which prominent
Congressmen, including Gandhi himself, became involved. The
princes became alarmed and began to doubt the wisdom of
joining a federation in which the Congress, now openly bent on
their destruction, would be the predominant political party.
Largely as a result of their hesitation, federation had not been
inaugurated by the outbreak of World War II and was then
postponed indefinitely.

Gandhi's presonal involvement arose from an agitation for
responsible government that was started in Rajkot, the small
state in Kathiawar of which his father had been diwan and
where he had received his early education. In December 1938
Vallabhbhai Patel, who was really directing the agitation, persuaded the ruler to appoint a committee of ten to draw up a
scheme of political reform, seven of whose members were to be
chosen on Patel's recommendation and three to be nominated
by the ruler. The ruler, or Thakore, as he was called, reneged
on this agreement and, on the grounds that representatives of
the minorities—Muslims, Bhayats, and Harijans—must be included in the committee, nominated four persons to represent
them without consulting Patel. Civil disobedience was started
to protest this breach of the agreement, and as part of the strategy Patel's daughter and Gandhi's wife, Kasturbai, entered the
state, courted arrest, and were imprisoned. At the end of February Gandhi himself went to Rajkot and, finding that the
Thakore was still unwilling to abide by the agreement and was
disputing its terms, he precipitately—although he believed it
was at God's bidding—embarked on a fast unto death unless

the Thakore lived up to the original agreement.

The news of the fast caused a commotion throughout the country. Gandhi, who had been seriously ill in 1936 with high blood pressure, was still in poor health and was not likely to survive a prolonged fast. It was felt, therefore, that urgent action was required to prevent or end the fast. The Congress ministries sent telegrams to the Viceroy asking him to intervene, and some of them threatened to resign unless effective pressure was put on the Thakore to compel him to abide by his promise. Gandhi also sent a message to the Viceroy, discreetly designed to prompt his intervention. Lord Linlithgow responded by proposing that the Chief Justice of India, Sir Maurice Gwyer, should adjudicate on the terms of the agreement between the Thakore and Patel. Gandhi accepted this suggestion and broke his fast, declaring that "this good ending is an answer to the prayers of millions."

On April 3 the Chief Justice gave his award, and it was a complete vindication of Gandhi and Patel: he held that the ruler was bound by the agreement to appoint Patel's seven nominees. The matter seemed to be at an end. But the Thakore and his astute diwan, Durbar Virawala, were not to be so easily defeated. At their instigation the minorities had been reminding Gandhi of their right to be represented on the committee, and on March 11—three weeks before the award was announced—had obtained a letter from him in which he assured them that the four representatives previously nominated on their behalf by the Thakore would certainly be given places on it. He had assumed that this could be done simply by enlarging the committee, not only adding these four but allowing Patel to nominate an additional member so that his nominees would still be in the majority. But when, after the decision had been announced, he proposed this arrangement to the Thakore, the latter blandly replied that the agreement "as observed by the Chief Justice, restricts the number of the Committee to ten."

Gandhi found himself cornered, and the minorities, egged on now by Jinnah and Dr. Ambedkar as well as by the Thakore and his diwan, closed in to make sure he did not escape. They said that he must either stand by his assurance or, if he disputed its meaning, refer his letter of March 11 to the Chief Justice for interpretation. Gandhi was in despair: "I never knew what it was to lose hope. But it seems to have been cremated in Rajkot. . . . The Chief Justice's award has become a halter round my neck. . . . It has been effectively used against me for accusing me of a breach of promise to the Muslims and Bhayats." Some of his intimates advised him not to give the appearance of avoiding a further judgment by the Chief Justice, but though Gandhi professed confidence that the decision would again go in his favor, he was not taking any risks. "I am defeated," he told Virawala, and shortly afterward he capitulated completely, renouncing the award and leaving the Thakore free to fill the committee as he wished.

He attributed his defeat to moral failings:

> I was weighed in my own scales at Rajkot and found wanting. . . . For me to rely on the Viceroy instead of God, or in addition to God, to act upon the Thakore Sahib, was an act of pure violence. . . . This was not the way of *ahimsa* or conversion. It was the way of *himsa* or coercion. My fast to be pure should have been addressed only to the Thakore Sahib, and I should have been content to die, if it could not have melted his heart or rather, that of his adviser Durbar Shri Virawala.

There was little chance of their hearts being melted, for they regarded the fast not as an exercise in moral suasion, but as a political maneuver. They prepared to outmaneuver it—and did so, inflicting on Gandhi the greatest humiliation of his public career.

Gandhi emerged from this humiliation at the hands of a petty ruler and his unknown diwan almost unscathed, politically. It did not affect his dominance in Congress; in fact, at this very time his dominance was being confirmed.* But the Rajkot defeat prompted him to call a halt to agitation against the states. To the dismay of Jawaharlal and the left wing, he advised state reformers to moderate their demands to what the

* See pages 209–210.

rulers might be expected to grant and to move slowly toward their goal, as the atmosphere was not propitious for self-government. This advice was taken and almost everywhere agitation subsided. But the princes were now convinced that Congress was their deadly enemy and that a federation controlled by Congress must be avoided.

The significance of Congress policy toward the states did not escape the notice of Muslim leaders. Jinnah termed it "a camouflage to secure numerical majority in the Central Assembly," and it was one of several factors that combined at this time (1937-39) to make the Muslims apprehensive of "Congress Raj" and to cause a revolution in Muslim thinking.

The new constitution had been accepted by the majority of Muslims with comparative equanimity. They felt that their interests were sufficiently protected by separate electorates, the "safeguards," and the participation of the states in the federation. Although the more radical Muslim elements, represented by Jinnah and the Muslim League, had, like the Congress, criticized the constitution because it did not concede full self-government, they had expressed no special anxiety at the prospect of a Hindu majority at the Center.

The Muslim League professed to be an All-India party, but it had a substantial following only among Muslims in the Hindu-majority provinces: in provinces where Muslims were in a majority it counted for little. In the Punjab and Bengal, Muslim League candidates had been decisively defeated in the 1936 elections by Muslims belonging to local parties, and in the Frontier Province, where the Muslims were in alliance with Congress, the League was virtually unknown. Its claim, therefore, to speak for the Muslims of India could not be sustained.

This was the situation at the beginning of 1937. A year later it had completely changed and Muslims all over India were ranged under the banner of the League to fight the threat of "Congress Raj." This remarkable transformation was largely the result of the ill-judged policy of Congress toward Jinnah and the League.

Jinnah had hoped that in Hindu-majority provinces the Congress, if successful in the elections, would join with the League in forming coalition governments, and the League's election manifesto had been drafted so as to be in broad accord with that of Congress. He no doubt envisaged the formation of a similar coalition government at the Center when the federal part of the new constitution came into operation. But Congress, flushed with its triumph in the provincial elections, felt that there was no need for coalitions with the League, and in the United Provinces, where the League was strongest, its members were informed that if they wished to find a place in a Congress ministry, they must join Congress and "cease to function as a separate group." In other words, the League was offered not partnership but absorption.

This was a rude shock to Jinnah and his lieutenants, and had immediate repercussions in the Muslim-majority provinces, for it seemed from this example that in due course "Congress Raj" at the Center would mean the extinction of all independent minority parties and that only Congress stooges would be allowed to have some share of power. In the autumn of 1937 the Muslim premiers of the Punjab, Bengal, and Assam joined the League with all their Muslim followers and accepted Jinnah as their leader, and Jinnah, enormously strengthened, began to employ all his considerable talents on vilifying Congress, whipping up Muslim feeling against it, and organizing the League to fight it. Congress rather than the British was represented as the principal enemy. "Muslims," he declared, "can expect neither justice nor fair play under Congress Government." It followed that "Congress Raj" at the Center was not to be tolerated, and in 1938, on the grounds that it would lead to just this, Jinnah and the League denounced the federal part of the new constitution, and the next year declared that Muslim India was irrevocably opposed to any federal objective. They were by then thinking along quite different lines, for the idea of "Pakistan" had already gained wide acceptance in League circles.

Congress leaders, including Gandhi, were slow to appreciate the revolutionary change that had taken place in Muslim opinion. While Muslims were talking among themselves of Pakistan, Jawaharlal blithely informed the world that "in India today no one, whatever his political views or religious persuasions, thinks in terms other than those of national unity." "Evidently," Jinnah wrote acidly to Gandhi, "you have not been following the course of events." But although strangely blind to realities, Congress leaders were disconcerted by Jinnah's anti-Congress propaganda and the consequent deterioration in Hindu-Muslim relations. Nor could they entirely ignore the new strength of the League. They therefore arranged for a meeting between Jinnah and Gandhi in the spring of 1938 to explore the possibilities of agreement.

Gandhi said that he approached the meeting in no political spirit but "in a prayerful and religious spirit. . . . I ask all lovers of communal peace to pray that the God of truth and love may give us both the right spirit and the right word and use us for the good of the dumb millions of India." It is not known in what spirit Jinnah approached the meeting, but the results of it and of a subsequent meeting with the Congress president, Subhas Chandra Bose, were negative. Jinnah bluntly told Gandhi that he should recognize the League as the one authoritative and representative organization of the Muslims in India and not look for guidance on Hindu-Muslim questions to Congress Muslims like Maulana A. K. Azad. Neither Gandhi nor Congress was prepared to do this, so Jinnah's anti-Congress propaganda continued and the growing rift between Congress and the League was not healed.

Jinnah complained that Gandhi "had destroyed the very ideals with which Congress started its career and converted it into a communal Hindu body." The complaint was not entirely ill-founded, for whatever Gandhi's intentions may have been, Congress under his leadership had become imbued with a marked spirit of Hindu revivalism. His own political aims were intimately bound up with his ideas of Hindu reform, and, without any sense of incongruity, he could pass from leading a campaign against the British to leading one against untouchability. The main themes of his public statements were all derived from Hindu rather than Muslim thought, and he himself proudly claimed that every fiber of his being was Hindu. All this inevitably made Muslims suspect that Congress was really nothing but a Hindu organization, inimical to Muslim interests and

aspirations. Jinnah assiduously fed their suspicions. Gandhi and
the Congress failed lamentably to allay them.

Congress policies had scared the Muslims and the princes
into opposition to the proposed federal scheme, and Congress
itself had rejected it all along. In 1938 it reiterated its outright
condemnation of the proposed federation and authorized the
All-India Congress Committee to determine the line of action
to be taken if an attempt was made to impose it. Did this mean
there would be another civil-disobedience movement? The British did not think so; they believed that, as in the case of the
provinces, Congress would compromise and agree to work the
federal scheme. Rumors began to spread among the left wing of
Congress that another surrender was contemplated, and Subhas
Chandra Bose, who, with Gandhi's approval, had held the office
of president in 1938, sought re-election on the grounds that
since influential Congress leaders had been advocating condi-
tional acceptance of the federal scheme, it was "imperative to
have a Congress President who will be an anti-federationist to
the core of his heart" and able to lead the country in resisting
its imposition. Gandhi and the majority of the Working Committee were opposed to Bose's re-election and supported a rival
candidate, Dr. Pattabhi Sitaramayya. But Bose, undeterred by
Gandhi's opposition, declined to withdraw and in January 1939
defeated his opponent by a narrow margin.

"I rejoice in this defeat," Gandhi declared—somewhat un-
truthfully, for he could scarcely conceal his anger. Congress, he
complained, had become, a "corrupt" organization in that it
had many "bogus members" on its registers, and with Congress
in such a condition he could "see nothing but anarchy and red
ruin in front of the country." He threatened that he and other
Congressmen who thought as he did might withdraw, as it was
plain that his principles and policy were not approved by the
delegates who had elected Bose.

In reality Gandhi and the Working Committee had no intention of withdrawing, but were determined to turn the tables
on Bose and drive him from the field. They proceeded with a
ruthlessness and cunning more in keeping with Gandhi's character as a politician than as a saint. Twelve out of fifteen

members of the Working Committee resigned, ostensibly to enable Bose "to choose a homogeneous cabinet and enforce his programme without let or hindrance," but really as a prelude to a showdown. For when Congress met in session at Tripuri in March, a resolution was introduced expressing confidence in the ex-members of the Working Committee, approving the policies followed by Congress under Gandhi's leadership, and calling on Bose to nominate his Working Committee in accordance with Gandhi's wishes. Faced squarely with a choice between Gandhi and Bose, Congress opted decisively for Gandhi and the resolution was passed.

Gandhi had not attended the Tripuri session, as he was deeply embroiled in Rajkot affairs at the time, and when Bose asked him to give him names for the Working Committee, he flatly refused, saying that he would not impose a cabinet on him. This refusal, which made Bose's compliance with the Congress resolution impossible, had the intended effect of forcing his resignation. He then formed a new group within Congress known as the "Forward Bloc," whose aim was said to be to "rally radical and anti-imperialist elements within the Congress." But this incipient revolt was quickly crushed. In July Bose was rash enough to organize public demonstrations against a resolution of the All-India Congress Committee to tighten Congress discipline, whereupon the Working Committee disqualified him from being president of the Bengal Congress Committee and from holding any office in Congress for a period of three years.

Thus on the eve of World War II Bose's career as a Congress leader was abruptly terminated. Gandhi had never liked him and had good reasons for wanting to suppress him, because Bose was no believer in nonviolence; he openly sympathized with Bengal terrorists and probably had links with them. He was also no believer in the "constructive program" and the Gandhian philosophy of village life and hand spinning. Like Nehru he was an extremist with socialist ideas, but he did not share Nehru's steadfast loyalty to Gandhi—he was one of those who had criticized him in 1933 and called for a change of leadership. And he had ambitions to assume functions that Gandhi considered peculiarly his own. Gandhi had launched and directed two national struggles in India and regarded it as his prerogative to do so in future. On the eve of Bose's triumphant election as president he had written: "Although I am not in the Congress, I have not ceased to be of it. Congressmen still expect me to give the call when, in my opinion, the time for action has come. What is more, if God so wills it, I feel that I have strength and energy to lead a battle more strenuous than I have fought." In 1939 Gandhi did not think it was the right time for another contest with the Government. Bose thought the opposite. With war threatening, Britain's difficulties should be exploited; now was the time to mount a fresh mass movement against the Government, when Britain was hard pressed by her enemies. He himself aspired to plan and lead it. He had been dissatisfied with Gandhi's halfhearted and largely improvised "noncooperation" and "civil disobedience" campaigns. He wanted an all-out onslaught on the Government with no holds barred, not a movement hampered and limited by Gandhi's moral scruples and reliance on God.

Bose had fascist leanings, and after the outbreak of war he escaped from India and joined the Axis powers. Gandhi knew or suspected these tendencies and disapproved of them, for Gandhi, like most Congress leaders, had no sympathy with Nazism and fascism, whatever his feelings might be toward Britain. Moreover, it was quite contrary to his character and his principles—and also his own inclinations—to make common cause with Britain's enemies.

The elimination of Bose was a decisive rebuff to the left wing of Congress and precluded the possibility of launching any mass movement against the Government during the war unless Gandhi was its leader.

XV ❧

War and the "Quit India" Rebellion

On September 3, 1939, the Viceroy proclaimed that India was at war with Germany. There was no consultation with the Central Legislature nor, constitutionally, was this necessary, but the Viceroy tried to make amends by immediately inviting Gandhi to come and see him. They met on September 5. Gandhi explained that he had no instructions from the Working Committee and that he could not represent the national will because of his complete belief in nonviolence, which others did not share; but he said that his own sympathies were with England and France from a purely humanitarian standpoint. As he pictured to himself the Houses of Parliament and Westminster Abbey and thought of their possible destruction, he was quite overcome and shed tears.

The great majority of Indians shared Gandhi's sympathies and were overwhelmingly on the side of the Allies at the outbreak of war. Hitler's enormities made a much greater impression on the intelligentsia of the country than had those of the Kaiser, and there was a more positive desire among Indians to play a part in Germany's defeat than there had been in 1914. Jawaharlal himself admitted that India's sympathies were inevitably on the side of democracy and freedom against fascism and aggression. He expressed the wish that India should throw all her resources into the struggle for a new order, and declared that Congress was not out to bargain and "did not approach the problem with a view to taking advantage of Britain's difficulties."

But to bargain was exactly what Congress intended. When the Working Committee met shortly after the outbreak of war, a resolution was passed asking the British Government to state unequivocally what its war aims were and how they would apply to India and be carried out, and in October the All-India Congress Committee demanded more curtly, as the price of support, that India be declared an independent nation and "present application . . . be given to this status to the largest extent possible."

Gandhi found himself alone in his belief that whatever support was to be given the British should be given unconditionally. This attitude appeared more generous than it really was, however, for it turned out that moral support was the only support that he and, in his view, Congress in accordance with its avowed principle of nonviolence could offer. During World War I he himself, although a believer in nonviolence, had acted as a "self-appointed recruiting sergeant" for the British, but he could not dream of doing so again. Even though his sympathies were "wholly with the Allies, [his] own personal reaction to this war [was] one of greater horror than ever before." He could therefore offer only unconditional moral support, and he thought that Congress should do likewise.

But the saint had to co-exist with the politician. The nonviolence of the members of the Working Committee, as he soon discovered, "had never gone beyond fighting the British Government with that weapon," and like most Congressmen they were "unprepared for non-violent defence against armed invasion." Thus it was vain to hope that Congress as a body would join with him in upholding nonviolence in all its purity. And so while Gandhi the saint proclaimed his message of nonviolence to the world—and to Hitler, to whom he had sent a letter of appeal on July 23—Gandhi the practical politician was content to let Congress ignore his message and offer the British a good deal more than nonviolent moral support—at a price; and he made it plain that the price Congress demanded was, in his view, reasonable.

It is probable that if the British had had the imagination to declare that a war fought for freedom could not but end in freedom for India, Gandhi and the right wing of Congress would have been quite satisfied and would not have worried too much about interim arrangements for making India independent "to the largest extent possible" while the war lasted. But the British were not in a mood for imaginative statements and their Viceroy, Lord Linlithgow, was not the man to make them. Nor were they particularly anxious to have Congress' active support in the prosecution of the war, for they knew that even without it they would get all they required in men, money, and physical resources from India. All they wanted from Congress was abstention from active opposition, and they were not inclined to make many concessions in order to achieve this end. So on October 17, after interviewing more then fifty Indian leaders of all shades of opinion, Lord Linlithgow issued an uninspiring statement to the effect that dominion status was the goal of British policy in India, that the scheme of government embodied in the Act of 1935 would be open to modification at the end of the war "in the light of Indian views"—and that in particular, full weight would be given to the opinions of minorities—and that meanwhile, in order to associate Indian opinion with the prosecution of the war, "a consultative group" would be established representative of all major political parties as well as the princes.

"The Viceregal declaration is profoundly disappointing," Gandhi commented, and the Working Committee hastily rejected it, declaring that it was in every way unfortunate—the reference to minorities seemed to them a deliberate encouragement of Muslim intransigence—and that in the circumstances Congress could not possibly give any support to Great Britain. The Congress ministers were directed to tender their resigna-

tions and by November 15 all of them, albeit with some reluctance, had complied. Thus the experiment in cooperation
—which had had Gandhi's full approval but not Jawaharlal's
and which had been conducted with such a large measure of
success over the past two years—was brought to an untimely
end.

Although cooperation was withdrawn, active opposition was
not started and Gandhi made it clear that for the present it
would not be. Announcing that the Working Committee had
entrusted him with the control and management of any civil-
disobedience campaign that might be launched, he said that for
a variety of reasons he was in no hurry to precipitate such a
movement. He feared that it would lead to Hindu-Muslim
riots, since the Muslim League now looked upon Congress as
the enemy; he was convinced that many Congressmen neither
believed in nonviolence as a principle nor would follow his
instructions implicitly; and finally, he did not want to embarrass the British! "Whilst by their own action the British Government have made it impossible for the Congress to cooperate
with them in the prosecution of the war, the Congress must not
embarrass them in its prosecution. I do not desire anarchy in
India." Once more he turned to the familiar recipe he always
adopted when there was a lull in political activity: "My pre-
scription to Congressmen, for the time being, is to consolidate
the organisation by purging it of all weakness. I swear by the old
constructive programme of communal unity, removal of untouchability and the *charka*."

Of these items communal unity was far the most pressing, as
it, rather than the struggle with the British, had already become
the prime national problem. But Gandhi and most of the foremost Congress leaders failed to see this, and until 1942, when
they were incarcerated, they made no real attempt to assuage
the Muslim League's distrust and hostility and reach an understanding with Jinnah.

At the outbreak of war Jinnah and the Muslim League had,
like Congress, declined to offer the British unconditional support, but they had agreed to the Muslim League provincial
premiers doing so and clearly had no intention of hampering

the war effort. For unlike Congress, they did not regard the British Government as their foremost enemy. They cast Congress in that role and their primary objective now was to unite all Muslims in opposition to it under the banner of the League. They therefore continued their violent anti-Congress propaganda, representing it as a purely Hindu body, inimical to Muslim interests, and bent on subjecting the whole of India to "Congress Raj"; and in all their discussions with the British authorities they stressed that only the League could speak for the Muslims and that no new constitution should be framed for India without the League's consent and approval. The Congress plan for a Constituent Assembly, long favored by Jawaharlal and suddenly and most inopportunely espoused by Gandhi, in November 1939, was scornfully rejected; Jinnah declared that the assembly would be nothing but "a packed body, maneuvered and managed by a Congress caucus." Finally, at a session in Lahore in March 1940, they adopted a resolution setting forth their own startling proposals for the future constitution of India. Asserting that Hinduism and Islam were not merely different religions but different social orders and that, in consequence, India was not one nation but two, they demanded that India be partitioned and the Muslim majority areas of the northwest and northeast formed into separate "independent states." Only in this way could Muslims hope to escape the heel of a Hindu Raj.

There was an immediate outcry in the Congress press against the proposed vivisection of Mother India, and Gandhi declared that he would employ every nonviolent means possible to prevent it and that he did not believe that Muslims, when they came face to face with partition, would find it practicable or really want it. In a long article in *Harijan* he attacked the League's thesis:

The "two nation" theory is an untruth. . . .Those whom God has made one, man will never be able to divide. . . . My whole soul rebels against the idea that Hinduism and Islam represent two antagonistic cultures and doctrines. To assert such a doctrine is for me the denial of God for I believe with my whole soul that the God of the Koran is also the God of the Gita.

Gandhi was utterly sincere, but what he said and wrote was tactless. An outright, uncompromising condemnation of the League's proposal without making any attempt to understand what grievances had prompted the Muslims to make such an extreme demand was hardly the way to induce them to consider some less drastic alternative. There was still ample room for negotiation and compromise. Muslims as a whole, including probably Jinnah himself, were not yet committed to partition. There was an obvious danger, however, that they would become so unless negotiations were begun and concrete alternatives examined for giving them the security they demanded against Hindu Raj. League leaders contended that the sole objective of Congress "under Mr. Gandhi's fostering care" was the revival of Hinduism and the imposition of Hindu culture on all Indians. This was a calumny, but Muslims believed it and Gandhi failed by word or action to refute it. An article in *Harijan* in which he implied that Congress alone would "take delivery" from the British seemed in fact to confirm it.

A first step toward promoting greater harmony that many Muslims would have welcomed at this time would have been the formation of Congress-League coalition governments in the provinces and the expansion of the Viceroy's Executive Council to include leaders of both the Congress and the League. But all such proposals foundered on the refusal of Congress to cooperate in the prosecution of the war, and discussion of any long-term settlement was blocked by its insistence on the plan for a Constituent Assembly, which Jinnah rejected.

A few of the Congress leaders, notably Maulana Abul Kalam Azad and C. Rajagopalachari, the highly successful ex-premier of Madras, were not as blind as Gandhi to the fatal chasm that was opening between Congress and the League. Realizing the need to close it before it became unbridgeable, Azad began corresponding with Sir Sikander Hyat-Khan, premier of the Punjab and a moderate Muslim Leaguer. But these approaches came to nothing. They were not backed by the Working Committee and were frowned upon by the Viceroy.

Thus by May 1940, when the war entered its more intense phase, Congress was firmly set in a policy of negation. It remained uncomprehending and inert toward the Muslim League and the new menace of partition. It remained noncooperative toward the British, reasserting in March 1940 at a session at Ramgarh (which Gandhi addressed after an interval of six years) that it could not, directly or indirectly, be a party to the war. It continued, under Gandhi's guidance, to discourage the extremists in its own ranks who advocated civil disobedience. It would not countenance civil disobedience merely for the sake of embarrassing Great Britain, and when a Congressman of great influence suggested that if a civil-disobedience campaign were launched the response would be staggering and the whole labor world would declare a simultaneous strike, Gandhi replied: "If that happened I should be most embarrassed and all my plans would be upset. . . . I hope I am not expected knowingly to undertake a fight that must end in anarchy and red ruin."

The collapse of France and Britain's extreme peril produced a slight change of attitude in Congress. Gandhi himself continued to preach pacifism and was filled more than ever before with "the utmost non-violence"; indeed, at this time he could think of little else and on July 6 issued an appeal to every Briton to fight Nazism without arms and to let Hitler and Mussolini "take possession of your beautiful island" if they wanted to. But the Working Committee did not share his pacifism. They felt that it would be a handicap at this juncture, when Britain's peril seemed to afford a favorable opportunity for fresh bargaining, since the nonviolent moral support that was all Gandhi would offer was of little value to the British. Moreover, in the event of Britain's defeat and the collapse of British rule in India, there might be need for Congress to take charge of the ruins, and it would then be difficult to practice the doctrine of nonviolence.

So the Working Committee decided to make what Gandhi described as the "tremendous sacrifice" of breaking with him. While recognizing and respecting his desire for Congress to be true to the creed of nonviolence and declare its unwillingness for India to "maintain armed forces to defend her freedom against external aggression or internal disorder," they felt themselves unable to go the full length with him. They therefore left him "free to pursue his great ideal in his own way" and absolved him from all responsibility for the program that the Congress was to pursue.

The Working Committee's program was, in part, to establish their own "parallel" organization throughout the country, for self-defense and maintenance of public order. Naturally, little or nothing came of it. But they also offered to cooperate with the British. In return for an immediate and unequivocal declaration of the "full independence of India"—whether to be granted right away or at the end of the war was not absolutely clear— they would take part in a national government at the Center, restore ministerial government in the provinces, and throw their "full weight into the efforts for the effective organisation of the defence of the country."

Gandhi was wholly opposed to this program and in particular he warned Congressmen against succumbing to the temptation to accept office once again. He need not have been anxious, for the British were neither going to grant immediate independence nor even promise it unequivocally at the end of the war. On August 8 the Viceroy made another statement of British policy toward India, but beyond expressing the British Government's concurrence in the Indian desire that a new constitution should be "primarily the responsibility of Indians themselves" and promising that after the war a representative Indian body would be set up for this purpose, it offered little more than had been offered before—and it contained the following passage, which although reassuring to the Muslim League, had the same effect on Congress as waving a red rag before a bull:

It goes without saying that the British Government could not contemplate transfer of their present responsibilities for the peace and welfare of India to any system of government whose authority is directly denied by large and

powerful elements in India's national life. Nor could they
be parties to the coercion of such elements into submission
to such a Government.

Congress was deeply disappointed. The President, Maulana
A. K. Azad, refused the Viceroy's invitation to discuss the statement with him; Gandhi said that it widened the gulf between
the Congress and England; and the Working Committee declared that the British Government had made the issue of the
minorities an insuperable barrier to India's progress and that its
rejection of the Congress proposals had shown its determination to continue to hold India by the sword.

Gandhi was now invited to resume leadership of Congress,
and he accepted. When the All-India Congress Committee met
on September 15 the President announced that there was now
"no difference whatsoever between Gandhi and the Working
Committee," explaining further that "there was nowhere any
intention to discard non-violence; only we did not feel sure if
we would be able to meet every internal and external emergency
without resort to force."

Gandhi seems not to have objected to the ambivalence implicit in this statement, and drafted a resolution for the committee which, although it included an escape clause for those
who were not "dreamers" like himself, expressed a firm belief
"in the policy and practice of non-violence not only in the
struggle for *swaraj*, but also, in so far as this may be possible of
application, in free India."

Gandhi was asked to guide Congress in the action that
should now be taken. The left wing of Congress and extremist
elements outside it wanted to organize a mass civil-disobedience
campaign and a national revolt. Gandhi ruled this out on the
grounds that "the spirit of *satyagraha* forbids the Congress from
doing anything with a view to embarrass" the British. He maintained, however, that Congress was free to pursue a policy based
on nonviolence, and although at the moment such a policy did
not permit agitating directly for independence, it did permit an
antiwar propaganda campaign: "I claim the liberty of going
through the streets of Bombay and saying that I shall have

nothing to do with this war, because I do not believe in this war and in the fratricide that is going on in Europe." If permission to do this were granted, there would be no civil disobedience, but if it were withheld, a strictly nonviolent civil-disobedience campaign would be started.

Gandhi met the Viceroy at the end of September to discuss his demand for freedom "to call upon people throughout the country to refrain from assisting India's war effort." His demand was rejected, and so he proceeded to launch his campaign of civil disobedience. It was frankly symbolic and fully met the requirement not to embarrass the British, for it caused them a minimum of anxiety and inconvenience. At the outset it was confined to a few selected individuals who shouted antiwar slogans in villages near Wardha, the first of whom was Shri Vinoba Bhave, one of Gandhi's earliest disciples. He was arrested and sentenced to three months' simple imprisonment. Jawaharlal was to have followed him, but before he could do so he was sentenced to a long term of imprisonment for making seditious speeches and a much less well-known Congressman took his place.

After a month the campaign was stepped up slightly and many prominent Congressmen, including most of the former Congress ministers, were authorized by Gandhi to shout antiwar slogans and were sentenced to varying terms of imprisonment. Humbler members of Congress were next enrolled as *satyagrahis* and by May 1941 the number of persons imprisoned reached a peak figure of fourteen thousand. But the movement caused no commotion and attracted little attention, partly because under the wartime "defense of India rules" newspaper accounts of it could be suppressed. To most people it seemed rather ridiculous, and after a few months even Congressmen were asking that it be called off. But Gandhi was deaf to these appeals—the campaign "must continue at all odds"; it was "a moral protest" and was not intended "to make an appreciable impression on the war effort."

So the movement dragged on for over a year. The numbers willing to become *satyagrahis* dwindled and few of those released from jail courted rearrest. Gandhi did not mind. If there were only ten—or even only two—*satyagrahis*, he said, they would represent the whole Congress. He would neither abandon the campaign nor expand it into a mass movement, since this would "embarrass" the government and, in the absence of communal unity, would be "an invitation to civil war." To critics who complained that his policy was really one of passive inaction he replied that Congressmen should continue the "constructive program."

One of the Congress leaders arrested early and like Jawaharlal given a long term of imprisonment for making a seditious speech was the Congress President, Maulana A. K. Azad. At the time of his arrest he was about to speak to Gandhi about the communal problem and perhaps urge that something more was required than idealistic preaching about communal unity. But whatever he had to say remained unsaid and the year 1941 passed without the slightest rapprochement between Congress and the Muslim League.

Satyagraha having virtually come to an end, the Government, feeling conciliatory, released all *satyagrahi* prisoners early in December 1941, including Nehru and Azad. Immediately afterward, Pearl Harbor and the rapid advance of the Japanese through Malaya and Burma brought the war to the gates of India. It was a moment of extreme peril comparable to the summer of 1940, but whereas then Britain had been threatened with invasion and the danger to India was only indirect, in the winter of 1941–42 their positions were reversed.

Once again, as in the summer of 1940, Gandhi withdrew from leadership and left the Working Committee free to frame its policy unfettered by the doctrine of nonviolence. It was not his wish, he said, for India to obtain independence under the shadow of war and at the price of playing a full part in the war effort. The Working Committee, on the other hand, was willing to accept independence at any time and wanted an independent India to join with "progressive forces of the world" in fighting fascist aggression. But the committee was not prepared on this occasion, as it had been in 1940, to propose terms for a settlement with the British. Only Rajagopalachari urged that Congress "must ever be ready for a settlement." The other members of the committee shared Jawaharlal's view that to talk of settlement with Britain "at this late stage" was out of the question, as no help could be given to "an arrogant imperialism which is indistinguishable from Fascist authoritarianism." They decided, therefore, to concentrate on setting up, as they had contemplated in 1940, their own parallel organization for self-defense in case the Japanese landed in India.

Though unwilling to make any move for a settlement itself, the Working Committee was not wholly averse to considering an offer by the British, if the terms were sufficiently attractive. Toward the end of January there were signs that the British, under pressure of American opinion and their own military defeats, were considering a new declaration of policy, which was finally made on March 11. Churchill announced that in order to rally all forces of the Indian population to defend the country from invasion, Sir Stafford Cripps, who was well known for his sympathy with Congress, was being sent to India to lay before political leaders new proposals for India's political advance. These proposals were designed "to convince all classes, races and creeds in India of our sincere resolve" that, as soon as possible after the war, "India should attain Dominion Status in full freedom and equality with this country and the other Dominions, under a Constitution to be framed by Indians themselves."

This unequivocal promise of dominion status immediately after the war, not hedged around with qualifications about minorities and allowing the right of secession from the Commonwealth, went considerably beyond any previous policy statement of the British Government. If it had been made two years earlier Congress leaders might have adopted a different attitude toward cooperation with the British in the war effort. Even at this late stage it nearly won their acceptance, for unqualified independence was promised—not, indeed, immediately, but as soon as hostilities ended and a new constitution had been framed.

The British proposed that a body elected by members of the provincial legislatures, to which the appropriate number of representatives of the princely states would be added, should have the responsibility for drawing up the new constitution. The Muslim objection that the Hindu majority in such a body would override Muslim interests in framing a constitution was met by providing that any provinces or Indian states unwilling to accept the new constitution could stay out of the proposed Indian Union and form separate unions of their own. Thus while Pakistan was not explicitly conceded, the possibility of partition through the nonaccession of some of the Muslim-majority provinces was publicly acknowledged by the British for the first time.

Constitutional change was considered impossible while the war was still in progress, but in order to secure the immediate maximum participation of Indian political leaders in the government of the country it was proposed that all members of the Viceroy's Executive Council except the commander-in-chief should be Indians, chosen not by the Viceroy but by the political parties they represented.

Negotiations went on for two weeks. At an early stage the British got the impression that if Congress accepted the proposals, Jinnah would too. Among the Congress leaders, Rajagopalachari favored acceptance while the two principal Congress negotiators, Azad and Nehru, seemed undecided for a few days; at any rate, they did not reject the proposals out of hand. With the scales so evenly balanced, Gandhi's influence was decisive. During his interview with Cripps he said that he represented only himself and not Congress. This was formally correct, and he left Delhi halfway through the negotiations, telling the members of the Working Committee to make up their own minds. Actually, however, his known views made up their minds for them; he had made no secret of his opinion that the proposals should be rejected.

Why was he so firmly in favor of rejection? The primary purpose of the mission, as Cripps repeatedly emphasized, was to rally the country to its own defense. This had no appeal for Gandhi, at least if the defense were to be conventional, as it would be under British guidance, and therefore not nonviolent. From the very outbreak of war, true to the principle of nonviolence, he had objected to India giving the British anything more

than moral support, and his objection was all the stronger now
that the Japanese seemed to be poised for invasion, because
supporting the British would mean violent resistance to the
Japanese on Indian soil, the last thing the apostle of *ahimsa*
would desire. And what were the British offering? In a memorable phrase that has been apocryphally attributed to him, "A
post-dated check on a failing bank." They were offering not
independence, but only prospective independence which it
might never be their privilege to grant, for they might themselves be driven from India by the Japanese as they already had
been from Burma and Malaya. As Gandhi had himself said, he
did not want independence, let alone prospective independence, at the price of full support of the war effort. Moreover,
even prospective independence was clouded by the shadow of
partition. He stated later that the British proposals were unacceptable to him "for the simple reason that they contemplated
almost perpetual vivisection of India." Other Congress leaders
agreed with him.

Gandhi is reported to have said to Cripps, "Why did you
come if this is what you had to offer? I advise you to take the
next plane home." In his heart, however, he knew that the
British could hardly have offered more. Earlier in the war he had
himself pointed out that in the midst of a life-and-death struggle the British could not be expected to transfer the complete
direction of India's war effort to people they did not trust. Yet
this is virtually what Azad and Jawaharlal demanded. They
wanted the Viceroy to become a constitutional monarch, losing
his ultimate right to overrule his proposed Indian Executive
Council, and it was on this point that the negotiations finally
broke down. To Gandhi, however, the fundamental objection to
the Cripps offer was that it would commit India to wholehearted cooperation with the British in violently resisting the
Japanese. This was exactly what he personally wished to avoid.

So Congress rejected the Cripps offer, whereupon Jinnah and
the Muslim League did likewise. The decision was widely criticized and among the critics was Rajagopalachari, who had been
a member of the Working Committee since 1921 and had close
personal ties with Gandhi, his daughter having married one of

Gandhi's sons. Since the outbreak of war their views had diverged and, as if to emphasize this divergence, in January 1942 Gandhi had publicly stated that Nehru, not Rajagopalachari, would be his political heir. Like most Congressmen, including Nehru, Rajagopalachari disagreed with Gandhi's pacifism; but, unlike Nehru, he had been among Congressmen the chief protagonist of cooperation, on acceptable terms, with the British and of seeking an accord with the Muslim League, and the Cripps offer had provided a golden opportunity for both. Rajagopalachari, displaying more insight than Gandhi, realized that in terms of Hindu-Muslim unity its rejection had been a dangerous mistake, and he tried to make amends. At the end of April he submitted to the All-India Congress Committee a resolution recommending the acceptance of Pakistan in principle as the basis of a settlement between Congress and the League. He was heavily defeated, for now that cooperation with the British in the war effort had once again been ruled out Gandhi was back in full command; and Gandhi, considering "the vivisection of India to be a sin," would not for a moment countenance a resolution that accepted it. A counterresolution was passed flatly repudiating any proposal to give a state or territorial unit the right of secession. Thus Gandhi became a party to rejecting the Muslims' right of self-determination—the one condition, as Rajagopalachari saw, on which Hindu-Muslim accord was at this stage possible. Unwittingly, by counseling the rejection of the Cripps offer, Gandhi had paved the way for Pakistan.

Gandhi now proceeded to follow to its logical conclusion his obsession that any resistance to a Japanese invasion of India must be purely nonviolent. The first step was to demand the immediate withdrawal of the British from India, for if they remained the Japanese were sure to attack, the British would certainly resist violently, and India would become the scene of a sanguinary conflict. On the other hand, "if the British left India to her fate, as they had to leave Singapore, non-violent India would not lose anything. Probably the Japanese would leave India alone." He developed this line of thought further in a resolution drafted for the All-India Congress Committee, which even Nehru considered too favorable to the Japanese. The resolution stated that "the Committee desires to assure the Japanese Government and people that India bears no enmity either towards Japan or towards any other nation. . . . If India were freed, her first step probably would be to negotiate with Japan."

But although Nehru modified Gandhi's draft, he and almost all the members of the committee had now fallen in line with Gandhi's views. Whereas in mid-April he had been talking of organizing guerrilla warfare against the Japanese, now, only two weeks later, he agreed that resistance must be nonviolent and proceeded to justify on practical grounds what Gandhi demanded on principle. With Gandhi as its prophet and Jawaharlal its scribe the committee resolved: "In case an invasion takes place, it must be resisted. Such resistance can only take the form of non-violent non-cooperation as the British Government has prevented the organisation of national defence by the people in any other way." The British Government, it seems, at least had the merit of forcing India to be nonviolent!

The committee also agreed with Gandhi that nonviolent resistance to the Japanese required the immediate withdrawal of the British from India, and since he had repeatedly declared that he did not wish to embarrass the British—and had hitherto consistently refrained from doing so, confining civil disobedience to harmless symbolic protest—it was necessary to show that it would not be embarrassing at all for the British to leave India at this juncture; in fact, it would positively benefit them. So the committee boldly asserted that "not only the interests of India, but Britain's safety and world peace and freedom, demand that Britain must abandon her hold on India."

Having persuaded himself that by demanding that the British withdraw he was doing them a favor, Gandhi could now with a clear conscience prepare for his "Quit India" campaign. The withdrawal of the British would also, he found, have another merit—it would make possible the Hindu-Muslim unity that he had so long sought, for he had come to the conclusion that "real heart unity, genuine unity is almost an impossibility unless British power is withdrawn and no other power takes its place "

The position that Gandhi had adopted led him during the next three months into a maze of inconsistencies and contradictions. His conduct and many of his statements had an air of desperation, possibly accounted for by "an emotional urge which gave second place to logic and reason or a calm consideration of the consequences." The basic cause of this perturbation was the threat of a Japanese invasion. Gandhi assumed that it was imminent and that, as in Malaya and Burma, the British would be unable to repel or contain it and that consequently India would become the scene of destructive and disastrous fighting. On these assumptions—which, although disproved by events, in April and May of 1942 were not unreasonable—he felt passionately that the one way of saving India from this calamitous fate was to get the British to withdraw. It is true that, granted his assumptions, this solution would have been in the best interests of the Indian people, for it would have enabled India to come to terms with the Japanese or at most to put up only a token nonviolent resistance, a policy that Thailand followed with conspicuous success. But unfortunately such a solution was essentially impracticable. There was no possibility of getting the British to withdraw voluntarily, especially since they were now no longer alone, but members of a worldwide alliance intent on retaining India as a military base for operations against the Axis powers. And to try to compel them to do so by using civil disobedience or other forms of insurrection would increase the danger of a Japanese attack and, if it came, intensify the anarchy and violence that would ensue.

Gandhi had certainly not thought out all the implications of his policy, but he was already deeply committed to it, emotionally and otherwise, and throughout May he continued to call for a British evacuation of India.

The time has come during the war, not after it, for the British and the Indians to be reconciled to complete separation from each other. . . . The presence of the British in India is an invitation to Japan to invade India. Their withdrawal removes the bait. Assume, however, it does not; free India will be better able to cope with invasion. Unadulterated non-cooperation will then have full sway.

American journalists soon began to ask him if the cause of China and the United Nations would not be hurt if India were abandoned as a base of operations, and Jawaharlal also tried to get him to see that he was ignoring important international considerations. Confronted with these issues, he had to confess that there had been a gap in his original thinking: "I could not guarantee fool-proof non-violent action to keep the Japanese at bay. Abrupt withdrawal of the Allied troops might result in Japan's occupation of India and China's sure fall. I had not the remotest idea of any such catastrophe resulting from my action." Therefore at the beginning of June he conceded that Allied troops might remain in India "under a treaty with the Government of a free India and at the allied powers' expense for the sole purpose of repelling a Japanese attack and helping China." Realizing that this concession negated his strict non-violence policy, he suggested that it would be sufficient if nonviolence, instead of taking the form of noncooperation with the Japanese, were expressed by India's ambassadors "going to the Axis Powers not to beg for peace, but to show them the futility of war."

Gandhi had lost touch with realities and was building castles in the air, while on the Hindu-Muslim problem he was urging counsels of despair. In the past, and again quite recently on the failure of the Cripps mission, he had said that the attainment of independence was impossible until the communal tangle had been solved. He was now saying just the reverse—that the British must first withdraw and then the communal problem would dissolve itself in anarchy: "Let the British entrust India to God, or in modern parlance, to anarchy. Then, all parties will fight one another like dogs, or will, when real responsibility faces them, come to a reasonable agreement. I shall expect non-violence to arise out of that chaos."

He was plainly heading for a direct collision with the Government, but under the pressure of Jawaharlal and American

critics he had shifted his ground. The demand for British withdrawal had originally been made on the grounds that it would
reduce the temptation to the Japanese to invade and, if they did
so, would enable India to resist them nonviolently. All this was
now forgotten and the withdrawal of the British was called for
on two quite different grounds—that India in bondage could
play no effective part in saving the world from Nazism and that
India's subjection was a moral burden that hampered the allied
cause. "If we have freedom to play our part," Gandhi optimisti-
cally asserted, "we can arrest the march of Japan and save
China. . . . The allies have no moral cause for which they are
fighting, so long as they are carrying this double sin on their
shoulders, the sin of India's subjection and the subjection of the
Negroes and African races."

When the Working Committee met at Wardha on July 6,
with Gandhi in attendance, nonviolence was relegated very
much to the background. The committee stressed its desire that
India should be enabled to resist aggression effectively, and this
did not mean nonviolently. To build up effective resistance, the
committee contended, the existing ill will against Britain must
be changed to good will. It therefore called for the immediate
end of British rule in India, insisting that the proposal was
made with "no desire whatsoever to embarrass Great Britain or
the allied powers in the prosecution of the war." Nevertheless,
if it was not accepted, Congress would be compelled to
utilize all its nonviolent strength for the vindication of political
rights and liberties, and "such a widespread struggle would inevitably be under the leadership of Mahatma Gandhi." A meeting of the All-India Congress Committee was fixed for August 7
for a final decision of these important issues.

The threat of some kind of mass civil disobedience unless the
Government abdicated was received throughout the country
with such dismay and disapproval that Congress President
Maulana Azad, who, like Nehru, had agreed to the "Quit India"
policy with some reluctance, hastened to explain that the Working Committee's resolution was not an ultimatum. But Gandhi
seemed to take a different view, telling journalists on July 14,
"There is no room left for negotiations in the proposal for

withdrawal. Either they recognise India's independence or they don't. After that recognition many things can follow." Plainly he felt that negotiations could follow but that they could not precede acceptance of the demand for the immediate end of British rule.

This demand was curtly condemned by Jinnah as an attempt "to coerce the British Government to surrender to a Congress Raj." He described the projected "Quit India" campaign as "a manifestation of an angered and desperate mentality" and sarcastically inquired if this was the best contribution that Gandhi could make to India in the evening of his life. The Muslim Premier of the Punjab, Sir Sikander Hyat-Khan, said that the Working Committee's resolution aimed at creating pandemonium and was a gross betrayal of the country and of the Indian soldiers fighting to preserve its freedom. More temperate, yet in some ways more forcible, criticism came from Congress supporters and sympathizers. In a letter to Gandhi, Rajagopalachari and three leading Madras Congressmen protested against the resolution:

> While there can be no difference of point of view on India's demand for complete freedom from foreign domination, the idea of the withdrawal of the government, to be automatically replaced by another government, is altogether impossible. . . . The withdrawal of the government without simultaneous replacement by another must involve the dissolution of the State and society itself.

They went on to point out that unless the two major political organizations, Congress and the Muslim League, could agree on some plan for a provisional national government that could take over power—and this had so far proved impossible—only chaos could follow abdication by the British and that the only ones to gain immediately would be the Japanese.

This was plain common sense, but Gandhi was not at this time open to common sense. In his own words, a fire was raging within his breast. This fire was driving him toward the biggest but most futile struggle of his life. Reason, logic, consistency, past statements were all thrown to the winds. "I want indepen-

dence now," he declared, and added in justification but contrary to all the evidence, that "that will help England win the
war."

While he was in this frenzied mood the reasoned reproaches
of the Congress sympathizer, Sir Stafford Cripps, went
unheeded.

> I remember Mr. Gandhi saying some years ago that, once
> given the certainty of Indian freedom in the future, he
> cared little how long the period of transition lasted. The
> certainty has now been given, and the period of transition
> has been reduced to "while hostilities last." Is it not then
> unreasonable to demand suddenly that there should be no
> transition at all, and to make that demand at a moment of
> peculiar difficulty for the United Nations?

It was, of course, unreasonable, and unreasonably Gandhi continued to harp on the untenable thesis that the demand was in
the interests of Great Britain and the allied powers. The chorus
of indignation from Britain and America would not, he declared,
deter the Congress from its purpose.

What *was* its purpose? Clearly a mass movement against the
Government was contemplated with a view to forcing it to
abdicate, but as usual Gandhi's plans for the movement were
hazy and he trusted to God and improvisation. In response to
questions by journalists he made a number of statements that
were hard to reconcile with one another. It would be a mass
movement of a strictly nonviolent character, but if, in spite of
precautions, violence occurred, it could not be helped. He
would do all he could to handle the movement gently, but
would not hesitate to go to the extremist limit if he felt it had
no impact on Great Britain or the allied powers. He wanted to
guard against an outburst of anarchy, but there might be fifteen
days of chaos. He intended to make the struggle as short and
swift as possible and conceded that a general strike would be
the quickest means of ending it and that this tactic was not
excluded. Since, however, the struggle was to be conducted in a
friendly spirit, not a hostile one, he would proceed with the

utmost caution—but, nevertheless, if a general strike became absolutely necessary he would not flinch from it.

Gandhi was still basically faithful to his old *satyagraha* principle and claimed to attach the same importance as ever to nonviolence, but undoubtedly he was less inhibited by it than in earlier days. He accepted outbreaks of violence and disorder as more or less inevitable and was no longer averse to the "anarchy and red ruin" against which he had protested in 1940. He outlined no regular program and made no organized preparations for mass nonviolent civil disobedience, possibly hoping that, as he had earlier been assured, the response to his call would be so staggering that the Government would immediately be paralyzed by a spontaneous, universal strike throughout the country. But is is difficult to believe that he was wholly ignorant of the preparations that were being made by others, many of them Congressmen, for mass action very far removed from nonviolent *satyagraha*.

The All-India Congress Committee duly met in Bombay on August 7 and on the following day, with little opposition, sanctioned a mass struggle on nonviolent lines on the widest possible scale under Gandhi's leadership and guidance. Nonviolence still retained, nominally at least, its sanctity against the British. But against the Japanese it was now openly discarded. In the course of its resolution the committee declared that the primary purpose of the provisional government of free India would be to cooperate fully with the allied powers in the defense of India with all the armed as well as other forces at her command. Gandhi, who subscribed to the resolution, was induced to swallow his principles and, forgetful of his exhortation to the British not to use weapons to fight the Nazis, to acquiesce in violent resistance to the Japanese. The politician (and patriot) had triumphed over the saint.

After the "Quit India" resolution had been passed, Gandhi addressed the committee both in English and Hindustani. Parts of the Hindustani speech were marked by a passion and eloquence unusual in his public utterances, for although outwardly calm and self-possessed, he was in a mood of patriotic fervor amounting almost to frenzy.

I want freedom immediately, this very night, before dawn, if it can be had. Freedom cannot wait for the realization of communal unity. . . . Congress must win freedom or be wiped out in the effort. Here is a *mantra*, a short one, that I give you. You may imprint it on your hearts and let every breath of yours give expression to it. The *mantra* is: "Do or Die." We shall either free India or die in the attempt; we shall not live to see the perpetuation of our slavery.

The call for freedom before dawn, if it could be had, was answered promptly by the Government of India. Early on the morning of August 9, Gandhi, the members of the Working Committee, and other Congress leaders were arrested and the All-India Congress Committee and the provincial Congress committees declared unlawful associations.

XVI ✑

Reconciliation:

The Cabinet Mission

In the course of his address to the All-India Congress Committee Gandhi had said that the actual struggle would not begin immediately and that he intended first to see the Viceroy and plead with him to accept the Congress demand. This, he thought, might take two or three weeks and he advised Congressmen to devote themselves in the meanwhile to the spinning wheel and the "constructive program." "After my last night's speech," he told his secretary, "they will never arrest me." He was therefore surprised and aggrieved when he was arrested in the early hours of the morning and unceremoniously hurried away to the Aga Khan's palace at Poona with only half an hour allowed to him for his morning drink of goat's milk and for hymn singing and recitations from the Koran. Accustomed to the latitude that had been granted him so amicably in the past, he failed to realize that, with the Japanese threatening invasion, even the tolerant, easygoing British were not inclined to allow him time to preach and organize what he himself described as "an open rebellion."

Up to the time of his arrest Gandhi's own plans and preparations for the mass movement that he was supposed to direct
had been more than usually tentative, but had followed well-
established precedents. Harking back to 1920, he had suggested
to the All-India Congress Committee that the campaign be
opened with a one day *hartal* during which all the people would
fast and offer prayers; meetings and processions were to be allowed only in villages where there would be "no fear of violence
or disturbance," not in towns and cities. Thereafter salt was to
be manufactured in defiance of the salt laws and the payment
of land revenue was to be refused; Congress members of the
legislature were to resign their seats, and everyone who desired
freedom for India and fully believed "in the weapon of truth
and non-violence" was to be invited to join in the struggle, even
if his name was not on the Congress register.

This program was never carried out. Before it could be implemented Gandhi and the members of the Working Committee
were arrested, and a campaign of quite a different character was
launched, a campaign of violence and sabotage directed princi-
pally against communications. Mobs set fire to railway stations,
signal boxes, and post offices, and organized gangs cut telegraph
and telephone wires and tampered with the railway track. Police
stations and other government buildings were also attacked;
government servants were intimidated and a few were murdered in cold blood.

The gravest and most extensive disorders occurred in Bihar
and the eastern part of the United Provinces, where for a while
whole districts were wrested from the Government's control
and communications were so badly disrupted that the eastern
provinces of Bengal and Assam and the armies guarding the
eastern frontier against the Japanese were entirely cut off from
northern India. Elsewhere, the disturbances were comparatively
limited, and nowhere was any large proportion of the population involved in them. The Government forces, police and military, remained completely loyal and struck back vigorously. By
the end of August the attacks on communications had been
effectively checked and by the end of September, in the words
of Gandhi's chief biographer, "the Government had apparently

succeeded in crushing both the non-violent and the violent attempts to compel them to quit India."

The Government claimed to have evidence that this violent campaign of lawlessness and sabotage was conducted under secret instructions issued in the name of the All-India Congress Committee. The committee's name must have been taken in vain, for the campaign was certainly not authorized by the Congress high command, much less by Gandhi. But some members of the Working Committee and some leading Congressmen at the provincial level were probably privy to it; well-known Congressmen, in spite of their stated belief in nonviolence, organized and incited acts of violence and even murder, and everywhere the Congress rank and file, supported by the hooligan element in the population, freely joined in sabotage and attacks on public buildings. Even Gandhi appears to have been less concerned than on previous occasions about preventing a mass movement from turning to violence, and his own words on the eve of his arrest had a decidedly militant tone. He spoke of "a fight to the finish in the course of which he would not hesitate to run any risk, however great," and his slogan—"Do or Die"— was hardly appropriate for *satyagrahis*, for if they remained really nonviolent they would have little scope for doing and none at all for dying.

Nevertheless, he was still—or certainly claimed to be—as great a believer in nonviolence as ever, and was therefore deeply affronted by the charge, made in a Government communiqué issued on the day of his arrest, that Congress had been preparing for violent activities. As the tale of violence and destruction unfolded and the Government continued to heap the blame for it on Congress, he became more and more aggrieved. In a lengthy letter, written as early as August 14, he protested against his precipitate arrest before he had even inaugurated mass action; and in a second letter, sent to the Government on September 23, he asserted that if they had waited for his planned letter to the Viceroy

no calamity would have overtaken the country. The reported deplorable destruction would most certainly have been avoided. In spite of all that has been said to the contrary, I claim that the Congress policy still remains unequivocally non-violent. The wholesale arrest of the Congress leaders seems to have made the people wild with rage to the point of losing self-control. I feel that the Government, not the Congress, are responsible for the destruction that has taken place.

The Government replied curtly or not at all to these communications, and Gandhi continued to nurse a grievance. His assumption that the disorders had arisen spontaneously on the arrest of the Congress leaders was, of course, far from accurate; the campaign of sabotage had been carefully organized—not, indeed, as the Government insinuated, by the All-India Congress Committee, but by revolutionary groups and left-wing elements among the lower echelons of Congress. Some high-ranking Congressmen had knowledge of it, and even Gandhi himself may not have been without some inkling of what was afoot. But the Government's unrelenting insistence that he and the Congress leadership were responsible, directly or indirectly, for the widespread outbreaks of violence rankled with him, and on the last day of the year he unburdened himself in a personal letter to the Viceroy:

I had thought we were friends and should still love to think so. However, what has happened since the 9th August last makes me wonder whether you still regard me as a friend. . . . Your arrest of me and the communiqué you issued thereafter . . . and much else I can catalogue go to show that at some stage or other you must have suspected my bona fides. . . . If I had not ceased to be your friend, why did you not, before taking drastic action, send for me, tell me of your suspicions and make yourself sure of your facts?

He went on to complain that he had been quite misjudged and that the statements made about him in Government quarters contained "palpable departures from truth." The Government had unjustly condemned him and his colleagues and "wronged innocent men." In such moments of trial, he concluded, the law of *satyagraha* prescribes a remedy:

> In a sentence it is "Crucify the flesh by fasting." That same law forbids its use, except as a last resort. I do not want to use it, if I can avoid it. This is a way to avoid it. Convince me of my errors, and I shall make ample amends.

Lord Linlithgow tried to convince him of his errors, but without success. Pointing out that he had not uttered a single word in condemnation of the violence that had resulted from Congress policy, he told him with all the frankness of a friend that he necessarily bore a heavy responsibility for it.

> There is evidence that you and your friends expected this policy to lead to violence; that you were prepared to condone it; and that the violence that ensued formed part of a concerted plan, conceived long before the arrest of the Congress leaders. . . . You may rest assured that the charges against the Congress will have to be met sooner or later and it will then be for you or your colleagues to clear yourselves before the world, if you can.

Finding that he could get from the Viceroy no "soothing balm for his pain," Gandhi felt driven to his last resort of a fast. On learning that this was his intention the Viceroy informed him rather harshly that he regarded "the use of a fast for political purposes as a form of political blackmail (*himsa* *) for which there can be no moral justification." Gandhi replied that it was "an appeal to the Highest Tribunal for justice which I have failed to secure from you." It would certainly seem that on this occasion Gandhi's fast was not designed to blackmail or coerce anybody, but to express, and convince the Viceroy of, his innocence. It was not a fast unto death, but "a fast according to capacity," which he assessed at three weeks. He had no wish to die, he told the Viceroy, but "if I do not survive the ordeal, I shall go to the Judgement Seat with the fullest faith in my innocence."

* Opposite of *ahimsa*: violence.

The Government immediately offered to release him "for the purpose and the duration of the fast," but he declined this limited offer of release, which was of obvious convenience to the Government but of no particular convenience to him, and undertook the fast in the confinement of the Aga Khan's palace. Facilities were given for his own physicians to attend him.

He was now seventy-three years old and, expert though he was at fasting, the prospects of his surviving the strain of a twenty-one-day fast at his age were uncertain. The fast began on February 10. Within a week there were disturbing symptoms of uremia and the medical bulletins became gloomy. A powerful agitation was started for his unconditional release and, when the Viceroy would not yield to it, three Indian members of his Executive Council resigned in protest. On February 20 the doctors reported a decided change for the worse and on the next day they said that unless the fast were ended without delay it might be too late to save his life. But Lord Linlithgow refused to be rattled. With remarkable courage and resolution he accepted the risk of Gandhi dying on his hands, correctly judging that the risk was not as great as it appeared. For Gandhi also possessed high courage and resolution and was determined, if possible, to get through the fast alive. On the advice of his doctors orange juice was added to his water in place of the citrus juice that he had taken from the outset to assist his system in absorbing water in sufficient quantities. The effects were immediately beneficial; after a day or two the medical bulletins became more reassuring, and the country heaved a sigh of relief. The last week passed without further alarming reports, and the fast was successfully completed on March 3 with the usual ceremonies. Kasturbai handed him a glass of orange juice, hymns were sung, and passages from the Gita and the Koran were recited.

This was the last occasion on which Kasturbai was to perform this ceremonial office at the end of one of Gandhi's fasts. She had voluntarily shared his confinement in the Aga Khan's palace, but it was as unwelcome as it was unexpected to her—he had assured her that he would not be arrested unless he actually courted arrest—and she fretted, fell sick, and died in February 1944, before his release. They had been married for sixty-two years. In Gandhi's own words they were "a couple outside the ordinary." His manner of life made it impossible for them to be otherwise. In the domestic sphere she gave him many lessons in nonviolent noncooperation, but as he grew in fame and stature she merged herself in him. Though she was literate in Gujarati and had picked up a few scraps of English, she remained to the end quite uneducated and Gandhi, who had tried to instruct her when they were both in their teens, was still engaged on the same task when in their seventies they were confined together in the Aga Khan's palace.

When the fast ended a number of non-Congress leaders, including the ex-Congressman Rajagopalachari,* issued a statement calling for Gandhi's release and a reconciliation between Congress and the Government. They expressed their conviction that Gandhi, if set free, would do his best to resolve the internal deadlock and that there need be no fear of any obstruction to the war effort. It is probable that the fast, undertaken to convince the Viceroy of his innocence, had induced in Gandhi himself some measure of repentance for the 1942 "rebellion" or at least a consciousness of the need to come to terms with both the Government and the Muslim League. But the Government was in no mood for negotiations and demanded guarantees and clearer signs of repentance and of "a change of heart and mind" than Gandhi was willing to offer. So throughout 1943 and the first four months of 1944 Gandhi remained in confinement in the Aga Khan's palace, reading Shakespeare, Browning, Marx, Engels, and Lenin and indulging, by letter, in a sterile controversy with the British authorities over the disorders of 1942.

The British were fully justified in believing these disorders to have been the natural and predictable consequence of Gandhi's declaration of open rebellion. Gandhi himself had been well aware that he was risking outbreaks of violence; indeed, the risk was far greater than in 1920 when he admitted that he knew he was playing with fire. But the British insinuation that the Congress high command had actually planned or authorized a campaign of sabotage was less firmly based, and the allegation that

* He had been compelled to resign from Congress because of his opposition to the "Quit India" resolution.

they were pro-Axis and deliberate saboteurs of the Allied struggle against Japan was essentially false, even though the mass
civil disobedience that they threatened might have been likely,
in practice, to favor the Japanese. At this time Smuts, his old
adversary in South Africa, issued a salutary reprimand to the
British press: "It is sheer nonsense to talk of Mahatma Gandhi
as a fifth columnist. He is a great man. He is one of the great
men of the world."

Nevertheless, in launching or threatening to launch a mass
movement against the Government in the midst of war Gandhi
made a grave mistake, which can be excused or explained only
by his exaggerated dread of a Japanese invasion and of India
suffering the same fate as Burma. He said that it was the last
and biggest struggle of his life; but it was also, as his loyal
friend, Rajagopalachari, realized, the most misconceived and
the most unprofitable. It furthered none of his aims: it did not
advance India's independence by a single day; it did not promote Hindu-Muslim unity—on the contrary, it emphasized
and increased the separateness of the two communities; and it
let loose violence in place of nonviolence.

The greatest gainers from the 1942 rebellion—apart from the
British authorities in India, who for the rest of the war were
spared harassment from Congress—were Jinnah and the Muslim League. The imprisonment of all the Congress leaders left
the political field free for Jinnah to dominate, and he exploited
it to the full, taking advantage of the opportunity for anti-
Congress propaganda provided by the fact that Congress had
become discredited among many non-Congressmen. The 1942
rebellion appeared so senseless that it became plausible to represent it, however falsely, as a crafty plot to coerce the British
into surrender to a "Congress Raj." Throughout the rest of the
war Jinnah and the League steadily consolidated their position
in the Muslim-majority provinces in which they had been weak-
est and by the end of the war they were able to substantiate the
claim that only the League could speak for the Muslims.

In May 1944, after a severe attack of malaria, Gandhi was
released unconditionally on medical grounds. He was thoroughly run down and was suffering from hookworm as well as

acute anemia. He went to the seaside at Juhu to recuperate and, to ensure rest, observed complete silence for two weeks.

In June he wrote to the Viceroy—Lord Wavell had by now succeeded Lord Linlithgow—asking for an interview and for permission to consult members of the Working Committee. The Viceroy refused these requests, but Gandhi was not to be easily put off. In an interview with a London journalist he indicated that he had retreated somewhat from the extreme position of the "Quit India" resolution. He had no authority, he said, to withdraw that resolution, but 1944 was not 1942, there was no longer any question of starting mass civil disobedience, and he would now be content with a national government controlling only the civil administration and with the Viceroy and commander-in-chief retaining complete control of military operations. And for the first time he expressed some qualified disapproval of the excesses of 1942: "Heroism, suffering and self-sacrifice of those who took part in the struggle are beyond praise; but weighed in the scale of truth and non-violence there are glaring defects in the popular demonstration." Reports of the interview drew complaints from extremists that "under the influence of moderates and moneyed men [Gandhi] had betrayed the cause of the country." Undeterred by this criticism, he continued to proffer his modest olive branch, promising the Viceroy the full cooperation of Congress in the war effort— nonviolence had now been totally discarded so far as the Axis powers were concerned—provided that a declaration of immediate Indian independence was made and a national government formed responsible to the Central Assembly, but without power to control military operations. The Viceroy replied that the proposal was "completely unacceptable" and pointed out once again that no constitutional changes such as those the contemplated national government would entail could be made until the war was over. The British were not much interested in Congress cooperation in any case. The majority of Indians were helping them to win the war out of sheer economic self-interest, regardless of what Gandhi and the Congress might say or do. In the British view, "not another shell, not another pair of boots, not another recruit, could be contributed by Congress support of the war effort."

Repulsed by the British, Gandhi applied himself to reaching an accord with Jinnah. He wrote to him: "Brother Jinnah, Let us meet whenever you wish. Do not regard me as an enemy of Islam or of the Indian Muslims. I have always been a servant and friend to you and mankind. Do not disappoint me." They met in Bombay and had talks from September 9 to 27. Rajagopalachari had at last induced Gandhi to accept the principle of Pakistan and had devised a formula that was the basis of the talks. The "Rajaji formula" was that if the Muslims endorsed the demand for national independence, Congress would agree to the demarcation of contiguous Muslim-majority areas in the northwestern and northeastern corners of India, the inhabitants of which would be allowed to decide by plebiscite whether they would remain in a free united India or form a separate state or states of their own.

Since Gandhi had previously described the "vivisection" of India as a sin, his acceptance of this formula indicated a marked change of attitude. If only he had been less vehement in his opposition to the proposal for Pakistan in 1940 or even 1942, he might have achieved the "proper heart-to-heart agreement" with Jinnah that he sought. Belated though it was, his conversion to Rajagopalachari's viewpoint seemed to augur well for the talks and they began amidst high hopes. Even Jinnah spoke more encouragingly than usual: "It has been the universal desire that we should meet. Now that we are going to meet, help us. We are coming to grips. Bury the past."

After the first day of the talks, when asked if he had brought anything from Jinnah, Gandhi replied, "Only flowers"; by the end of the talks he had obtained nothing more substantial. He and Jinnah were temperamentally so antipathetic that even in the most favorable circumstances agreement between them would have been difficult. There was, in any case, no possibility that at this stage Jinnah would accept the "Rajaji formula." The Pakistan of his conception was not "a bundle of contiguous areas" but comprised the whole of six provinces. The "Rajaji formula" offered him only "a shadow and a husk, a maimed, mutilated and moth-eaten Pakistan." This is what he ultimately had to be content with, but he was not willing at the very outset of the negotiations to accept half a loaf rather than none, and Gandhi was not prepared to offer more.

Furthermore, Gandhi insisted, both then and later, that any division of India must take place by mutual agreement *after* the British had left India and not before. Jinnah insisted that the "division" should precede the "quitting," knowing full well that once the British had gone the Hindus would never agree to division and that the Muslims, if they wanted Pakistan, would have to fight a civil war for it in which they would be at a disadvantage. Gandhi's insistence on the postponement of division appeared to Jinnah a sly way of evading it altogether—as perhaps subconsciously it was. He told Gandhi, with some measure of truth, "The question of the division of India, as Pakistan and Hindustan, is only on your lips and does not come from your heart." Gandhi's statements, both during the talks and after, confirm this judgment, and a particular statement he made at the time discloses how far he was from conceding to Pakistan the independence that Jinnah demanded: "If it means utterly independent sovereignty, I hold it is an impossible proposition. That means war to the knife. The separation should be within ourselves and not separation in the face of the whole world."

Finally, Jinnah questioned Gandhi's credentials. He himself had authority to speak for the Muslim League, whereas Gandhi had no authority to speak for Congress. Gandhi admitted that he represented only himself, but he aspired to represent all the people of India. Jinnah was not interested in his aspirations and told him brutally: "It is quite clear that you represent nobody but the Hindus, and as long as you don't realise your true position and the realities, it is very difficult for me to argue with you."

The talks failed. Both leaders expressed the hope that this was not the end of their efforts. But it proved to be.

Gandhi, having been unsuccessful in his attempts at reconciliation with both the British and the Muslims, took no further initiative, but he remained in a conciliatory frame of mind. He advised political workers, who had gone underground in order to elude arrest, to give themselves up; and when Subhas Chandra Bose, commander-in-chief of the "Indian National Army," which had been formed by the Japanese from Indian military personnel captured in Malaya and Singapore, hailed Gandhi from Rangoon on his seventy-fifth birthday as the "father of our nation" and invoked his blessings and good wishes for the success of the "holy war for India's liberation," Gandhi remained silent, giving no sign of encouragement. He disapproved of Bose's policy and in spite of what he had permitted to be done in the name of Congress in 1942, he still held that "India can come to her own fully by truth and non-violent means."

The British made no move to end the political deadlock until June 1945 when the war in Europe was already over. The members of the Working Committee were then released and leaders of both Congress and the League were invited by Lord Wavell to a conference at Simla to discuss proposals for the formation of an interim government representative of the principal political parties. Congress was in a chastened mood and ready to accept proposals that it had previously rejected with contumely. As in 1942, the British felt that the Viceroy's Executive Council should continue to function under the existing constitution, but that all its members except the Viceroy himself and the commander-in-chief should be Indian political leaders. A new feature was that equal representation was proposed for Muslims and for caste Hindus, that is, Hindus other than Untouchables. This was a concession to Jinnah and the Muslims, and the Congress leaders had the good sense to agree to it. But Jinnah wanted more; he demanded that no Muslim should be given a place on the council unless he was a member of the League, and on this issue the conference broke down. Thus Lord Wavell's well-meant attempt to promote Hindu-Muslim cooperation quickly ended in failure. Yet in one respect his initiative had been successful. Congress leaders had been induced to return to the path of cooperation and were sufficiently impressed by Wavell's sincerity to wish to stay on it.

Gandhi was not a delegate to the Simla conference, but he had been in touch with the Working Committee and the Viceroy, and although he objected to the distinction drawn

between caste Hindus and Untouchables, he did not use this as
an excuse for withholding cooperation. It was beginning to
dawn on him, and, other Congress leaders, notably Vallabhbhai
Patel, that the British meant to honor their promise of independence after the war. The coming to power of a Labor Government at the end of July confirmed this impression. Two
weeks later the Japanese surrendered, ending the war, and soon
afterward the Labor Government announced that it sought "an
early realisation of self-government in India." As a first step new
elections were to be held for the central and provincial legislatures; thereafter a constitution-making body would be convened. The Labor Government appeared to mean business.

Congress entered the elections and met with overwhelming
success in Hindu areas. More significant, however, was the success of the Muslim League. It won all the Muslim seats in the
Central Assembly and 446 out of a total of 495 Muslim seats in
the provincial assemblies. Muslim parties other than the League
were virtually eliminated and Jinnah's claim that he alone spoke
for the Muslims of India was at last irrefutably established.

The crucial question now was not the independence of India,
but whether India should remain united or be divided. Jinnah
declared:

We could settle the Indian problem in ten minutes if Mr.
Gandhi would say, "I agree that there should be a Pakistan; I agree that one-fourth of India, composed of six provinces—Sind, Baluchistan, the Punjab, the North-west
Frontier Province, Bengal and Assam—with their present
boundaries constitute the Pakistan state."

But neither Gandhi nor Congress would say anything of the
kind. Gandhi still shrank instinctively from the partition of
India, and even realists in Congress like Vallabhbhai Patel still
thought that Jinnah was bluffing and would in the end, accept
something less than Pakistan. In any case they were not going
to make him a present of six whole provinces.

While still unwilling to meet Jinnah halfway, Congress recognized that with independence within its grasp the time was
past for antigovernment agitation, for Congress itself would

soon be the government. They therefore began to calm the excitement and moderate the discontent that swept through the country in the months following the conclusion of hostilities. Shortages of food and cloth, rising Hindu-Muslim feeling, the ill-judged trial of three officers of the "Indian National Army" on charges of treason, and finally in February 1946 a mutiny in the Royal Indian Navy brought huge crowds into the streets and sparked off serious riots in several of the big cities. To combat these disorders the doctrine of nonviolence was once more pressed into service. In a resolution drafted by Gandhi himself the Working Committee reaffirmed that "the policy of non-violence continues unabated" and explained that "non-violence does not include burning public property, cutting of telegraph wires, derailing trains and intimidation." Emphasis was again laid on the "constructive program" and to underline one of its aims—the removal of untouchability—Gandhi began to stay in the Harijan quarter instead of in the palatial residence of some wealthy admirer when visiting Bombay and Delhi.

The general unrest greatly perturbed Gandhi and other Congress leaders, and Vallabhbhai Patel personally intervened to quell the naval mutiny and to prevent strikes in sympathy with it. Gandhi reproached the mutineers for "setting a bad and unbecoming example" and said their mutiny was "not in any sense of the term non-violent action." And he warned the country:

> Now that it seems we are coming into our own, indiscipline and hooliganism ought to go, and calmness, rigid discipline, cooperation and goodwill must take their place. . . . The rulers have declared their intention to "Quit." Let not the action be delayed by a moment because of the exhibition of this distressful unrest.

While the naval mutiny was still in progress, the British Government gave a further indication of its desire to hasten the day of Indian independence. It announced that three British cabinet ministers—Lord Pethick-Lawrence, Secretary of State for India; Sir Stafford Cripps; and A. V. Alexander—would be sent to India to assist the Viceroy in negotiations with the political parties to try to secure agreement on the method of framing a constitution and on the formation of a new and representative executive council that would run the government in the meanwhile. The Cabinet Mission arrived in Delhi in March and at once began lengthy discussions with representatives of political parties, the Indian states, the Sikhs, the Harijans, and, not least, with Gandhi. He claimed, as usual, to speak only for himself, but the British ministers requested him to keep in touch with them during the whole progress of the negotiations. He established himself with due publicity in the Harijan quarter of New Delhi.

The only two political parties that really mattered were Congress and the League, and their proclaimed aims were contradictory. The League contended that there were two nations in India and that there must therefore be two national states. Congress maintained the opposite. Since these two parties were unable themselves to arrive at any agreed basis for framing a constitution, the Cabinet Mission put forward a plan of their own. They proposed a three-tier federal constitution consisting of a Union (embracing both British India and the princely states) limited to foreign affairs, defense, and communications; three groups of provinces and states dealing with such common subjects as the units within the groups might decide; and the individual provinces and states in which all residuary powers would be vested. To draw up a constitution on these principles they proposed that a Constituent Assembly be elected by the members of the provincial legislatures; and to meet Jinnah's objection that a single Constituent Assembly would be dominated by Hindus they proposed that after a preliminary meeting the assembly should be divided into three sections corresponding to the proposed groups of provinces—section A consisting of the representatives of the six Hindu-majority provinces; section B of the representatives of the Punjab, the North-West Frontier, and Sind; and section C of the representatives of Bengal and Assam. These sections would draw up constitutions for the provinces included in them and also decide what subjects, if any, should be dealt with at group level. Finally, the Constituent Assembly would meet again as a whole to settle the details of the Union constitution.

This ingenious attempt to reconcile contradictory aims was well received. It was universally accepted as evidence of the British Government's genuine desire to end British rule in India. Speaking at one of his prayer meetings, Gandhi said that the Cabinet Mission had accomplished something of which it had every reason to be proud; and some days later, when doubts had begun to assail him, he still expressed appreciation: "After four days of searching examination my conviction abides that it is the best document the British Government could have produced in the circumstances." The more he studied it, however, the less he liked it, for he saw in it the seeds of separatism.

For this same reason it appealed to Jinnah. Although the Mission had decisively rejected partition, he realized that their plan did not exclude the possibility of the *ultimate* establishment of a completely sovereign Pakistan comprised of five or, if Baluchistan were included, six whole provinces. And so on June 6 he persuaded the League to accept the plan and to agree to join the projected Constituent Assembly.

No final verdict on the proposals had yet been passed by the Working Committee of Congress. At Gandhi's insistence it had tried to persuade the Mission to admit an interpretation of the proposals that would make it optional for the individual provinces to join the sections in which they had been placed. Since the League did not command a majority in the Punjab, Assam, or the North-West Frontier, these provinces could frustrate the grouping that the League desired by refusing to join. The Mission rejected this interpretation of their proposals; it was mandatory for the provinces to sit in the appropriate sections, for this was an essential feature of the plan. Only *after* the constitutional arrangements had become effective would a province, by the vote of its legislature, be able to opt out of a group. Rebuffed, Gandhi and the Working Committee withdrew for a rest to the cool climate of Mussouri and continued to postpone their decision.

Meanwhile the Viceroy had been vainly trying to bring the two parties to agree about the formation of a new Executive Council. The League claimed "parity" with Congress and the right to nominate all the Muslim members. Congress rejected both claims. No agreement could be reached, and it became clear that in this matter also the Viceroy and the Mission would have to offer compromise proposals of their own and hope that both parties would accept them.

Gandhi was in a dilemma. His oft-repeated advice had been to grant the Muslims the concessions they wanted. He ought therefore to have tried to persuade the Working Committee to concede the League's claims to "parity" and to the sole right to nominate the Muslim members. But acceptance of the latter claim would have meant virtual abandonment of Congress' own claims to represent everybody—Muslims as well as Hindus. How could Gandhi agree to do this? His own solution was typically original and impractical. He wrote to the Viceroy and Sir Stafford Cripps telling them to choose one horse or the other, as they would never succeed in riding two at the same time. They should choose either the names submitted by Congress or the names submitted by the League: "For God's sake do not make an incompatible mixture and in trying to do so, produce a fearful explosion."

But the British were trying to act as honest brokers; they could not come down wholly on one side or the other, as Gandhi suggested, and so they attempted to gain acceptance for the mixture that he deprecated. After consulting with the Mission, in mid-June the Viceroy issued invitations to fourteen persons to serve as members of a new Executive Council, or Interim Government as it was now being called. Six were Hindu members of Congress (including one Harijan), five were members of the League, and the remaining three were a Sikh, a Parsee, and an Indian Christian. Jinnah's claim to "parity" with Congress was rejected, but his claim to veto non-League Muslims was respected.

These proposals were acceptable to Jinnah, although he did not publicly say so until after Congress had spoken. Some Congressmen wanted to substitute a Congress Muslim for one of the Congress Hindus, but it was generally believed that this point would not be pressed and that Congress too would accept these proposals as well as the long-range constitutional

plan. It seemed that after years of barren controversy Congress
and the League were about to be successfully coaxed into an
interim coalition government and into a Constitutent Assembly
that would frame a constitution on a mutually acceptable basis.
A cartoon appeared showing the Cabinet Mission packing to go
home under the caption "All's well that ends well."

The optimists were reckoning without Gandhi. At the critical
moment he intervened decisively—and disastrously. Congress,
being a national party with a Muslim president, could not, in
his view, agree to the omission of a Congress Muslim from the
Interim Government even as a temporary expedient to insure
the cooperation of the League. He felt that a principle was
involved which Congress could not give up. It mattered not to
him that the principle had ceased to have practical significance
now that Jinnah had won almost all Muslims to his side. It
mattered not that insistence on it would frustrate the chances
of agreement that were now almost within sight. Such common-
sense considerations did not appeal to Gandhi; and his views
prevailed. The Viceroy's proposals for an Interim Government
were rejected by the Working Committee.

The Congress decision was a tremendous blow to all the
hopes that had been aroused and psychologically was a turning
point in these delicate negotiations. But in their disappointment the Mission drew consolation from the fact that the
Working Committee, while declining to join the Interim Government, had at last made up their minds to accept the long-
term constitutional proposals. The failure to form an Interim
Government was, the Mission said, regrettable, but after a short
interval the Viceroy would try again, and they expressed happiness that "constitution-making can now proceed with the consent of the two major parties."

The happiness was ill-founded, for in reality there was no
agreed-upon basis for drawing up a constitution. Jinnah's acceptance of the Mission's proposals had been genuine, but Gandhi
had advised the Working Committee not to accept them at all,
and although the committee rejected this advice, under his well-
intentioned but baleful influence its acceptance was qualified
and ambiguous. It persisted in its own interpretation of the

provisions regarding grouping—an interpretation that the Mission had repudiated. Jinnah complained that the acceptance was disingenuous, but the Mission, thankful to save something from the wreck of all their hopes, were willing to accept it without too close a scrutiny.

Hardly two weeks after the Cabinet Mission had left India Jawaharlal himself confirmed the correctnes of Jinnah's complaint. The Congress, he told a press conference on July 10, in accepting the Mission's long-term plan, had "agreed to go into the Constituent Assembly and . . . to nothing else"; and in regard to grouping, which the Mission had said was an essential feature of the plan, he volunteered the view that there would probably be no grouping at all.

It was now plain that Congress had not really accepted the constitutional plan. Jinnah and the League retaliated by withdrawing their acceptance of it and declared that they would take "direct action" to achieve Pakistan. "Today," said Jinnah, "we bid goodbye to constitutional methods. . . . We have forged a pistol and are in a position to use it. . . . Why should I sit with folded hands? I am also going to make trouble now."

This militant mood was something new and quite unexpected by the members of the Congress Working Committee. Some of them realized that the outlook was radically altered and began to feel that partition in some form could perhaps not be averted except by civil war. Gandhi was thinking along other lines—partition must be averted, but by some form of *satyagraha.*

XVII ⌒

Pilgrim's

Progress

Early in August, Nehru, who had succeeded Azad as president
of Congress,* was invited by Lord Wavell to form an Interim
Government—with the cooperation of the Muslim League, if
possible. Nehru approached Jinnah but without success, and so
went ahead alone, and on September 2 the Congress nominees
took office as members of the Viceroy's Executive Council with
Nehru as its vice president.

Meanwhile on August 16, which the League had decided to
celebrate as "Direct Action Day," there was a fearful outbreak
of communal rioting in Calcutta, far exceeding in scale and
intensity anything of the kind that had been known before.
According to official estimates four to five thousand people were
killed and fifteen thousand injured. Lord Wavell, impressed
more than ever by the need to bring Congress and the League
together so that communal frenzy could be checked, tried to

* Patel, who had the largest measure of support from the provincial Congress committees, was persuaded by Gandhi to withdraw
his candidature.

induce Gandhi and Nehru to reassure the League and secure its cooperation by signing a statement clearly accepting the grouping arrangements of the Cabinet Mission's plan. They refused to do so. Gandhi, failing to appreciate the full gravity of the situation and the sincerity of Lord Wavell's endeavors, indulged in legalistic quibbles and later complained that Lord Wavell's manner had been "minatory"—as well it might be, for the communal frenzy that he was trying to check soon spread to East Bengal, first to Dacca and then to the remoter districts of Noakhali and Tipperah. Muslim gangs killed or forcibly converted Hindus, destroyed and pillaged Hindu property, and abducted Hindu women. Many Hindus fled in terror to West Bengal and Bihar.

Gandhi, quite unaware of his own responsibility for these disorders, was deeply shocked by them. All his life he had believed in nonviolence and Hindu-Muslim unity, but now, on the threshold of independence, Hindus and Muslims were at each other's throats. His own doctrine of *ahimsa* was failing, or at least it did not seem to answer in the matter of Hindu-Muslim relations. A few months earlier he had told an interviewer, "I do not want to die as a failure but as a successful man. But it may be that I may die a failure." He was conscious now of failure and impending disaster. The *swaraj* that was coming seemed likely to bear little resemblance to the *swaraj* of his dreams. Nevertheless, all the energy he still possessed—and it was considerable—must be thrown into the service of the people. He therefore resolved to go to Noakhali and "bury himself in East Bengal until such time as the Hindus and Muslims learnt to live together in peace and harmony."

Friends tried to dissuade him. His health was none too good; his presence was required in Delhi by the new Congress government; Jinnah had just been persuaded by Lord Wavell to nominate five Muslim Leaguers to the Executive Council and their entry would create problems on which his advice would be essential. But Gandhi had made up his mind to go to East Bengal: "I do not know what I shall be able to do there. All that I know is that I won't be at peace unless I go." And to an American who inquired, "Will the Muslims listen to you?" he replied, "I don't know. A man who goes to do his duty only expects to be given strength by God to do his duty."

He was now seventy-seven and had expressed a desire to live to be one hundred twenty-five. Still in full possession of his faculties, he was wonderfully alert and vigorous for his years. But advancing age and the approach of independence were beginning to affect his role in the political life of the country. Antigovernment agitation, in which he had specialized and which it had been his prerogative to direct, was not wanted now, and even if he had launched another *satyagraha* campaign, most of his old colleagues in Congress, with their hands on the levers of power at last, would not have responded to his call to go into the wilderness again. Nor were his visionary, idealistic solutions of practical problems very helpful to men who now daily had to grapple with realities. In important matters he was still usually consulted, but not always; his advice was listened to with respect, but not always followed—already his advice to reject in toto the Cabinet Mission's constitutional plan had been overruled. With the formation of the Interim Government the real direction of Congress policy was passing from him to Nehru and Patel, and he, as though by a natural instinct, was drifting away from the seats of power to devote himself to direct service to the people. The remaining fifteen months of his life, although politically ineffectual, were morally the crown of his career. The politician gave way to the saint.

Gandhi had reached Calcutta on his way to Noakhali when the tales of woe told by Hindu refugees from East Bengal provoked reprisals in Bihar. Thousands of Muslims were butchered with revolting savagery by Hindus, and many others were driven from their homes. The Congress government of Bihar seemed unable to control the situation. Nehru and one of the newly appointed Muslim League ministers flew to Patna, the capital of Bihar, and threatened to resort to aerial bombing to quell the disturbances, and Gandhi threatened to fast until death if peace were not restored at once. Neither threat was implemented; the disorders subsided. Gandhi sent a message to the people of Bihar reproaching them for their misconduct. Although he felt he should go there, he decided not to interrupt his program and continued his journey to Noakhali.

At the outset of his mission he was given every facility and encouragement by the Muslim League government of Bengal, which believed that he would be of assistance in restoring confidence to the demoralized Hindus. His own ambition was "to wipe every tear from every eye." After traveling for some days from one place to another, trying to induce the terror-stricken Hindus who were huddled in temporary refugee camps to return to their homes, he settled for several weeks in the village of Sirirampur—from which all but three out of two hundred Hindu families had fled—and dispersed his entourage in neighboring villages so that their efforts to promote peace and harmony might be diffused as widely as possible. His presence helped to ease tension and assuage angry feelings, but he soon found that it was not easy to get the two communities to resume normal peaceful life: "My present mission is the most complicated and difficult one of my life. I can say with 100 per cent of truth 'The night is dark and I am far from home, lead Thou me on.' " He decided to suspend all other activities. Putting aside the affairs of his *ashram* at Sevagram and of the nature clinic that he had recently started near Poona, entrusting to others the editing of *Harijan* (which had been discontinued in 1942 but revived in February 1946), and curtailing his enormous correspondence, he devoted himself wholeheartedly to his mission in Noakhali, having a lesson in Bengali every day, receiving visitors and deputations, holding prayer meetings, preaching to the people about fearlessness and forgiveness, and preparing himself by daily walks for the more extended village-to-village tour that he was planning to undertake on foot. In his gloom he still nursed the hope that if Hindus and Muslims could be persuaded, after the recent upheaval, to live in good will and amity in Bengal, then the whole of India might be saved and partition avoided.

Soon, however, his own mission began to be suspect. The Muslim press saw in it "a deep political game" and even the Bengal Chief Minister, H. S. Suhrawardy, who had welcomed him at first, became critical of his protracted stay. Muslims began to ask him why he did not go to Bihar to help the

Muslim victims of Hindu violence. He replied that he would go there when directed by the inner voice. But the criticism hurt him and he wrote the following in his diary on January 2: "God's grace alone is sustaining me. I can see there is some grave defect in me somewhere which is the cause of all this. All round me is utter darkness. When will God take me out of the darkness into his Light?"

On that same day he set out on his projected tour on foot, stopping at a different village every day. Nehru had been urging him to return to Delhi, and friends told him that he was trying to still the tempest by preventing the forest leaves from rustling, but they could not keep him from his pilgrimage. Walking barefoot, he covered a hundred and sixteen miles and visited forty-seven villages in seven weeks. His progress was not without its comic side, which he, with his keen sense of humor, would have appreciated. An eyewitness says:

> First in the procession would come a party of police constables whose presence was due not to any apprehension of Gandhi but to the concern of the Provincial Government for his safety. After the police party, and at a decent interval, came the main body—Gandhi himself, members of his entourage, press correspondents, and such local people as might join in the walking tour. There was again a decent interval and then at the rear of the procession would come a porter carrying the Mahatma's portable commode! That the use of a commode was entirely commendable and civilized did not somehow lessen the ludicrous effect of its being borne on the head of a porter at the rear of this solemn procession!

Almost every afternoon, at whatever village he had reached, he would hold a public prayer meeting at which he would discourse not only on the current topics of communal amity and good neighborliness, but also on many social and political problems. In the mild winter weather of Bengal he would sometimes discourse on such matters while taking a mud bath. A witness reports seeing him lying in the afternoon sun covered with mud from head to foot. I came upon him thus one afternoon in the courtyard of a village house. But he was not alone. He was receiving a deputation that had come to seek his advice on rural reconstruction and uplift. Questions were being asked and answers were coming out of the mud as if from a Delphic oracle.

While Gandhi was thus nobly striving to promote communal harmony in Noakhali, antagonism between Congress and the Muslim League was mounting to crisis proportions in Delhi. The League nominees had joined the Interim Government not, as Gandhi had hoped, "to work as brothers" but to prevent Congress getting a firm grip on power at the center. Instead of a coalition government there was a government of two bitterly hostile blocs, each trying to thwart the other and consolidate its own power.

There was also still no agreement about framing a new constitution. When the League members joined the Interim Government, Jinnah told Lord Wavell that the League would once again accept the Cabinet mission's constitutional plan and cooperate in the work of the Constituent Assembly if the Congress would also accept the plan unequivocally, which, he maintained with some justice, they had not yet done. Lord Wavell and later, in December, the British Government tried hard to extract from Congress an unequivocal acceptance of the plan as the Cabinet Mission intended it rather than as Congress wished to interpret it, and in January the All-India Congress Committee finally approached a genuine acceptance of it. But the committee still had some qualifications, while Gandhi, away in East Bengal, openly advised the Assam Congress committee not to go into their section as provided in the plan, and said that he would give the same advice to the Sikhs. In these circumstances the League decided that Congress' acceptance of the plan had not been genuine, and refused to take part in the Constituent Assembly. Nehru and Patel then demanded that the League members of the Interim Government be made to resign and threatened to resign themselves if the League

members were retained. Either alternative was likely to lead to
widespread disorders.

The British Government, despairing of getting the parties to
agree and fearing further communal clashes and a drift into
chaos or civil war, now made a bold decision. On February
20 the Prime Minister, Clement Attlee, announced that it was
His Majesty's Government's definite intention to transfer
power to responsible Indian hands by no later than June 1948.
All parties were urged to resolve their differences, but it was
made plain that there would be no postponement even if the
differences remained. If by the date fixed no constitution had
been agreed upon, the British Government would have to consider

> to whom the powers of the Central Government in British
> India should be handed over, on the due date, whether as a
> whole to some form of Central Government for British
> India, or in some areas to the existing Provincial Govern-
> ments, or in such other way as may seem most reasonable
> and in the best interests of the Indian people.

Mr. Attlee also announced that Lord Mountbatten would replace Lord Wavell as Viceroy.

Partition within the next seventeen months was now inevitable, for because of the Congress-League feud there could be
no central government capable of exercising power over the
whole of British India to which the powers of the existing Government of India could be transferred. Among Congress leaders,
Patel was well aware of this and had for some time been reconciled to partition. His experience in the Interim Government
had convinced him that it would be impossible to secure cooperation from the League in building up the strong united
India that Congress desired, and that rather than risk civil war
for the achievement of this ideal or acquiesce in a loose federation of antagonistic states with divergent aims and interests, it
would be better to let Jinnah and the League have the areas
that they could indisputably claim—the mutilated, moth-eaten
Pakistan that Rajagopalachari had offered him. By February 20
Nehru and most other Congress leaders were also coming

around to this view. Jinnah too, on his side, realized that Congress was never going to accept the weak, easily divisible Union of India that he desired and that he would have to be content with the mutilated Pakistan, without Assam and with only the half of Bengal and the Punjab to which the League was entitled on a population basis. This was the solution toward which all parties were now to be skillfully shepherded by Lord Mountbatten.

Gandhi continued his mission in Noakhali until the end of February. Because the Muslim press was clamoring for him to leave and he received a message from one of the Congress ministers in Bihar that his presence there would help the suffering Muslim minority, the "inner voice" was prompted to tell him to transfer his activities to that province, and by the second week of March he was holding prayer meetings in Patna and collecting money from the Hindus for the relief of Muslim sufferers. He had not, it seems, grasped the full implications of Mr. Attlee's announcement of February 20 nor was he in touch with the latest thinking of the Congress leaders in Delhi. Therefore when he read in the papers that the Working Committee had passed a resolution on March 8 proposing the division of the Punjab, he was aghast—he had been neither consulted nor forewarned and he rightly saw the resolution as a prelude to the acceptance of partition. He wrote to both Patel and Nehru saying that he could not understand the resolution and asking them to explain it. Patel replied drily that it had been "adopted after the deepest deliberation," but that if Gandhi disagreed with it he was, of course, entitled to say what he felt to be right. Nehru replied that it was necessary to press for division "so that reality might be brought into the picture" and that this was the only answer to partition as demanded by Jinnah.

The Working Committee's resolution had been prompted partly by the outbreak of serious communal rioting in the principal cities and some of the rural areas of the Punjab on March 4. The strife continued for about two weeks, after which there was an uneasy lull, but the province seemed ready for further rioting at any moment, and there were also signs of trouble in the North-West Frontier Province.

Lord Mountbatten reached Delhi on March 22 and immediately invited Gandhi to come and see him, offering to send his private plane for him. Gandhi declined the offer and returned to Delhi by third-class railway coach. He advised Lord Mountbatten, as he had previously advised Lord Wavell and Sir Stafford Cripps, to give up the attempt to please both parties simultaneously. He proposed that the Interim Government should be dissolved and that Jinnah should be invited to form and lead a government. Congress would guarantee to give him sincere support as long as he acted in the interests of the whole Indian people. In the event of any dispute about this, Lord Mountbatten was to be the sole umpire. If Jinnah declined the invitation, then the same offer should be made to Congress.

Lord Mountbatten told Gandhi that he found the proposal "attractive." What he really thought of it is not recorded, but a member of his staff described it is "an old kite flown without disguise." Jinnah's reactions are also unknown, but it may be surmised that he would have ridiculed it. Nehru saw "at least one fatal objection" to it, and Patel was wholly opposed to it. Gandhi soon realized that he could not carry the Working Committee with him and that it no longer shared his basic opposition to any partition under British aegis. "There is wide and frequent divergence of views between us," he confessed to Patel, and on April 11 he wrote to the Viceroy virtually abdicating general direction of Congress policy.

I could not convince [the Working Committee] of the correctness of my plan, from every point of view. Nor could they dislodge me from my position. . . . Thus I have to ask you to omit me from your consideration. Congressmen who are in the Interim Government are stalwarts, seasoned servants of the nation, and therefore so far as the Congress point of view is concerned, they will be complete advisers.

The next day he returned to his peace mission in Bihar—the province where thirty years earlier he had made his entry into Indian politics as champion of the oppressed tenants in Champaran. Since then he had transformed the whole political scene in India and for a quarter of a century had held the center of the stage. But the Gandhian era in politics was drawing to a close, and he knew it. A few weeks later he was lamenting:

Who listens to me today? . . . I am being told to retire to the Himalayas. Everybody is eager to garland my photos and statues. Nobody really wants to follow my advice. . . . Neither the people nor those in power have any use for me.

During April and May Lord Mountbatten succeeded in evolving a plan for the partition of the country to which all the principal parties were willing to agree. Power was to be transferred to two successor states, India and Pakistan, but Pakistan was to be of the mutilated "contiguous area" variety with both the Punjab and Bengal partitioned. Elaborate arrangements were agreed upon for giving the division of the country the seal of democratic approval and it was also decided to advance the date for the transfer of power from June 1948 to August 15, 1947.

Gandhi could see nothing but evil in the partition plan. He opposed it in the Working Committee, at a meeting with Jinnah, and in correspondence with the Viceroy. The British, he told Lord Mountbatten, should take the risk of leaving India to chaos or anarchy and hand over power either to the Muslim League or to Congress, he did not care which, but it would be a blunder of the first magnitude for them to be a party to the division of India. If it had to come, it should come after British withdrawal, "as a result of understanding between the parties or an armed conflict." Lord Mountbatten felt some anxiety lest Gandhi might successfully intervene at the last moment and induce the Working Committee to retract its acceptance of the plan. But Nehru and Patel had at last shaken themselves free from Gandhi's influence in this matter and were their own masters. It was they who were guiding the Working Committee, and Patel assured the Viceroy that Gandhi would loyally abide by any decision the Working Committee might make.

And so it turned out. When the Working Committee's resolution in favor of the plan for partition came before the All-India Congress Committee for confirmation, Gandhi himself urged its acceptance on the ground that it was a recommendation of old and tried leaders who could not be replaced, although he was quite unconvinced of its merits. "The very idea of the vivisection of India still made him shudder" and he felt that partition was being accepted at bayonet point because of fear of civil war. He personally "would rather let the whole country be reduced to ashes then yield an inch to violence," but he had been unable to make his views prevail.

Some of his followers expected him to try to avert partition by some bold, dramatic step. When the partition had first been suggested, he had said that he would oppose it with all the nonviolent forces at his command and even at the cost of his life, and as late as April 1947 he had told Azad that if Congress accepted partition it would be over his dead body. Why then did he give in to it without more of a struggle? It seems that he did contemplate launching another *satyagraha* campaign, but he felt that at seventy-seven he did not have the strength for it, especially without the support of his most trusted lieutenants, Nehru and Patel; and it had no prospects of success. A fast unto death would also be futile. It might end in his death, but it could not prevent partition. Gandhi did not believe in being a futile saint and martyr, nor was he one to waste time on fruitless sorrowing. Partition was, in his view, a calamity, but since this calamity could not be averted, he began to think how it could be mitigated or even turned into a blessing.

XVIII ✑

Independence

Gandhi announced that on August 15, the day fixed for the transfer of power, he would be in Noakhali, where the Hindus feared that there would be fresh disturbances when Pakistan was established. But on reaching Calcutta on August 9 and "listening to the woes of the city" he decided to stay for a while. Calcutta had never returned to normal after the appalling communal rioting of August 1946, and although H. S. Suhrawardy, the Bengal Chief Minister, who had been blamed for that outbreak, subsequently took maximum precautions, scarcely a day passed without some incident of stabbing, looting, or arson, and from time to time these incidents flared up into major riots. The Hindu and Muslim populations of the city had become so obsessed with fear and hatred of each other that the baser elements in both were sure of support and applause for any atrocity they might commit.

In April Lord Mountbatten had persuaded Gandhi and Jinnah to sign a joint appeal to the country, deploring recent acts of "lawlessness and violence," renouncing the "use of force to achieve political ends," and calling on all communities to refrain from violence in any form. The appeal had a negligible effect in general and no effect at all in Calcutta. There was serious rioting in July, and on August 8, the day before Gandhi's arrival, a Hindu mob stopped a train, dragged out ten Muslim passengers, and slaughtered them.

How were these mad passions to be exorcised and the city restored to sanity? This was the problem to which Gandhi, on the eve of independence, tried to find an answer. He had said a year earlier that he had never had the chance to test his non-violence in the face of communal riots. The chance had now come, and he grasped it.

On August 10 he held a prayer meeting at which he told a vast crowd that all of them, and not merely *goondas,** were responsible for the widespread violence. They must "turn the searchlight inwards" and realize that "crude open *goondaism* was a reflection of the subtle *goondaism* they were harbouring within." The next day Suhrawardy came and implored him to stay in Calcutta at least until after independence. In a flash Gandhi perceived that to bring back peace and good will to the embittered communities of the city, he and Suhrawardy— whom the Hindus regarded as the arch-villain—must be seen visibly working together in the closest collaboration. He suggested therefore that they should live together, unprotected by the police or the military, in an abandoned Muslim house in Balliaghata—a section with a mixed Hindu-Muslim population and one of the most riot-torn and filthy quarters of the city— and move about among the people in "brotherly fashion," calming their fears and assuaging their angry feelings.

Earlier in May there had been a suggestion that Gandhi and Suhrawardy work together. Suhrawardy had proposed that Bengal, instead of being partitioned and assigned half to India and half to Pakistan, should remain undivided as a third sovereign state alongside India and Pakistan. Gandhi, attracted by the idea, had volunteered to help further it as Suhrawardy's "honorary private secretary" and to live under his roof. Suhrawardy had dismissed this suggestion as "a mad offer," but now he did not reject so hastily Gandhi's hardly less extraordinary suggestion that they should live together in the shambles of Balliaghata, "a notorious den of gangsters and hooligans." After

* Hooligans.

twenty-four hours' consideration he accepted it without qualification.

They moved into the deserted house, Hydari Mansion, on the afternoon of August 13. The effect was miraculous. At first hostile Hindu demonstrators threw stones and broke windows. Gandhi confronted them, reasoned with them kindly, and they dispersed; the next day Hydari Mansion became a place of pilgrimage. Thousands of Calcutta's citizens flocked to visit him and seek his advice. The tension of the preceding weeks and months was suddenly broken and at the independence celebrations on the fifteenth there was unprecedented communal fraternization. Hindus and Muslims shook hands, marched about arm in arm, danced happily in the streets, and joined in shouting *"Ek hogaya"* ("We are one") and *"Jai Hind"* ("Victory to India"). It was a transformation that amazed everyone.

In a message to the nation on August 15 the President of Congress, Acharya Kripalani, saluted Gandhi as the "Father of the Nation" and claimed that "never before was so great an event, transforming the destiny of many millions of men and women, consummated with such little bloodshed and violence." The claim was hollow and no one was more aware of it than Gandhi. Indians had on the whole practiced nonviolence against the British and in achieving freedom had shed little British blood. But their nonviolence, as Gandhi now recognized, was "the non-violence of the weak." They had pretended to resist the British nonviolently, but in their hearts they had nursed feelings of violence and ill-will, and these feelings were now manifesting themselves in violence against each other and the shedding of their own blood. Peace had returned for the time being to Calcutta, but in the Punjab, with the coming of independence, the fires of communal frenzy that had been smoldering ever since the outbreaks in March, had once more burst into flame.

Gandhi could not therefore bring himself to share in the general rejoicing of August 15. It should be a day, he said, for prayer and deep heart-searching and not for rejoicing, since the minorities in both the new dominions contemplated it with heavy hearts. He himself spent the day fasting and spinning. When asked to give a message to the nation, he said that "he had run dry," and when he was pressed further and told that it would not be good if he gave no message he replied, "There is no message at all; if it is bad, let it be so."

The communal fraternization in Calcutta did, however, bring him some comfort, recalling the far-off Khilafat days when Hindus and Muslims had publicly embraced each other. "We have drunk the poison of mutual hatred," he wrote on the sixteenth, "and so this nectar of fraternization tastes all the sweeter." Throughout August the nectar flowed. Huge crowds gathered at his evening prayer meetings, Hindus and Muslims mingling together without fear and rejoicing in the restoration of peace and good will. Glowing tributes came to him from all over the country for the "miracle" he had wrought. Even the Muslim League expressed its "deep sense of appreciation." Lord Mountbatten pointed to the contrast between Bengal and the Punjab: "In the Punjab we have 55,000 soldiers and large-scale rioting on our hands. As a serving officer, as well as an administrator, may I be allowed to pay my tribute to the One Man Boundary Force, not forgetting his Second in Command, Mr. Suhrawardy?"

Eyewitnesses agree that Gandhi's presence and the reverence felt for him by the mass of the population was one important cause of the explosion of communal good will in Calcutta at this time, but there were also other reasons for it. One was the ending of British rule, an event that momentarily united the two communities, reminding them of their occasional joint resistance to the British in the past. Another was the resignation of the Muslims to their fate. It was now irrevocably settled that Calcutta was to be included in India and not in Pakistan and that the Muslims there would be a helpless minority. Their instinct therefore was to lie low and not invite repression by a Hindu government unless provoked beyond endurance. Gandhi's influence was largely exercised in persuading the Hindus to refrain from provocation.

The good will did not last long. Toward the end of the month tales of the hideous atrocities that Sikhs and Muslims were perpetrating on each another in the Punjab caused fresh restiveness in Calcutta, and on the evening of August 31 a crowd of Hindus created a scene at Hydari Mansion, alleging (falsely) that a Hindu youth had been stabbed by a Muslim and calling on Gandhi for redress. He was unable to pacify them and police had to intervene to stop them from hurling brickbats and trying to break into the house. This incident was followed the next day by a recurrence of rioting in which about fifty people were killed.

The charm had been broken and the situation was once more critical. "What was regarded as the 'Calcutta Miracle,'" Gandhi wrote to Patel, "has proved to be a nine days wonder. I am pondering what my duty is in the circumstances." He did not take long to decide. When Rajagopalachari, now Governor of West Bengal, visited him on the evening of September 1, Gandhi announced that he was going to fast until sanity returned to Calcutta. "Can one fast against the *goondas?*" Rajagopalachari asked. Gandhi replied:

> I want to touch the hearts of those who are behind the *goondas*. The hearts of the *goondas* may or may not be touched. It would be enough for my purpose if they realize that society at large has no sympathy with their aims or methods and that the peace-loving element is determined to assert itself or perish in the attempt.

His fast was therefore an appeal to the better, peace-loving elements in society, an attempt to impress on them their social duty to control the *goondas* by withdrawing support and sympathy for them. It was directed primarily against the Hindus, for it was Hindu *goondas* who were now the aggressors. When urged by Rajagopalachari to delay the fast for a while, he replied that he must undertake it at once. "The minority community cannot be left in a perilous condition."

Supplemented by stringent military precautions and very heavy rain, which dampened the enthusiasm of rioters, the fast had achieved complete success by the third day. Rioting had ceased and deputations of Calcutta citizens were thronging Hydari Mansion with offers to help maintain order. Fanatical

Hindus surrendered to Gandhi illicit arms they had collected, and a gang of *goondas* came to him and offered to submit to any penalty he might impose. Finally, leading members of all three communities—Hindu, Muslim, and Sikh—pledged themselves, now that quiet had been restored, never to allow communal strife in the city again and to strive unto death to prevent it. Gandhi was satisfied with this pledge and broke his fast, and there was no more communal trouble in Calcutta. "Gandhi has achieved many things," Rajagopalachari commented, "but there has been nothing, not even independence, which is so truly wonderful as his victory over evil in Calcutta."

Gandhi left Calcutta on September 7, not to relax or recuperate, but intending to go to the Punjab and carry on the same noble work there. In Calcutta, aided by favorable circumstances, he had worked a "miracle." He could not do the same in the Punjab—not because he lacked the courage, will, and determination, but because the Sikhs and Muslims of that province were so determined to take revenge on each other that they would not have paid the slightest heed to him if he had appeared. The Punjab massacres could not be brought to an end by prayer and fasting, but only by military measures or—as actually happened—by the physical separation of the two communities as a result of massive migrations.

Gandhi never went to the Punjab because when he reached Delhi he found the city ablaze with communal strife and felt that there was no point in going further. "I must do my little bit," he said, "to calm the heated atmosphere." So while the Government deployed police and military to quell the riots, he set about the more difficult task of "purging violence from the hearts of the people." The Harijan quarter where he usually stayed was so crammed with refugees that he had to be accommodated in Birla House, the palatial residence of an industrial magnate. Refugee camps had been established in and around the city, some containing Sikhs and Hindus who had been forcibly expelled from their homes in West Punjab, others containing Muslims who had been chased out of their homes in Delhi by murderous Hindu mobs. Gandhi began to hold prayer meetings nearly every day and to visit the refugee camps, comforting, encouraging, and admonishing the depressed but often revengeful refugees and listening to their grievances. It was dispiriting work, for there was not much he could do to alleviate their distress and his advice to them to forget and forgive, to bear no malice or hatred, and to endure their sufferings with fortitude and patience fell on unwilling ears. However, he persevered and promised not to rest until peace ruled again in Delhi.

He did not rest, but he was sad and disillusioned. On his birthday on October 2 he confessed that he no longer had any wish to live a hundred and twenty-five years. He wished to live only if he could render service to the people, but this was impossible if the people would not listen to him. He felt that his words had ceased to carry weight and that it would be best if God took him away from "this vale of tears." But he wanted to die in harness and with God's name on his lips.

His erstwhile colleagues, now immersed in great affairs of state, still sought his counsel from time to time, but often found it too idealistic to be acceptable. Aware that Congress was being corrupted by power, he advised it to disband as a political organization now that its political objective of independence had been secured, and reorganize itself as a *lok sewak sangh* * that would be rooted in the village *panchayat*, unconcerned with political power and devoted only to social, moral, and economic reform and the "constructive program"—*khadi*, village industries, basic education, and the removal of untouchability, to all of which he turned once more after he had been settled in Delhi a few weeks. Naturally, his advice had little appeal to men like Nehru and Patel, who, after years of struggle, had at last realized their ambition of running the affairs of the country.

One of Gandhi's special aims at this time was to undo what the migrations had done and enable all the refugees to return in safety and honor to their own towns and villages—a laudable but impractical aim which, if actively pursued, was likely to start a fresh holocaust. Gandhi's wishes in this matter had to be ignored.

More attention was paid to his desire for the removal of

* Organization for the service of the people.

wartime controls on food grains, cloth, and other necessities. His instinct to be rid of them was right, for they were a source of corruption and harassment to the people, but, so far as food grains were concerned, they were a necessary evil. Nevertheless, Gandhi attacked them and the officials who advised their continuance, in his most trenchant style:

> Must the voice of the people be drowned by the noise of the pundits, who claim to know all about the virtue of controls? Would that our ministers, who are drawn from the people, listened to the voice of the people, rather than of the controllers of red tape which, they all know, did them infinite harm when they were in the wilderness! The pundits then ruled with a vengeance. Must they do so, even now? Will not the people have any opportunity of committing mistakes and learning by them?

His influence, combined with the prejudice against officials, was sufficient to persuade Congress ministers to remove the controls. They had to be reinstated some months later.

Although the police and military restored peace in Delhi, Gandhi felt that it was "the peace of the grave, not a peace symbolising the union of hearts." Muslims in Delhi complained to him that they still felt insecure and that they were being harassed by militant Hindu groups whose aim was to drive all Muslims from India. Patel, who was now Minister of Home affairs and Deputy Prime Minister, was alleged to sympathize with this aim. This view seemed to be confirmed by some blunt speeches he made early in January to the effect that Muslims who were disloyal or only half loyal—and he implied that they were a majority—would have to leave Hindustan. These sentiments were at variance with Gandhi's views, and Nehru also was unhappy about them.

After some thought, Gandhi decided once again to fast. He announced his intention at his prayer meeting on January 12:

> I have no answer to return to Muslim friends, who see me from day to day, as to what they should do. My impotence has been gnawing at me. It will go immediately this fast is

undertaken. I have been brooding over it for the last three
days. . . . The fast will end when I am satisfied that there
is a reunion of hearts of all communities, brought about
not by outside pressure, but from an awakened sense of
duty.

The fast began the next day. Past experience had taught Nehru,
Patel, and other friends not to try to dissuade him from fasting,
but Patel in particular was very upset, feeling that the fast was
in some sense directed against him. This was also the popular
view, and a newspaper reporter asked Gandhi whether "the fast
is more intended to bring about a change of heart in Sardar
Patel and thereby amounts to a condemnation of the Home
Ministry." Gandhi firmly repudiated the suggestion and emphasized that he, Nehru, and Patel all stood together. Patel was,
in truth, one of Gandhi's oldest and most loyal lieutenants and
as an administrator the ablest of all Congress leaders. But inevitably at this time there was some lack of harmony between
Patel's practical realism—which was in tune with the popular
mood—and the idealism of Gandhi and Nehru.

Patel sent word to Gandhi that he would do anything Gandhi might want him to. What Gandhi wanted him to do was
rather embarrassing. A sum of more than 500 million rupees
(about 112 million dollars) was due to be paid to Pakistan
in accordance with an agreed division of united India's cash
assets, but the Indian Cabinet had unanimously decided to
withhold payment in view of the hostilities that had broken out
between the two countries over Kashmir. Gandhi denounced
this decision as a breach of agreement and told Patel that first
priority must be given to paying Pakistan. In deference to his
wishes, on the third day of the fast the Indian Cabinet reversed
its previous decision and as a gesture of good will paid Pakistan
the amount due. Thus Gandhi's last fast, undertaken at the age
of seventy-eight, immediately produced a tangible result, but
one that was more appreciated in Pakistan than in India. To
most of the Hindu population of India it seemed that he was
fasting for the benefit of the Muslims and Pakistan and, as
India and Pakistan were virtually at war, this provoked criticism

and even anger. One evening a party of Sikh and Hindu refugees from West Punjab paraded outside Birla House shouting, "Blood for blood," "We want revenge," "Let Gandhi die."

The Indian Government's gesture of good will did not immediately bring the fast to an end. Something more was required. Gandhi wanted the people to "dethrone Satan from their hearts and reinstate God"—a wish rather difficult to fulfill. In Calcutta, however, Gandhi had ultimately been satisfied with pledges given by the leaders of the several communities, and the same method was now employed in Delhi to end the fast. Leaders of all the communities in Delhi pledged themselves to restore communal peace and amity by their own personal efforts and, if necessary, at the sacrifice of their lives. On being assured that this pledge would be kept, Gandhi broke his fast on the sixth day.

Allowing himself scarcely a moment to recover his strength, he plunged again into his usual activities, expounding at length in *Harijan* his proposals for converting Congress into a *lok sewak sangh* based on the village *panchayat* and resuming his evening prayer meetings in the grounds of Birla House. At one of these meetings soon after he had broken his fast, a crude bomb was thrown. It exploded on the lawn without causing any injury, but furnished further evidence of the violent hostility that his fearless championing of the Muslims had aroused. The police guards on Birla House were increased, but in spite of Patel's personal entreaties Gandhi would not permit the police to search those attending the prayer meetings. "If I have to die I should like to die at the prayer meeting," he said. "You are wrong in believing that you can protect me from harm. God is my protector."

Besides the question of his own protection there was another serious topic to discuss with Patel. During the fast, Patel had written Gandhi expressing a wish to resign, since his outlook and statements seemed to be displeasing to Nehru, Azad, and some of his other colleagues. At first Gandhi said that either Patel or Nehru should withdraw from the Cabinet, but later, after a talk with Lord Mountbatten, he changed his mind and on the afternoon of January 30 he told Patel, who came to see him at Birla House, that the presence of both of them in the Cabinet was essential. Patel, whose feet were firmly planted on the ground, was an ideal and necessary partner for Nehru, whose head was in the clouds. It would be disastrous if they were drawn apart. Patel accepted Gandhi's advice and assured him that he would support Nehru loyally.

As soon as Patel had left, Gandhi got ready to go to his prayer meeting on the terrace of Birla House. It was due to begin at 5:00 P.M., and he was ten minutes late. Accompanied by two granddaughters, he stepped out of his room and walked slowly toward the congregation awaiting him. As the crowd parted to make way for him to pass through to the dais and as he was raising his hands to answer their salutations, a man suddenly elbowed his way forward and, bending down before Gandhi as though to touch his feet, fired three shots in quick succession at point-blank range. At the second and third shots Gandhi collapsed and died, uttering the words *"Rama, Rama."* The apostle of nonviolence had fallen, a victim to violence; but his wish to die in harness with God's name on his lips had been fulfilled.

XIX ❧

Summing Up

When Gandhi made his debut as a political leader in India during World War I, the movement for Indian freedom had already been in progress for about thirty years, and even without him it would have proceeded to its appointed end of independence soon after the close of World War II. He cannot therefore truthfully be acclaimed as the author of India's freedom. But it was under his leadership that India became free; it was he who, for better or worse, dominated and directed the national struggle from 1920 until the eve of its final triumph, and it was his personality which, although not the cause of India's freedom, decisively influenced the manner in which it was achieved.

There are many who think that this influence was harmful to India's interests and that if he had followed the constitutional path of Gokhale, accepting whatever political concessions the British offered and promptly asking for more, independence would have been achieved just as soon and with much less disturbance and disorder, perhaps even without the disaster of partition. It is undeniable that his policies did some harm. Defiance of authority, however nonviolently it was done, bred habits of disorder that have proved an evil legacy for independent

India. The appeal to mass feeling aroused the communal passions that existed at mass level and so thwarted Gandhi's own
goal of Hindu-Muslim unity. But whether a more moderate,
constitutional line of conduct would have produced better over-
all results is a might-have-been of history on which no sure
conclusion can be reached.

Those who deplore the fact that Gandhi was not another
Gokhale and who argue, plausibly enough, that his unconstitu-
tional methods gained little and lost much, are apt to forget
that after World War I moderate leadership of India's freedom
movement had less of a chance than it had earlier of commanding general assent. It is true that the majority of educated
Indians, although eager for independence and irked by British
delay, did not as yet have any desire for direct conflict with the
Government, while the illiterate rural masses were unmoved by
political issues. But by this time there was a powerful extremist
wing in the national movement, typified by such youthful firebrands as Jawaharlal Nehru and Subhas Chandra Bose, and it is
very doubtful whether these extremists could have been controlled by the Gokhale type of leadership. Gandhi's personality
combined with his positive program of nonviolent action had
sufficient appeal to keep all of them, except a handful of terrorists, within the Congress fold and to confine their energies,
except in 1942, within the relatively innocuous limits of nonviolent defiance of the government. If Gandhi's leadership had
been more moderate, this group would have broken away and
resorted to violent, revolutionary methods, bringing down upon
themselves and others stern repression by the British authorities
with consequences that are incalculable. Indo-British relations
would probably have become much more embittered, but
whether the general outcome would have been better or worse
than the actuality is a matter of conjecture. Gandhi's leadership
of the freedom movement had certain merits; it also had some
obvious defects—but it was the idealistic leadership of a unique
personality without parallel in the modern age.

Gandhi's influence on India's achievement of independence
may be considered under three main heads—his reorganization
of Congress as a mass movement, his impact on Hindu-Muslim

relations, and his theory and practice of nonviolence. In some respects his influence had effects very different from those he intended.

Gandhi basically changed the character of Congress in 1920 and 1921. He converted it from a small, upper-middle-class Westernized institution into an extensive political organization with an essentially Indian character and a strong appeal to the lower middle class. Under his leadership it became the spearhead of a mass movement insofar as it attracted the support or at least the sympathy of a majority of literate Hindus throughout the country and, in urban areas, of many of the illiterates also. But it was the mass movement of a minority. In the rural areas illiterate villagers venerated Gandhi but showed little interest in the political activities of Congress except for occasional brief periods in limited localities. The vast majority of the population remained neither hostile to the British Raj nor particularly in favor of it, but just indifferent. This inertia of the masses posed a problem for the national movement that was never overcome, and even the success it achieved in rousing and sustaining national feeling among the literate classes would probably have been impossible without Gandhi's religious and moral appeal. The immense value of this appeal was appreciated not only by Congress politicians—and partly accounts for his long dominance of Congress—but even more by the industrial and commercial magnates who supplied Congress with funds, for they realized that Gandhi's power to stir the masses, which was useful against the British, was not associated with views likely to be dangerous to their interests. He was neither a socialist nor a revolutionary; he had no desire to do away with capitalists and landlords or to turn society upside down and precipitate "red ruin." His regressive ideals of the self-contained village and the simple life were conservative, cranky, and harmless. He appealed to the masses, but was a check on mass forces, so that under his direction large-scale agitation was least likely to imperil the established social order.

Successful agitation, as Gandhi's South African experience had taught him, requires numbers and organization, and he refashioned Congress primarily in order to make it an effective instrument of political agitation against the British. Independence was the goal—an orthodox political end—and the Congress organization a means thereto. But Gandhi's conception of the purposes of Congress was also in part nonpolitical, unorthodox, and idealistic. Aside from political agitation, he felt that the function of Congress and of the ancillary organizations he added to it was to serve the people through the "constructive program"—*khadi,* village industries, social and moral reform. These organizations, such as the All-India Spinners Association, served as training grounds for workers who could be "political" as well as "constructive." But the "constructive program" was not a mere camouflage for political activity; Gandhi believed in it in and for itself, and once independence had been won it became for him the *raison d'être* for Congress. By this time, however, Congress had become a powerful party machine adapted to such normal political ends as fighting elections and capturing and consolidating political power. Increasingly divorced by now from the "constructive program," it was devoted to serving the politicians rather than the people, and there was not the slightest chance that it would dissolve itself in deference to Gandhi's visionary aims. Building on foundations that Gandhi had laid in the early twenties, realist political bosses like his lieutenant, Vallabhbhai Patel, had made it by far the strongest political organization in the country. Its unquestioned dominance was one of the main reasons why parliamentary democracy functioned smoothly in India for twenty years after independence. This was not at all what Gandhi had visualized.

Gandhi, being a Hindu to the depth of his being, inevitably, though perhaps unconsciously, imparted his own Hindu bias to Congress when he remodeled it. In so doing he accentuated tendencies that could be observed in the national movement before his advent. C. F. Andrews, the English missionary and Congress sympathizer who became Gandhi's close friend and one of his principal contacts with the British, drew attention to this trend as early as 1908 in a letter written to the Viceroy's private secretary: "There is a rapid Hinduising of 'national' ideas going on among the younger men. The boycott spirit follows inevitably as a consequence. The religious element becomes mingled with the political . . . and a Hindu religious colouring is given to National ideas." This "Hinduizing" of the national movement, which Gandhi's leadership promoted and symbolized, was injurious and ultimately fatal to Hindu-Muslim unity. But Gandhi failed to see the danger. Conscious only of his own good will toward the Muslims, he was obstinately blind to the adverse effects on Muslim opinion of his own pronounced Hinduism. His basic concepts, his moral values and ideals, even his fads and foibles, were of Hindu origin; in his writings and speeches he constantly employed language, imagery, and symbolism undisguisedly derived from Hindu sources; and he often appeared to be as interested in the reform of Hinduism as in the attainment of independence, and indeed more or less to equate them. Naturally, Muslims were alienated rather than attracted, and yet with regrettable vanity Gandhi persistently aspired to represent them and insisted that Congress *did* represent them, even though this was demonstrably false. The truth is that except for a brief period during the Khilafat agitation he was never in tune with the Muslim population. His opportunist allies, the Ali brothers, soon denounced him as a leader of purely Hindu nationalism who had no regard for the interests of Muslims—unfair criticism, no doubt, but it shows the impression that he unwittingly conveyed—and Jinnah, a key figure on the Muslim side, was estranged at an early date. As we have seen, he withdrew from Congress at the time Gandhi became its leader—"that Hindu revivalist," Jinnah contemptuously called him.

Steeped in Hindusim and set in his ways and outlook when at the age of fifty he began to dominate Congress, Gandhi could hardly have avoided intensifying its Hindu complexion. This was an unfortunate but inevitable consequence of his whole personality. But at the more conscious level of political bargaining he can be blamed for his repeated failure to come to terms with leaders of Muslim opinion. His Congress colleagues must share the blame and, of course, blame also attaches to the Muslim politicians and, to some extent, to the British who at a crucial time showed little interest in bringing the parties together. But the largest share of responsibility for the failure to reach an agreement that could have preserved Indian unity appears to fall on Gandhi and Congress, even though it was they who most wanted to preserve it. On more than one occasion Gandhi said that the way to effect Hindu-Muslim unity was for the majority community to yield to the demands of the minority, but again and again he neglected his own advice. A conspicuous instance was in 1928 when Motilal Nehru's report was being debated. Jinnah, whose section of the Muslim League had fully cooperated with Congress in the boycott of the Simon Commission and in the discussions that led to the Nehru report, was scornfully brushed aside when he pressed for modifications of that report. That wise liberal, Sir Tej Bahadur Sapru, voiced at that time the very principles Gandhi had advocated. "Give Jinnah what he wants," he said, "and be finished with it, even if he is a spoiled child; the first and last question should be to bring about unity." But Sapru was not supported from the Congress side.

Subhas Chandra Bose said of Gandhi that at times he was as obstinate as a fanatic, which certainly characterized his attitude to the demand for Pakistan, and it proved disastrous. From 1937 to 1946 the policy of Gandhi and Congress could hardly have been more misjudged or better calculated to bring about the result they most wished to avoid. Gandhi "shuddered at the vivisection of India" as though it really were the cutting up of a living creature. This emotional outlook, which prevented him from calmly discussing the Pakistan proposals in the early stages when Jinnah's own ideas were still fluid, and later caused him to reject the Cripps offer and to wreck the Cabinet Mission plan, was largely responsible for the absolute division of India that ultimately took place. Almost to the end, he doggedly continued to oppose division, but with a growing sense of his own impotence, until he was finally obliged to abandon in despair all thought of launching a *satyagraha* struggle against it and to resign himself to the realization that his dream of Hindu-Muslim unity had ended in partition and mutual slaughter. This was the tragic irony of his career, implicit, although unknown to him, in his own character and conduct. In good will and good intentions he had not been lacking, but from the early

Khilafat days his approach to the Hindu-Muslim question had been emotional at the expense of the sober, rational compromises that were needed to resolve the conflict between Hindu and Muslim interests. The visionary, the idealist, and the saint did not have the instinct and judgment necessary for political bargaining and failed where a man of less elevated character might have succeeded.

The Hindu-Muslim conflict made a mockery of nonviolence. In the last two years of Gandhi's life, India, which he believed was destined to carry the message of nonviolence to the world, gave to the world an exhibition of violence such as had seldom been seen before. It seemed that all his teaching had been in vain. He was forced to recognize that Congress' nonviolent struggle against the British had been little better than a sham. Nonviolence had been on their lips but not in their hearts. He himself specifically attributed the Bihar massacres of 1946 to the example of violence that his own Congressmen had set in 1942, and in general he confessed that all the looting, arson, and murder of 1946–47 was "because our struggle was not non-violent."

This was a sad confession of failure and went rather farther than was justified. Whatever the defects of nonviolent *satya-graha*, it did help to keep terrorism in check and to prevent the freedom movement, or at least an important section of it, from becoming violent and murderous. Moreover, from a practical point of view as a weapon against the British it was fairly effective. For this reason many Congressmen who had no belief in it as a principle were willing to accept Gandhi's leadership and adhere to nonviolence during the freedom struggle. The sincerity of his own belief in it not merely as a tactic but as a principle is unquestioned. But as a practical politician he gave in to his colleagues' open departure from it during the war, and on at least one occasion—in connection with resistance to the Japanese—he was ready to depart from it himself. Also, three times—in 1920–21, 1930, and 1942—he unleashed mass movements which, though ostensibly nonviolent, he knew were likely to lead to violence, and in 1942 he seemed himself almost to invite violence. Moreover, his own castigation of the British

Government was at times so intemperate as to be inconsistent with the preaching of nonviolence and love. Such conduct, it may reasonably be contended, was pardonable in a politician and understandable even in a saint, for most saints who have been called to operate in the world of affairs have failed to keep their principles inviolate, and even the Founder of Christianity was unable to square all His words and actions with the Sermon on the Mount. Gandhi sometimes fell far short of his own standards but was usually well above ordinary ones.

There is, however, no doubt that Gandhi deceived himself both about the nature of the nonviolence he employed and about the real attitude of his colleagues toward it. He had said that *satyagraha*, "the Force which is born of truth and Love or non-violence . . . postulates the conquest of the adversary by suffering in one's own person." But whatever it might have been in its ideal purity, in practice it was likely to be only another form of coercion, and that is how it was generally regarded by those against whom it was directed. Gandhi's most celebrated fasts did not melt the hearts of Dr. Ambedkar, Durbar Virawala, or Lord Linlithgow, who looked upon the fasts, however mistakenly, as a form of blackmail. Similarly, the mass civil-disobedience movements, though to some extent effective as demonstrations of the strength of national feeling, were viewed by the British as an ingenious form of political agitation; they were not impressed by the "sufferings" of the participants. Tagore, who disapproved of civil disobedience, drew attention to the moral dangers and distortions inherent in Gandhian techniques. In its struggle for freedom India needed all the moral force that Gandhi represented but it was wrong, Tagore said, "to transpose moral force into force," and he felt that "martyrdom for the cause of truth [might] degenerate into fanaticism for mere verbal forms, descending into self-deception that hides itself behind sacred names." This was valid criticism, but seems to have been lost on Gandhi.

The ambiguous attitude toward nonviolence of most of his colleagues was well known to him, yet he chose to shut his eyes to it. In the case of his Khilafatist allies he was under no illusions; they stated explicitly that they adopted nonviolence merely as a tactic and he did not expect more of them, recognizing that *ahimsa* had little appeal for Muslims. But for Congress under his leadership nonviolence was supposed to be a principle. True, when he put the matter to the test of a resolution in 1924, he secured only a small majority, but nevertheless nonviolence was the avowed principle of Congress and was paraded before the world as a merit. Did Gandhi think that his followers genuinely believed in it? It seems that this was one of the matters in which, in Lord Irwin's phrase, he was "the victim of unconscious self-deception." He knew quite well that they did not, but he repeatedly allowed himself to think, wishfully, that they did. The real attitude of most Congressmen to nonviolence was starkly revealed by Nehru in the following statement:

> We have not the material or the training for organised violence, and individual or sporadic violence is a confession of despair. The great majority of us, I take it, judge the issue not on moral but on practical grounds, and if we reject the way of violence it is because it promises no substantial results. But if this Congress, or the nation at any future time, comes to the conclusion that methods of violence will rid us of slavery, then I have no doubt it will adopt them.

These remarks were made in 1929. Yet ten years later, just after the outbreak of the war, Gandhi expressed surprise at discovering that the Working Committee's belief in nonviolence had never gone beyond using it as a tactic to fight the British Government. Not long afterward he said that he would not identify himself with civil disobedience unless he was convinced that Congressmen believed in nonviolence with all its implications. Was he really convinced that they believed in it in 1942?

The truth is that there was a considerable element of humbug in Congress' nonviolence, and Gandhi, perhaps unconsciously, connived at it. Congress claimed moral virtue for the adoption of a principle in which most of its members had no genuine belief. Their nonviolence was no more than "the weapon of the weak"; it was not the genuine "nonviolence of the brave."

Fully realizing this at the end of his life, Gandhi said that if he had known it earlier he would not have launched the freedom struggle. But he returned to India, he said, "intoxicated by [his] success in South Africa," and this, combined with initial success in India, blinded him to the real facts. There are few politicians, and not many saints, who have frankly confessed to such a fundamental misjudgment.

Nonviolence was central to Gandhi's career as a politican; it was the method he employed to achieve his overriding political aim—the emancipation of India from British rule. This aim meant so much to him that in pursuing it he was ready to run the risk of violence, and he even said that he would prefer to "see India freed by violence than enchained like a slave to her foreign oppressors." But he did not believe that violent methods could ever set India free; nonviolence was his chosen method.

Gandhi had been dedicated to the goal of a free India since boyhood, although then it was only a vague aspiration. That goal—and his desire to play a leading role in attaining it—seems to have crystallized during his stay in South Africa, where he discovered his capacity for public work, and thereafter, although he stayed in the Transvaal for many years, he never wavered from this ambition, which became the principal motivating force behind all his actions. His avowed intention on returning to India was to work as Gokhale's lieutenant, but within five years he himself had emerged as the foremost Indian political figure and had revolutionized the political life of the country. Under his guidance Congress literally and metaphorically put on a new dress and accepted in practice, if not in principle, his novel method of nonviolent agitation. For twenty-five years he retained his mastery and held Congressmen to at least outward allegiance to both nonviolence and the "constructive program." Throughout this period he was the symbol of India's fight for freedom. He enjoyed the veneration of the masses and the respect and devotion of highly gifted Indians of such diverse character as Jawaharlal Nehru, Rajagopalachari, Vallabhbhai Patel, Dr. Rajendra Prasad, and Maulana A. K. Azad. And finally independence was won—in such circumstances, it is true,

that it gave him more sorrow than joy, but the struggle against
the British had been conducted in the main nonviolently and
even amicably. Moreover, in one important respect it bore the
fruit that he desired. He had always hoped that the deliverance
of India from the English yoke would inspire the deliverance of
the "weaker races of the earth from the crushing heels of Western exploitation." Within twenty years of Indian independence
the colonial empires of the European nations had been virtually
liquidated.

All this was a tremendous political achievement, in no way
diminished by the fact that neither Congress, India, nor the
world accepted his teaching, and that only vestiges of it now
remain. He himself wished to leave no sect after him and
claimed, not quite correctly, that there was no such thing as
"Gandhism." Yet such is the honor in which his memory is
held that, although his principles and most of his social policies
have been rejected, the Government of India still feels compelled to pay some token homage to them. In deference to
nonviolence India refrains from making an atomic bomb, and
in deference to the "constructive program" the Government, in
the midst of gigantic efforts to industrialize the country, subsi-
dizes hand spinning.

At Gandhi's behest Cogressmen wore *khadi*, but most of
them had even less faith in the Gandhian philosophy of the
charkha than they had in nonviolence. Deeply moved by the
poverty of the Indian villagers, which he sometimes wrongly
attributed to English oppression, Gandhi thought that by hand
spinning and weaving they could add a few rupees to their
meager incomes, but he had no plan and no wish radically to
alter the character of their lives and the level of their material
prosperity. The simplicities of village life and the curtailment
rather than the multiplication of material wants were the Gandhian ideal of which the *charkha* was a symbol.

The traditional old implements, the plough and the spinning wheel, have made our wisdom and welfare. We must
gradually return to the old simplicity. . . . I do not believe
that multiplication of wants and machinery contrived to

supply them is taking the world a step nearer the goal. . . .
India's salvation consists in unlearning what she has learnt
in the last fifty years. The railways, telegraphs, hospitals,
lawyers, doctors, and such like all have to go; and the so-
called upper classes have to learn consciously, religiously
and deliberately the simple peasant life, knowing it to be a
life giving true happiness. . . . You cannot build nonviolence on factory civilisation; but you can build it on self-
contained villages.

Only a handful of his closest followers, mostly the residents of
his *ashram*, accepted this philosophy. Many Congressmen ritu-
ally performed their quota of spinning, but they did not believe
that the traditional implements and the *charkha* were the
means of building a better society. They put their faith in ma-
chines, industrialization, and all the apparatus of the Western
world that was anathema to Gandhi, rejecting his view that
factory civilization and large-scale production are evils. "Mys-
tics," wrote Subhas Chandra Bose, "would always hold an hon-
oured place in India, but it is not their lead that we shall have
to follow if we are to create a New India, at once free, happy
and great. . . . We have to live in the present. . . . Gandhism
will land Free India in a ditch." And so immediately after
independence the Congress government devoted its energies,
along with huge amounts of American and Russian aid, to an
attempt to change India into a modern industrialized society
which, if ever it comes into being, will be the exact antithesis of
the ideal envisaged by Gandhi.

Allied to Gandhi's objection to industrialization was his objection to socialism. Obviously socialism had little relevance to
his old-fashioned concept of self-sufficient villages administering
their affairs through their own self-appointed *panchayats*. But
aside from the irrelevance of socialism to his own ideal, Gandhi
believed in reforming society not through the coercive power of
the state but through self-reform of the individual. Rich men
and capitalists should be approached with sympathy and love
and persuaded to refrain voluntarily from exploitation and to
become "trustees" of the poor. Moral suasion rather than state

intervention was the key to the improvement of society. Men could be brought of their own volition to reduce exploitation to a minimum but, said Gandhi, "I look upon an increase in the power of the State with the greatest fear, because, although while apparently doing good by minimising exploitation, it does the greatest harm to mankind by destroying individuality, which lies at the root of all progress."

The Gandhian philosophy of the *charkha*, the bullock cart, and village life still influences Indian thought, still has a small body of fervent adherents, and still exacts from an unbelieving Indian government tribute in the form of large grants for *khadi* and village industries. But its practical effect has so far been slight and will continue to dwindle unless modern civilization follows its instinct for self-destruction to a catastrophic end. In that event the survivors, if any, whether in India or elsewhere, might recall and revive the Gandhian philosophy.

In much the same way a few faithful disciples still cling to Gandhi's doctrine of nonviolence, and his policy of fasting has been copied in recent years by some who could hardly claim to be disciples. But in general, nonviolence, whether as a principle or as a tactic, has been losing ground since 1942. In the form of passive resistance rather than of the pure *satyagraha* of Gandhi's conception it has had a long history in India; a hundred and fifty years ago Bishop Heber noted that it was a Hindu method of opposing anything considered to be wrong or unjust. It has also been employed from time to time in various other parts of the world, as it was during World War II against the Nazis in some countries of occupied Europe. It is possible that in the future passive resistance will be used to counter foreign aggression and will be the only weapon open to the ordinary mass of citizens for combating the tyranny of an authoritarian state. If so, Gandhian precedents and practice may have an influence beyond the boundaries of India, but it will not be quite the same message of nonviolence as that which Gandhi believed it was India's mission to carry to the world.

Most of Gandhi's teachings were accepted only temporarily in India. But one item in the "constructive program"—the removal of untouchability—had a lasting effect on Hindu society and places Gandhi in the ranks of the great social reformers of modern times. He described himself as "a reformer through and through," but at the same time he claimed that he rejected none of the essential tenets of Hinduism. He professed faith in the Vedas, Upanishads, and other Hindu scriptures; he believed in reincarnation and the transmigration of souls; he believed in the caste system; and he shared, but rationalized, the Hindu veneration for the cow.

Through the cow, according to Gandhi, man is made aware of his identity with all that lives, and the protection of the cow stands for "the protection of the whole dumb creation of God." His zeal in this matter was shown at the time of the Khilafat agitation. He did not want to bargain directly with the Muslims for concessions regarding the slaughter of cows in return for support of the Khilafat cause, but, in typically Gandhian fashion, he hoped that some *quid pro quo* would, in fact, be forthcoming—through divine intervention. "My prayer ascends daily to God Almighty that my service to a cause I hold to be just may appear so pleasing to Him, that he may change the hearts of the Mussalmans and fill them with pity for their Hindu neighbours and make them save the animal the latter hold as dear as life itself." The prayer was not answered.

Gandhi accepted and defended the four fundamental divisions of the caste system—Brahmans, Kshatriyas, Vaisyas, and Sudras—on the basis of the Hindu belief in reincarnation. If a Brahman did not live properly he would be reincarnated in a lower division, and vice versa. On the other hand, he rejected with indignation, as a "blot on Hinduism," the fact that some sections of the community were regarded as "untouchables." When as a boy he was told by his parents that he must not touch the "sweeper" who came to their house to clean the latrines, he dutifully obeyed, but he protested to them that untouchability could not be sanctioned by religion. Later he took the position that untouchability was not part of true Hindusim.

I know no argument in favour of the retention of untouchability, and I have no hesitation in rejecting Scriptural authority of a doubtful character in order to support a sinful institution. Indeed, I would reject all authority if it is in conflict with sober reason or the dictates of the heart.

So strong were his feelings on this subject that he went so far as to assert that if it were proved to him that untouchability was really fundamental to Hinduism, he would advise Hindus to convert to Islam or Christianity. But he was convinced that all passages in the Hindu scriptures which appeared to support untouchability were later interpolations, a "device of Satan."

He attributed to the sin of untouchability not only the Bihar earthquake, but all the humiliations to which India had been subjected at the hands of Britain and the West.

> Our being treated as social lepers in practically the whole world is due to our having treated a fifth of our own race as such. . . . We have driven the pariah from our midst and have thereby become the pariahs of the British Empire. . . . With eyes red with rage we push them out of railway carriages. Has the English Government ever inflicted anything worse on us? Indeed there is no charge that the pariah cannot fling in our faces and which we do not fling in the face of Englishmen.

The ending of untouchability was for Gandhi an aim second only to that of ending British rule in India, and he often asserted that the latter was dependent on the former. This proved to be an overstatement. British rule ended in 1947, but untouchability, although abolished by the Constitution of India and its practice in any form forbidden, still continues. Its end is, however, in sight. Gandhi's campaign against it was effective, and his success in stirring the conscience of Hindu society to recognize it as an evil was one of the great achievements of his life. He met with fierce opposition from orthodox Hindus, but most of his Congress colleagues, even if they did not share his crusading zeal or admit the connection that he saw between the removal of untouchability and the attainment of political independence, accepted this item of the "constructive program" wholeheartedly, with none of the mental reservations they had about the *charkha* and nonviolence. They knew that in this matter Gandhi was right.

Gandhi's onslaught on untouchability was part of a wider movement for the reform of Hindu society. Other abuses, such as child marriage, temple prostitution, the harsh treatment of widows, and the subjection of women generally, called for remedy. Gandhi, a reformer through and through and a keen believer in the emancipation of women, gave support and impetus to the efforts made to cure these ills; and after his death Nehru's government did whatever could be done by legislation to remove these age-old abuses of Hinduism. But Gandhi will above all be remembered and held in honor as a social reformer for his fight against untouchability.

Swaraj, according to Gandhi's conception of it, demanded more than the reform of the worst abuses of Hinduism; it demanded the reform of Indian character. In his first public speech in South Africa he had impressed on his audience the importance of truthfulness and cleanliness, and thereafter one of his constant themes was that if Indians aspired, as they should, to independence and equal rights with other nations, then they should strive to be worthy of their aspirations and not incur contempt by dirty, slovenly habits, cringing subservience, and lack of proper pride in their own traditions and culture. Centuries of autocratic rule, mostly by foreigners, had demoralized much of the population, especially the Hindu portion of it which had been longest under foreign domination, and fostered timidity and submissiveness. One of the virtues that Gandhi preached incessantly and practiced conspicuously in his own life was fearlessness. By his exhortations, by his own example, and by organizing disciplined movements of defiance of the government, he did more than any one man to instill in the Hindus self-confidence, self-respect, and a readiness to stand up for themselves. For this as much as for the actual attainment of independence he deserves the title of Father of the Nation.

The deliverance of India from British rule, which admittedly was Gandhi's chief political aim, would appear also to have been the dominant purpose of his life. He himself would have denied this. Religion and politics were for him inseparable, and he was brought to politics by religion. In 1925 he wrote the following:

> What I want to achieve, what I have been striving and pining to achieve these thirty years is . . . to see God face to face, to attain *moksha*.* I live and move and have my being in pursuit of this goal. All that I do by way of speaking and writing, and all my ventures in the political field, are directed to this same end.

The search for God required him, he said, to identify himself with the whole of mankind and love the meanest creature as himself, and this in turn meant that he could not keep out of any field of life, least of all politics. The search for God was, therefore, the mainspring of all his actions.

This analysis may have been somewhat faulty; certainly to outward appearance what first roused him to action and set him on a public career was not the search for God but resentment at the contempt shown for Indians in South Africa and a consequent desire to remove the stigma of inferiority. But he believed his own analysis of the motivation of his action to be true, and partly true no doubt it was. In any case, his "experiments in the spiritual field" gave him, as he himself said, the power that he possessed for working in the political field. Gandhi the politician would have been a failure without Gandhi the saint.

* Literally, freedom from birth and death; salvation.

Note on Fasting

On the last day of his seven-day fast in November 1925 Gandhi wrote a detailed account of his fasting technique for publications in *Young India* and concluded by laying down the following rules "for all those who may wish to fast on any account whatsoever":

1. Conserve your energy both physical and mental from the very beginning.
2. You must cease to think of food whilst you are fasting.
3. Drink as much cold water as you can, with or without soda and salt, but in small quantities at a time—water should be boiled, strained and cooled. Do not be afraid of salt and soda, because most waters contain both these salts in a free state.
4. Have a warm sponge daily.
5. Take an enema regularly during fast. You will be surprised at the impurities you will expel daily.
6. Sleep as much as possible in the open air.
7. Bathe in the morning sun. A sun and air bath is at least as great a purifier as a water bath.
8. Think of anything else but the fast.
9. No matter from what motive you are fasting, during this precious time think of your Maker, and your relation

to Him and His other creation, and you will make discoveries you may not have even dreamed of.

With apologies to medical friends, but out of fulness of my own experience and that of fellow cranks I say without hesitation, fast (1) if you are constipated, (2) if you are anaemic, (3) if you are feverish, (4) if you have an indigestion, (5) if you have a headache, (6) if you are rheumatic, (7) if you are gouty, (8) if you are fretting and foaming, (9) if you are depressed, (10) if you are overjoyed; and you will avoid medical prescriptions and patent medicines.

Eat only when you are hungry and when you have laboured for your food.

Glossary

ahimsa—abstention from doing injury; nonviolence.
ashram—hermitage: retreat; home for community living.
bagh—garden.
bania—merchant; shopkeeper; moneylender.
bhangi—scavenger; sweeper.
brahmacharya—observance of chastity or continence in quest of God.
chaddar—sheet.
charkha—spinning wheel.
crore—one million
dal—legumes.
darshan—sight of venerated person or deity.
dhoti—loincloth; a long piece of cloth worn by Indians.
diwan—Chief Minister of the ruler of an Indian state before independence.
faqir—Muslim ascetic and recluse.
ghani—oil press.
goonda—hooligan.
gur—molasses.
Harijan—a child of God; a term coined by Gandhi for Untouchables.
hartal—suspension of work as a mark of protest or mourning; strike.
himsa—opposite of *ahimsa*; violence.
jai—victory.

Jai Hind—Victory to (Long Live) India.

khadi or *khaddar*—hand-spun and hand-woven cloth.

Khilafat—the institution of the Khalifa (Caliph), the theocratic head of the Muslim world.

lok sewak sangh—organization for the service of the people.

mahatma—great soul.

mantra—religious formula or incantation.

maulana—title of respect applied to Muslim scholars and divines.

moksha—freedom from birth and death; salvation.

navajiwan—new life.

panchayat—village council of five persons.

pundit—learned Hindu teacher; honorific term applied to Brahmans.

purdah—veil; the custom of keeping women in seclusion.

purna swaraj—complete self-rule or independence.

raj—rule.

Rama—God.

rishis—sages, seers.

sabha—association; society.

sadhu—Hindu recluse; holy man; mendicant.

sardar—nobleman; an honorific term.

satyagraha—force born of truth or nonviolence; nonviolent resistance.

satyagrahi—one who practices *satyagraha*.

swadeshi—belonging to, or made in; one's own country.

swaraj—self-government; self-rule.

taluk—a subdivision of a district.

Thakore—title given to some rulers of small principalities.

tinkathia—system under which tenants had to plant three (*tin*) out of every twenty *kathias* (about one-twentieth of an acre) with indigo.

Bibliography

Ashe, G. *Gandhi: A Study of Revolution*. Heinman Imported Books.

Birla, G. D. *In the Shadow of the Mahatma*. Orient Longmans, India.

Bolitho, H. *Jinnah*. John Murray, London.

Doke, J. J. *M. K. Gandhi: An Indian Patriot in South Africa*. G. A. Natesan & Co., Madras.

Fischer, L. *The Life of Mahatma Gandhi*. Harper & Brothers, New York; Jonathan Cape, London. (Also available in two paperback editions: New American Library; Collier.)

Gandhi, M. K. *An Autobiography or The Story of My Experiments with Truth*. Navajivan Press, Ahmedabad. (Also available as *Gandhi's Autobiography*; Public Affairs.)

Gandhi, M. K. *Collected Works of Mahatma Gandhi*. Government of India Publications. Fifty volumes are contemplated of which twenty-four have appeared. (Nineteen volumes are available in the United States; Heinman Imported Books.)

Gandhi, M. K. *Hind Swaraj or Indian Home Rule*. Navajivan Press, Ahmedabad.

Gandhi, M. K. *Satyagraha in South Africa*. S. Ganesan, Madras.

Gopal, S. *The Viceroyalty of Lord Irwin, 1926–1931*. Oxford Clarendon Press.

Jack, H. A., ed. *The Gandhi Reader*. Dennis Dobson, London.

Majumdar, S. K. *Jinnah and Gandhi*. K. L. Mukhopadhyay, Calcutta.

Mukerjee, H. *Gandhi: A Study.* National Book Agency, Calcutta.

Nanda, B. R. *Mahatma Gandhi: A Biography.* Allen & Unwin, London. (Also available as *Shapers of History: Mahatma Gandhi*; Barron's.)

Nehru, J. *An Autobiography.* The Bodley Head; Paragon.

Pyarelal. *Mahatma Gandhi: The Last Phase,* 2 vols. Navajivan Press, Ahmedabad.

Tendulkar, D. G. *Mahatma: Life of Mohandas Karamchand Gandhi,* 8 vols. Vitalbhai K. Jhaveri and D. G. Tendulkar.

Index

Cripps mission, 223–26
Gandhi's symbolic civil-disobedience campaign, 220–22, 227
nonviolent resistance to Japanese resolved, 227
parallel-organization policy, 219, 223
"Quit India" campaign, 227–39
See also: Gandhi, Mohandas K.
Indian Opinion (journal), 43–45, 47, 49, 52, 57, 75
Indian Relief Act (South Africa), 72
Indigo planters, Gandhi's campaign for tenants of, 80–81
Interim Government, see Viceroy's Executive Council
Irwin, 1st Baron, of Kirkby Underdale (*later* Earl of Halifax)
attempted assassination of, 148
on Gandhi, 168, 284
as viceroy
Bardoli civil disobedience, 142
Gandhi's noncooperation campaign, 151, 153, 159
meetings with Gandhi, 138, 148, 165–72
release of Congress leaders (Jan. 1931), 164, 165
Round-Table Conference, 145–49, 160–73
Simon Commission, 138, 139, 145, 162
Islam
Gandhi's study of, 28
See also: Muslims

Jains, influence on Gandhi of, 11–12
Jallianwala Bagh massacre (1919), 104–7, 126
Japan, Congress attitude to (World War II), 224–30, 233
Jawaharlal, see Nehru, Jawaharlal
Jayakar, Mukund Ramrao, 161, 165
Jinnah, Mohammed Ali, 75, 134, 204
accepts limited Pakistan, 261
as "Ambassador of Hindu-Muslim unity," 116
Congress ministries and, 206–7
on cows, 91

Gandhi and, 12, 280
1938 meeting, 208
1944 talks, 244–45
Montagu-Chelmsford reforms and, 107
Nehru Report (1928) rejected by, 144, 281
1946 position of, 247, 250–52
noncooperation and, 112, 114, 116
proposed as head of Interim Government by Gandhi, 262
Round-Table Conference and, 148
Simla conference and, 246
Simon Commission and, 139
World War II and, 215–17, 242
Cripps proposals rejected, 225
on "Quit India" campaign, 231
See also: Muslim League
Johannesburg
Gandhi in, 42–43, 45, 49
registration certificates burned in, 61–62
Juhu, 129

Kaira district, 82–84, 86
Kaisar-i-Hind gold medal, 78
Kallenbach, Hermann, 65, 71
Kashmir hostilities (1948), 273
Khadi (*khaddar*), 117, 146, 190
defined, 78, 296
See also: Spinning
Khilafat movement, see Caliphate movement
Kitchlew, Saif-ud-din, 102–3
Kohat, 1924 Hindu-Muslim riots in, 133
Kripalani, Acharya, 267
Kruger, Oom Paul, 42

Labor
in Ahmedabad, 85
indentured, 79–80
Labor Party (Great Britain), 145, 165, 177, 178
granting of Independence by, 247
Lajpat Rai, Lala, 139, 150
Lal, Magan, 76
Laughton, Mr., 33
Law courts, boycott of, 113
"Lead Kindly Light," 57

Satyagraha (continued)
   comparison with Ganges, 59–60
   "Himalayan miscalculation"
      statement, 100
   needs to be confined to one per-
      son, 189
   objectives, 67–68
   as sovereign remedy against gov-
      ernment, 79
   Gandhi's adoption of, 52–53
   long history in India of, 288
   recognized as practical method of
      fighting British, 83, 84
   against Rowlatt Acts, 96–100
   in South Africa, 53–72, 75
   trained leaders needed for, 100–1,
      136, 278–79
   violence as result of, *see* Violence
   women and, 68–69, 155
   See also: Noncooperation
Satyagraha Ashram (Sabarmati), 76–
      78, 100, 137
   dissolved, 195
   spinning in, 77–78
Satyagraha Sabha, 96
Satyapal, Dr., 102–3
Schools, boycott of, 113
Selborne, 2nd Earl of, 54, 55
Servants of the Untouchables Society,
      195
Sevagram, 195, 257
Sèvres, Treaty of, 123
Sexual restraint, Gandhi's vow to ob-
      serve, 46–47
Shaw, George Bernard, 180
Sherwood, Marcella, 103, 104
Shraddhanand, Swami, 137
Sikhs, 104, 117, 130, 179, 259, 270
Simla conference, 246
Simon, Sir John, 139
Simon Commission, 138–40, 145–46,
      147, 162, 281
Sind
   Cabinet Mission proposal on, 249
   in proposed Pakistan, 247
Singh, Bhagat, 172–73, 174
Sirirampur, 257
Sitaramayya, Pattabhi, 209
Slocombe, George, 161
Smuts, Gen. Jan Christiaan, 54–59,
      63, 70–72

Gandhi's 1908 agreement with, 55–
      59
Gandhi's "ultimatum" to, 61
on Gandhi, 72, 242
Gokhale's meeting with, 66, 67
Socialism, Gandhi's objection to, 287–
      88
Socialist left wing of Congress, 193,
      195, 200, 211, 277
"Soul-force," 52
South Africa
   Asiatic Department in, 41, 43
   Chinese in, 54, 55
   discrimination against Indians in,
      25–27, 42–43
   annual tax, 31–32, 66–72
   Congress resolution against, 38
   effect of Gandhi's work, 72
   invalidation of non-Christian
      marriages, 68, 72
   Gandhi in, 25–37, 40–72
   assaulted by Pathans, 56–57
   Boer War, 35–36
   Durban mob incident, 32–34
   Gandhi's resolution to redress
      wrongs of Indians, 26
   his achievements, 74–75
   imprisonments, 54–55, 63, 70–
      71
   Indian Opinion, 43–45
   Natal Indian Congress formed,
      31
   Phoenix settlement, 45, 46
   satyagraha, 49–72, 75
   Tolstoy Farm, 65–66
   Zulu rebellion, 45–46
Spinners Association, All-India, 136–
      37, 279
Spinning, 77–78, 108, 115, 132
   Congress and, 115, 131, 135–37,
      194
   in India today, 286, 288
   See also: Khadi
States, princely
   in Act of 1935, 192
   Congress policy toward, 202–6
   Gandhi's Rajkot fast, 203–5
   at Round-Table Conference, 162–
      63, 202
Suhrawardy, Hussein Shaheed, 265
   Gandhi and, 257, 266–68

DATE DUE	BORROWER'S NAME

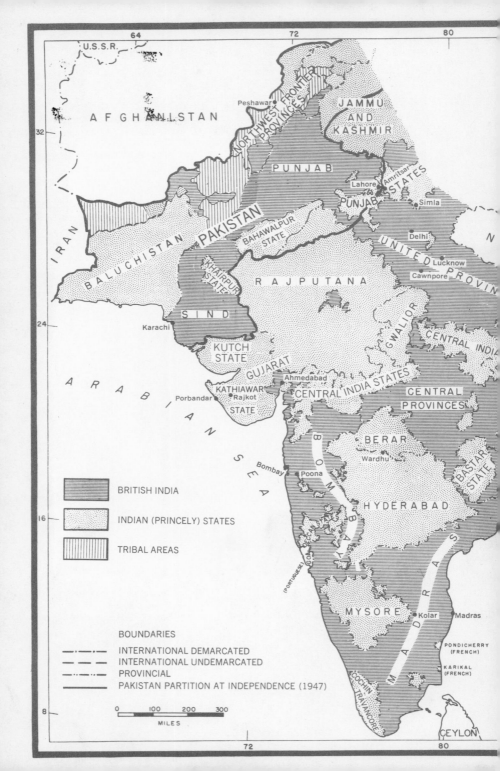